PE Connections

Helping Kids Succeed
Through Physical Activity

Thomas M. Fleming

Lisa Bunting

**HUMAN
KINETICS**

Library of Congress Cataloging-in-Publication Data

Fleming, Thomas M., 1941-
 PE connections : helping kids succeed through physical activity / Thomas M. Fleming, Lisa Bunting.
   p. cm.
 Includes bibliographical references.
 ISBN-13: 978-0-7360-5910-7 (soft cover)
 ISBN-10: 0-7360-5910-5 (soft cover)
 1. Physical education and training--Curricula. 2. Curriculum planning. 3. Sports for children--Health aspects. I. Bunting, Lisa. II. Title. III. Title: Physical education connections.
 GV363.F574 2007
 372.86--dc22
                    2006020015

ISBN-10: 0-7360-5910-5
ISBN-13: 978-0-7360-5910-7

The Web addresses cited in this text were current as of May 25, 2006, unless otherwise noted.

Acquisitions Editor: Bonnie Pettifor; **Developmental Editor:** Ragen E. Sanner; **Assistant Editor:** Carmel Sielicki; **Copyeditor:** Joan Dunayer; **Proofreader:** Sarah Wiseman; **Permission Manager:** Dalene Reeder; **Graphic Designer:** Nancy Rasmus; **Graphic Artist:** Dawn Sills; **Photo Manager:** Sarah Ritz; **Cover Designer:** Keith Blomberg; **Photographer (cover):** Sarah Ritz; **Photographer (interior):** Sarah Ritz, unless otherwise noted; **Art Manager:** Kelly Hendren; **Illustrator:** Denise Lowry; **Printer:** Versa Press

Printed in the United States of America   10   9   8   7   6   5   4   3   2   1

Human Kinetics
Web site: www.HumanKinetics.com

United States: Human Kinetics
P.O. Box 5076
Champaign, IL 61825-5076
800-747-4457
e-mail: humank@hkusa.com

Canada: Human Kinetics
475 Devonshire Road Unit 100
Windsor, ON N8Y 2L5
800-465-7301 (in Canada only)
e-mail: orders@hkcanada.com

Europe: Human Kinetics
107 Bradford Road
Stanningley
Leeds LS28 6AT, United Kingdom
+44 (0) 113 255 5665
e-mail: hk@hkeurope.com

Australia: Human Kinetics
57A Price Avenue
Lower Mitcham, South Australia 5062
08 8372 0999
e-mail: liaw@hkaustralia.com

New Zealand: Human Kinetics
Division of Sports Distributors NZ Ltd.
P.O. Box 300 226 Albany
North Shore City
Auckland
0064 9 448 1207
e-mail: info@humankinetics.co.nz

To everyone who works to improve the health and well-being of young people

Contents

Activity Finder

Activity	Page	Content connections	Asset action	Coordinated school health links
Chapter 5—Superstarters				
1, 2, 3, Go	40	• Warm-up • Aerobic health • Muscular endurance • Flexibility • Basketball dribbling • Volleying	• Caring • Honesty	Parental involvement
15-Second Skill Challenge	41	• Agility • Speed • Aerobic health • Muscular endurance	• Parent involvement in schooling • Honesty	PE and classroom teacher cooperation
Body Shape Bonanza	42	• Warm-up • Flexibility • Body shapes • Balance	Self-esteem	Parental involvement
Countdown	43	• Warm-up • Aerobic health • Muscular endurance • Rhythms • Jumping	• Other adult relationships • Caring school climate	PE/classroom/recess connections
In and Out	44	• Warm-up • Aerobic health • Muscular endurance	• Interpersonal competence • Cultural competence	Connection between physical health and mental, emotional, and social health
Instant Replay	45	• Locomotor skills • Aerobic health	• Interpersonal competence • Cultural competence	Parental, classroom, and school personnel involvement
Match Play	46	• Warm-up • Aerobic health • Throwing • Catching • Coordination	• Interpersonal competence • Personal power	Intellectual health
Mickey's Mambo	47	• Listening • Following directions • Aerobic health • Muscular endurance • Coordination	Cultural competence	Intellectual and social health
Mingle and Move	48	• Warm-up • Throwing • Catching • Muscular endurance • Flexibility	• Interpersonal competence • Cultural competence	• Intellectual and social health • PE/health integration

(continued)

(continued)

Activity	Page	Content connections	Asset action	Coordinated school health links
Chapter 5—Superstarters				
Operation Cooperation	49	• Aerobic health • Muscular endurance • Flexibility • Locomotor skills	• High expectations • Achievement motivation • School/learning engagement • Personal power • Positive view of personal future	• PE and classroom teacher cooperation • PE/health integration
Partner Jump and Jive	50	• Aerobic health • Muscular endurance • Locomotor skills • Jumping patterns	Interpersonal competence	• Lifetime health and fitness • Parental involvement • PE/health integration
Partner Mix-up	51	• Locomotor skills • Flexibility • Rhythms • Aerobic health • Muscular endurance	Cultural competence	• Alternative classroom activity • PE and classroom teacher cooperation
Run and Rap	52	Aerobic health	• Cultural competence • Interpersonal competence • Youth as resources • Positive peer influence • Caring • Healthy lifestyle • Sense of purpose	• Intellectual health • Parental and classroom involvement • PE/health integration
Scramble	53	• Cooperation • Aerobic health	• Achievement motivation • School/learning engagement • Bonding to school	PE and classroom teacher cooperation
Side by Side	54	• Agility • Quickness • Locomotor skills	Planning and decision making	Social health
Starting off Right	55	• Warm-up • Aerobic health • Coordination • Ball manipulation • Beanbag manipulation • Jumping rope	• Empowerment • Responsibility	Parental, classroom, and school personnel involvement
Trading Places	56	• Locomotor skills • Directions • Pathways • Levels	• Cultural competence • Interpersonal competence	Teacher tip—parental involvement
Tri-Color Action	57	Warm-up	Teacher tip—support, positive identity, commitment to learning	PE/classroom/recess connections
Whistle While You Work Out	58	• Aerobic health • Muscular endurance • Flexibility	School boundaries	Parental involvement

Activity	Page	Content connections	Asset action	Coordinated school health links
Chapter 6—Let's Get Physical Cards				
Exercise Exchange	60	• Aerobic health • Muscular endurance • Flexibility	• Empowerment • Social competencies	• Physical health • PE/health integration
Exercise Excitement	61	Health-related fitness	• Caring • Responsibility	• PE and classroom teacher cooperation • Alternative classroom activity
Exercise Parade	62	• Aerobic health • Muscular strength • Flexibility	Positive view of personal future	• Physical health • PE and classroom teacher cooperation • PE/health integration
Fitness Four Square	63	• Throwing • Catching • Underhand tossing • Bounce passing • Muscular endurance • Flexibility	• Caring • Personal power • Interpersonal competence	• Physical health • PE/health integration
Flexibility Frenzy	64	• Flexibility • Chasing • Dodging	• Honesty • Responsibility	• Physical health • PE/health integration
Locomotor Interval Training	65	• Aerobic health • Muscular endurance • Flexibility	Responsibility	Connection between physical health and mental health
Lots of Lottery	66	• Aerobic health • Muscular endurance • Flexibility	• Self-esteem • Personal power	Social health
Partner Pathways	67	• Locomotor skills • Pathways	Teacher tip—leadership, creativity, social competencies	Alternative classroom activity
Rectangle Romp	68	• Aerobic health • Muscular endurance • Flexibility	Responsibility	• Alternative classroom activity • Physical health • PE/classroom/recess connections
Tag Team Fitness	69	• Aerobic health • Muscular endurance • Flexibility	• Positive values • Social competencies	• PE and classroom teacher cooperation • Social health
Tag Training	70	• Aerobic health • Muscular endurance • Chasing • Dodging • Fleeing	• Planning and decision making • Achievement motivation	• Physical, emotional, and social health
Team Card Combo	72	• Aerobic health • Muscular endurance • Flexibility • Rhythm • Cooperation	• Interpersonal competence • Cultural competence • Creative activities	• Physical, intellectual, and social health • Parental involvement

(continued)

ALL THINGS ARE CONNECTED

(continued)

Activity	Page	Content connections	Asset action	Coordinated school health links
Chapter 6—Let's Get Physical Cards				
Terrific 10s	73	• Warm-up • Aerobic health	School/learning engagement	Physical health
You Make the Call	74	• Flexibility • Aerobic health • Muscular endurance	• Responsibility • Interpersonal competence • High expectations • Achievement motivation • Personal power	Physical health
Chapter 7—Deck of Cards				
Bank Tag	76	• Aerobic health • Chasing • Dodging	Caring	Social health
Card Collection	77	• Aerobic health • Flexibility	Caring school climate	Physical health
Card Run 21	78	• Aerobic health • Game skill development	• Other adult relationships • Personal power	• Physical health • Parental involvement
Card Suit Fitness	80	• Health related fitness • Aerobic health • Muscular endurance • Flexibility • Jumping rope	• Youth as resources • High expectations • Parental involvement in schooling	Parental, classroom, and school personnel involvement
Dealer's Choice	82	• Aerobic health • Cooperation • Muscular strength • Muscular endurance	• Planning and decision making • Interpersonal competence • Caring	Physical health
Digit Draw	83	• Aerobic health • Muscular endurance • Flexibility	School/learning engagement	PE and classroom teacher cooperation
Flash Card Fitness	84	• Aerobic health • Muscular endurance • Flexibility	School/learning engagement	• Alternative classroom activity • Parental involvement • Activity student can do on own
Lottery Tag	85	Aerobic health	Healthy lifestyle	Parental involvement
Stock Exchange Tag	86	• Chasing • Dodging • Locomotor skills	Teacher tip—support	Teacher tip— PE and classroom teacher cooperation
Two for the Road	87	Aerobic health	Teacher tip—social competencies	• Physical health • Lifetime health and fitness

Activity	Page	Content connections	Asset action	Coordinated school health links
Chapter 8—Balls				
10-Minute Ball Fitness Workout	90	• Ball handling • Fitness • Muscular endurance • Muscular flexibility	Teacher tip—commitment to learning	PE/classroom/recess connections
Asteroids	92	Overhand throwing	Teacher tip—support, adult relationships	PE/health integration
Ball Bombardment	94	• Overhand throwing • Throwing accuracy	Honesty	PE/health integration
Ball Bonanza	96	• Ball manipulation • Dribbling • Passing and catching	Teacher tip—support, encouragement, environment	Parental involvement
Bazooka Ball	98	• Throwing • Fitness	Caring school climate	• PE/health integration • Alternative classroom activity
Beach Ball Blast	99	Volleying	Integrity	Connection between physical health and mental, emotional, and social health
Come and Get It	100	• Skill-related fitness • Quickness • Changing direction • Agility	Peaceful conflict resolution	Social health
Dribble Mania 1	101	• Coordination • Ball manipulation • Dribbling skills	• School boundaries • Planning and decision making	• PE and classroom teacher cooperation • PE/classroom/recess connections
Dribble Mania 2	102	• Ball handling • Ball manipulation • Dribbling	• Caring school climate • Youth as resources • School/learning engagement	• PE and classroom teacher cooperation • Intellectual health
Globetrotter Games	103	• Ball manipulation • Rhythm • Dribbling	• Caring • Youth as resources	• Intellectual health • Physical health
Healthy Kid Tag	104	• Chasing • Dodging • Fleeing	• Healthy lifestyle/restraint • Planning and decision making	• Lifetime health and fitness • School personnel involvement
Hoop Shoot	105	Basketball shooting	Caring	PE and classroom teacher cooperation
Movin' on Up	106	• Passing • Catching • Throwing • Teamwork	• High expectations • Caring school climate • Caring • Self-esteem	Teacher tip—linking classroom to community

(continued)

(continued)

Activity	Page	Content connections	Asset action	Coordinated school health links
Chapter 8—Balls				
Partner Ab Fitness	108	• Cooperation • Muscular endurance	Cultural competence	Physical health
Score Five	109	• Passing • Catching • Throwing • Teamwork	Achievement motivation	Intellectual, social, and physical health
Star Wars Battle	110	• Accuracy • Throwing • Eye–hand coordination	Teacher tip—positive values	Physical health
Team Keep-Away	111	• Throwing • Catching • Cooperation	Cultural competence	Parental involvement
Throw and Go	112	• Overhand throwing • Throwing accuracy	Honesty	Physical health
Throwathon	114	• Throwing • Catching	Teacher tip—support relationships	• PE and classroom teacher cooperation • Alternative classroom activity
Chapter 9—Hoops				
Beanbag Tic-Tac-Toe	116	• Tossing • Throwing accuracy • Muscular endurance • Body shapes	School/learning engagement	Physical health
Fitness Hoopla	117	• Locomotor skills • Aerobic health • Muscle endurance • Flexibility	Safety	Physical health
Hoop Battle	118	• Coordination • Aerobic health • Hula hooping	• Peaceful conflict resolution • Youth as resources	• Social health • Parental involvement
Hoop It Up	119	• Agility • Tossing • Reaction time • Speed	Cultural competence	PE and classroom teacher cooperation
Hoop Scooting	120	• Chasing • Dodging • Fleeing • Cooperation	• Responsibility • Peaceful conflict resolution	• Physical health • School personnel involvement
Hooping It With Wipeout and YMCA	121	• Hula hooping • Coordination • Fitness	Self-esteem	Social health
Hula Hoop Tag	122	• Rolling hoops • Dodging	Caring school climate	• Lifetime health and fitness • Physical health

Activity	Page	Content connections	Asset action	Coordinated school health links
Hula Palooza	123	• Coordination • Body control • Aerobic health • Muscle endurance • Relationships	• Personal power • Creative activities	• Intellectual health • PE and classroom teacher cooperation
Musical Hoop Exchange	124	• Locomotor skills • Basketball dribbling	• Interpersonal competence • Cultural competence	Physical health
Up, Down, All Around	126	• Flexibility • Cooperative warm-up or cool-down	• Interpersonal competence • Cultural competence	• Connection between physical health and mental, emotional, and social health • Parental, classroom, and school personnel involvement
Chapter 10—Jump Ropes				
Blast Off	128	• Jumping • Landing • Fitness • Aerobic health	Teacher tip—community values youth, youth as resources	Physical health
Bump Up	129	• Jumping rope • Aerobic health • Muscular endurance	Teacher tip—parent involvement in schooling	Parental involvement
High and Low, Here We Go	130	• Jumping • Landing • Aerobic health	• Caring school climate • Youth as resources	Teacher tip—intellectual health
Jump!	131	• Jumping skills • Aerobic health • Muscular endurance	Teacher tip—empowerment	• Alternative classroom activity • Parental involvement
Jump and Jog	132	• Jumping • Landing • Coordination • Aerobic health	• Sense of purpose • Achievement motivation	Teacher tip—PE and classroom teacher cooperation
Jumpathon	133	• Jumping rope • Aerobic health • Muscular endurance • Teamwork	• School/learning engagement • Honesty • Personal power	• Connection between physical health and mental, emotional, and social health • Healthy school environment
Mouse Tails	135	• Chasing • Fleeing • Dodging • Aerobic health	Teacher tip—empowerment	Social, emotional, and physical health
Partner Party	136	• Jumping tricks • Aerobic health • Muscular endurance	• Empowerment • Positive identity	Physical health
Wild Over Webs	138	• Jumping • Landing • Rhythms	Personal power	• Lifetime health and fitness • PE/health connections

(continued)

(continued)

Activity	Page	Content connections	Asset action	Coordinated school health links
Chapter 11—Beanbags				
Bank the Beanbag	140	Underhand throwing	Cultural competence	PE and classroom teacher cooperation
Beanbag Addition	142	• Tossing • Throwing accuracy	• Integrity • Honesty	Social health
Beanbag Barrage	143	Throwing accuracy	Teacher tip—social connections	• Lifetime health and fitness • Alternative classroom activity
Beanbag Fitness Challenges	144	• Muscular endurance • Eye–hand coordination • Flexibility	High expectations	• Parental involvement • PE/health integration
Beanbag Rotation	145	• Muscular endurance • Aerobic health	Teacher tip—social competencies	• Lifetime health and fitness • PE/health integration
Beanie Bag of Tricks	147	• Tossing • Catching • Throwing • Eye–hand coordination	• Interpersonal competence • Cultural competence	• Activity student can do on own • Parental involvement
Fleet Feet	149	• Rolling skills • Throwing accuracy • Dodging	Peaceful conflict resolution	• Emotional health • Social health
Four-Color Tag	150	• Chasing • Dodging • Fleeing • Tagging	• Integrity (fairness) • Responsibility	• Physical health • PE/health integration
Hasty Helpers	151	• Aerobic health • Tossing • Catching	• Caring school climate • Community values youth • Safety	Physical health
Hot Potato	152	• Tossing • Catching	• Interpersonal competence • Cultural competence	• Lifetime health and fitness • PE and classroom teacher cooperation
Stop, Bop, and Drop	153	• Eye–hand coordination • Tossing • Catching • Muscular endurance	Teacher tip—support, adult relationships, healthy lifestyle	• Parental involvement • Activity student can do on own
Trading Spaces	154	• Reaction time • Dodging • Agility	Achievement motivation	PE/classroom/recess connection
Chapter 12—Dice				
Alphabet Soup	156	• Balance • Flexibility • Shapes	Positive peer influence	Social health

Activity	Page	Content connections	Asset action	Coordinated school health links
Dice Jump-Off	157	• Jumping rope • Jumping • Landing	Peaceful conflict resolution	• Intellectual health • PE and classroom teacher cooperation
Dice Multiples	158	• Aerobic health • Muscular endurance • Flexibility	Caring school climate	• Intellectual health • PE and community connection
Dice Trios	159	• Aerobic health • Muscular endurance	• Achievement motivation • School/learning engagement	• PE and classroom teacher cooperation • Alternative classroom activity
Dice-Ercise	160	• Aerobic health • Muscular endurance • Flexibility	Teacher tip—empowerment	Parental involvement
Exercise Surprise	161	• Aerobic health • Muscular strength • Flexibility	Teacher tip—commitment to learning, environment	• Physical health • Parental involvement
Four-Sided Fitness	162	• Aerobic health • Muscular endurance • Flexibility	Adult role models	Parental involvement
Odds and Evens	163	• Aerobic health • Muscular endurance	Planning and decision making	• Lifetime health and fitness • Alternative classroom activity
Roll 15	164	• Aerobic health • Muscular endurance • Flexibility	• Interpersonal competence • Responsibility	• Social health • Activity student can do on own
Chapter 13—Copy 'N' Go				
Alpha Action	166	• Physical activity featuring verbs and adverbs • Locomotor skills • Flexibility • Aerobic health • Muscular endurance	School/learning engagement	• Intellectual health • PE and classroom teacher cooperation
Cardio Challenge	167	• Aerobic health • Muscular endurance • Flexibility	Healthy lifestyle/restraint	• Physical health • Parental involvement
Fitness Frolic	168	• Listening • Following directions • Aerobic health • Muscular endurance	Teacher tip—positive values, responsibility	Teacher tip—school environment, school personnel involvement
Heart Smart	169	• Aerobic health • Muscular endurance	Healthy lifestyle/restraint	• PE and classroom teacher cooperation • Alternative classroom activity

(continued)

(continued)

Activity	Page	Content connections	Asset action	Coordinated school health links
I Say Go	170	• Aerobic health • Muscular endurance • Agility • Coordination • Following directions • Sequencing	• Creative activities • Personal power	Alternative classroom activity
Lucky Draw	171	• Aerobic health • Flexibility • Strength	Cultural competence	• Activity student can do on own • Parental involvement
Summer Shuffle	172	• Aerobic health • Flexibility • Muscular endurance • Cooperation	• Interpersonal competence • Cultural competence	PE/health integration
Winter Wonderland	173	• Aerobic health • Quickness • Flexibility • Muscular endurance • Cooperation	Cultural competence	Physical health
Chapter 14—Spinners				
Color Detectives	176	• Locomotor skills • Spatial skills • Aerobic health • Flexibility • Muscular endurance • Cooperation	• Responsibility	• Alternative classroom activity • Activity student can do on own • Community connections
Go Loco	177	• Aerobic health • Locomotor skills • Muscular strength • Endurance	Teacher tip—safe, caring environment	PE/health integration
Obstacle Options	178	• Aerobic health • Locomotor skills • Muscular endurance	• Interpersonal competence • Peaceful conflict resolution	• Physical health • PE/health integration
Run and Gun	179	• Jogging • Sprinting • Aerobic health • Basketball shooting and passing	• School/learning engagement • Achievement motivation • Responsibility	• Physical health • PE/health integration
Strive to Survive	180	• Locomotor skills • Muscular endurance • Flexibility	Healthy lifestyle/restraint	• Lifetime health and fitness • PE/health integration
Wheel of Fitness	181	• Locomotor skills • Muscular endurance	• Bonding to school • Achievement motivation	Community/after school connections

Activity	Page	Content connections	Asset action	Coordinated school health links
Zone Fitness	182	• Locomotor skills • Aerobic health • Muscular endurance • Flexibility	Responsibility	Connection between physical health and mental, emotional, and social health
Chapter 15—Poly Spots				
Body Boogie	184	• Warm-up • Flexibility • Muscular endurance	• Achievement motivation • School/learning engagement • Bonding to school	Caring school environment
Connect the Dots	186	• Aerobic health • Muscular endurance • Agility • Kicking • Throwing • Catching • Dribbling	• High expectations • Achievement motivation • Personal power	PE/health integration
Dot Dash	187	• Chasing • Fleeing • Dodging • Tagging	Peaceful conflict resolution	• Lifetime health and fitness • PE/health integration
Dot Duos	188	• Locomotor skills • Muscular endurance • Flexibility • Aerobic health	• Interpersonal competence • Cultural competence • Adult role models	Connection between physical health and mental, emotional, and social health
Dot to Dot	190	• Aerobic health • Muscular endurance • Flexibility	Honesty	• Social health • Parental involvement
Hot Spot	191	Aerobic health	Adult role models	Parental, community involvement
Spots Are Wild	192	• Cooperation • Ball rolling • Bowling	• Caring • Honesty	• Lifetime health and fitness • PE/health integration
Stop the Clock	194	• Aerobic health • Muscular endurance	• Personal power • Caring	• Lifetime health and fitness • PE/health integration
Stretch City	196	• Flexibility • Aerobic health	Peaceful conflict resolution	Physical health
Target Fitness	197	• Tossing • Throwing • Aerobic health • Muscular endurance • Flexibility	Honesty	Teacher tip—connection between physical health and mental, emotional, and social health

(continued)

(continued)

Activity	Page	Content connections	Asset action	Coordinated school health links
Chapter 16—Food Labels and Pictures				
Food Fact Fitness	200	• Aerobic health • Muscular endurance • Flexibility • Healthy eating	Teacher tip—positive values, support structure	• Parental involvement • Lifetime health and fitness
"Go Away, Fat" Relay	202	• Aerobic health • Muscular endurance • Reading nutrition labels	Healthy lifestyle/restraint	• Lifetime health and fitness • School personnel involvement
Inside the Pyramid	203	• Aerobic health • Classifying foods	Healthy lifestyle/restraint	• Lifetime health and fitness • Parental involement
Junk Food Dodge	204	• Chasing • Dodging • Tagging • Healthy eating	• Positive family communica-tion • Parent involvement in schooling	• Lifetime health and fitness • School personnel involement
Label Locomotion	205	• Locomotor skills • Nutrition	Positive family communication	• PE and classroom teacher coop-eration • Lifetime health and fitness
Nutriball	206	• Ball handling • Throwing • Catching • Nutrition	Interpersonal competence	• Lifetime health and fitness • School personnel involvement
Nutrient Treasure Hunt	207	• Aerobic health • Muscular endurance • Identifying nutrients in foods • Reading and analyz-ing labels	• Healthy lifestyle/restraint • Achievement motivation • Parent involvement in schooling	• Activity student can do on own • Parental involvement • PE and classroom teacher coop-eration • School personnel involvement
Nutrition Addition	208	• Analyzing foods' nutritional value • Jumping	Planning and decision making	• Parental involvement • School personnel involement
Strive for Five	209	• Aerobic health • Flexibility • Healthy eating	Healthy lifestyle/restraint	• PE and classroom teacher coop-eration • Activity student can do on own • Alternative classroom activity • Parental involvement • School personnel involement

Preface

Physical education is anchored by such traditional concepts as teaching basic movement patterns, fitness, and social interaction skills. PE can meet the challenges of the obesity epidemic and the other medical problems associated with a sedentary society. However, to fulfill its potential, physical education must embrace new instructional approaches that meet the needs of all students. The activities and instructional choices presented in this book reflect such approaches.

Schools are realizing that their mission and responsibility must change if all students are to have a chance at success. Schools and physical educators are expanding their vision so that it includes a joint effort by families, schools, and communities to enrich the lives of all children. The instructional choices and activities in *PE Connections: Helping Kids Succeed Through Physical Activity* are based on current research on adolescent development and offer guidance toward quality PE that helps young people succeed.

What Can Schools Do?

The Carnegie Council on Adolescent Development has stated, "Schools could do more than perhaps any other single institution in society to help young people, and the adults they will become, live healthier, longer, more satisfying, and more productive lives" (Carnegie Council on Adolescent Development, 1989).

How can schools and communities best help students succeed in school and in life? What ideas and interventions will maximize students' chances of academic, physical, emotional, and social success? We believe that the instructional choices presented in this book will help PE teachers provide students with a wider spectrum of opportunities and positive experiences.

Objectives of This Book

1. Offer PE teachers, classroom teachers, and after-school providers of students aged 4 to 14 quality health and PE activities that the authors have used successfully in their classes and staff development workshops.

2. Use the physical activity setting as the basis for developing new instructional strategies. Chapters 3 and 4 describe two such strategies: developmental assets and coordinated school health.

3. Provide PE teachers with an integrated instructional approach designed to meet changing educational demands while addressing student health needs.

4. Provide valuable resource and background information for anyone interested in adolescent development. Part I (chapters 1 to 4) and the appendixes can be used by teachers, supervisors, parents who wish to be more involved in their child's schooling, public school systems or university preservice teachers interested in program expansion, or anyone else concerned with school health programs and student success.

Who Can Use This Book

This book can be used both inside and outside of PE settings. The activities provide students with a sound physical activity experience. Incorporating the concepts of developmental assets and coordinated school health into these activities expands students' possibilities of success.

We hope that readers will use this book to introduce the power of developmental asset building and coordinated school health to schools, parents, and communities. Both concepts are based on the premise that parents, schools, and community organizations must work together to provide the supportive environment that all children need for healthy development.

What Makes This Book Different?

The activities in *PE Connections*

- are easy to implement,
- encourage sustained activity,

- foster student enjoyment and success (see pages 8-9 for our criteria for student success in a physical activity), and
- can be adapted to different ages.

PE Connections offers the following useful and unique features:

- Three instructional approaches
- Enjoyable activities and teaching strategies that go beyond the objectives of movement skill, fitness, and social competency
- Activities grouped by equipment type
- Specific suggestions for making activities more or less challenging
- Easy-to-reproduce flash cards and exercise pictures
- An activity finder

Instructional Choices

PE Connections offers a new approach to teaching physical education. Part I describes instructional choices:

- Teaching quality physical education (chapter 2)
- Building developmental assets (chapter 3)
- Establishing coordinated school health (chapter 4)

Part II presents 136 health and physical education activities that provide a foundation for each of the three instructional choices. A PE teacher can use these instructional choices in planning and delivering instruction.

Summary

Commenting on the natural world's beauty and complexity, Chief Seattle of the Suquamish people once said, "All things are connected." As reflected in this book's title, we agree. The connections in *PE Connections* are links between physical activity and adult support that improve young people's chances of success. The instructional strategies presented are also connected. Quality physical education programs, developmental assets, and coordinated school health are connected by the common goal of enriching young people's health and well-being. Coordinated support from many different adults within a school community is much more likely to make a positive difference in the lives of youth than good programs working independently.

One form of connection familiar to PE instructors is the use of partners in PE activities. Having students form pairs or small groups fosters cooperation, goal setting, an ability to make friends, and an ability to accept others' differences. Further benefits result when adults from the school community partner and work together to help kids. In a school setting, such partnerships improve the school environment and student health. Changing a school environment into one in which young people feel supported and valued helps them feel better about school and do better in school. The best physical education instruction recognizes and builds connections. Let the journey begin.

Acknowledgments

We are indebted to all of the health and physical education professionals who encouraged us to compile our workshop and in-service material in book form. Many people, especially teachers, made valuable recommendations regarding activities and instructional strategies that were incorporated into this book.

This book would have remained incomplete without the assistance of individuals too numerous to mention. To each person who devoted his or her time in support of our efforts, we are very grateful.

Instructional Approaches to Physical Education

The primary objective of educators, including physical educators, is to help young people experience success. Traditionally, success in physical education has meant improved physical fitness, greater skill, and increased social competency. Chapters 1 through 4 explain how PE settings can enable students to experience success in a much broader sense.

Chapter 1 introduces the book's principles. Chapter 2 presents the first of three instructional approaches: quality physical education based on an instructional philosophy, introduced in the 1980s, called "New PE." Chapter 3 presents the second instructional approach: quality PE plus the building of developmental assets. Integrating asset building into physical education provides extra opportunities for students to experience success and reinforces positive values learned in other settings, such as the home. This instructional approach can become a school-, district-,

or community-wide endeavor. Chapter 4 presents the third instructional approach: adding health content to quality PE and asset development. Integrating health content into physical education is a major step toward coordinated school health in which school personnel, students' families, and the community collaborate to improve the school environment and provide students with the experiences and support that they need to develop into responsible adults.

Chapters 2 through 4 each discuss the background and philosophy of the instructional approach that they address and contain a section titled "What a Teacher Can Do," which tells teachers how to apply the theoretical information to a physical activity lesson plan. Whichever instructional approach a teacher uses, the combination of theory and practical application provides a basis for student experiences and outcomes not typically associated with physical education.

Developing a Successful Physical Education Program

© Human Kinetics

This book is about helping young people succeed in a much broader sense than is usually associated with a physical education class.

3

As teachers, we want our students to succeed in our physical education classes. We want them to acquire the knowledge and skills that provide a foundation for an enjoyable, physically active lifestyle. We want them to understand the relationship between physical activity and health. We also want the PE experience to be fun so that our students will enjoy physical activity now and for the rest of their lives. Today all of this is possible. Many physical education teachers have made the transition from an old sport-driven style of PE instruction to a contemporary style that meets the needs of all students and provides new opportunities for student success.

We want even more for children. We want them to succeed in every way. We want them to develop intellectually and do well in school; express their emotions constructively; cope with the demands of daily life; have healthy social lives and good relationships with friends, family, and teachers; avoid risky behaviors; and overcome adversity. We want them to develop positive qualities, referred to as "assets," that will guide them to responsible adulthood.

Can schools do a better job of helping young people to succeed in school and in life? Can physical education classes do more to enrich students' lives? We think so. This book explores new approaches to teaching physical education.

Need for New Approaches in Physical Education

Before we discuss methods of teaching quality PE (often called "New PE" or "Contemporary PE"), let's consider the aspects of old-style instruction that necessitated a new instructional model. The Key Points box summarizes four factors that contributed to the decline of traditional physical education.

KEY POINTS

Factors Leading to the Decline of Traditional Physical Education

- The failure of traditional PE to work for all students
- Acknowledgment of the relationship between physical activity and health
- 1996 report of the surgeon general
- Escalating obesity epidemic

The Failure of Traditional PE to Work for All Students

It was inevitable that another instructional model eventually would replace traditional PE, which didn't work for most students. In old-style physical education, success was limited to students with athletic skills. Old PE was based on an athletic or team-sport model with weak instructional strategies.

Within the old PE framework, athletes succeeded whereas nonathletes did not. Physical education may have been fun for athletes, but

© Human Kinetics

Traditional physical education that focuses mainly on sport instruction can leave students feeling frustrated and sitting on the sidelines.

other students often found PE classes frustrating, even humiliating (Adler, 1998). Rather than influencing the lives of young people in positive ways, in many schools the old PE impeded student success and created negative perceptions that have persisted for decades. Some schools have confronted PE's image problem by adopting a more contemporary instructional philosophy and developing programs that provide a rich variety of experiences and many opportunities for success.

The philosophy behind the new style of PE is to make sure that all students experience a variety of movement forms, rather than limiting the PE experience to traditional team sports and games such as softball, touch football, and basketball.

Acknowledgment of the Relationship Between Physical Activity and Health

A sedentary lifestyle is now considered a major risk factor for preventable diseases that shorten Americans' lives. It is important that physical education focus on physical activity and be enjoyable while improving health.

Before 1968, prevention generally received little attention, and biomedical professionals considered physical activity an unimportant health topic. That all changed when the concept of aerobics was introduced to the world.

The impetus to get people moving in this country, and around the world, began after the 1968 publication of the best-selling book *Aerobics* by Dr. Kenneth Cooper, founder of the Cooper Aerobics Center in Dallas, Texas. Equally important, research conducted by the Cooper Aerobics Center and published in the *Journal of the American Medical Association* (Blair et al., 1989) confirmed that moderate physical activity substantially reduces the risk of premature death from some leading causes of death in the United States. Called the Aerobics Center Longitudinal Study (ACLS), the study followed thousands of Cooper Clinic patients to determine factors associated with health and longevity. Dr. Steven Blair, the Cooper Institute's president and CEO, as well as the study's principal investigator, has explained the health ramifications of the ACLS, which used an objective measure of physical fitness through maximal treadmill stress testing: (Fleming, 1989, p. 56):

Most of the studies in the exercise epidemiology area have related self-report on physical activity habits or, as in earlier studies, occupational physical activity was related to risk of disease, usually cardiovascular. But one of the surprising things from the ACLS study is that it doesn't take a whole lot of fitness to provide what appear to be optimal levels of protection.

The old PE emphasized high-level fitness, acquired through vigorous activities such as jogging and running. The ACLS study provided the first "proof" that moderate activity could improve health dramatically. The new PE activities in this book provide moderate intensity activities that kids enjoy.

The 1996 Report of the Surgeon General

The ACLS also influenced the 1996 surgeon general's report *Physical Activity and Health* (U.S. Department of Health and Human Services). In fact, Blair served as senior scientific editor for the report, which noted that 40 percent of U.S. deaths are caused by behavior patterns that could be modified.

The 1996 surgeon general's report summarized findings from decades of research on the relationship between physical activity and health. These were the two most important findings:

1. Physical activity need not be strenuous to confer health benefits.
2. Inactive people can improve their health and well-being by becoming moderately active on a regular basis.

The report indicated that getting people to move from low- to moderate-level physical activity by walking would reduce their chances of premature death by 50 percent. Despite the proven benefits of physical activity and assurances from medical professionals that regular physical activity generally prolongs life, more than half of U.S. adults don't engage in sufficient physical activity to reap health benefits.

The Escalating Obesity Epidemic

The surgeon general's 1996 report, published as new PE, was gaining momentum in the United States and emphasized that physical inactivity is a major factor in the obesity epidemic. As reported in a special issue of *Time* magazine devoted to the subject of obesity, "It's hardly news anymore that Americans are just too fat, and our individual weight problems have become a national crisis" (Lemonick, 2004, p.59).

A combination of factors has caused the epidemic, but the two main culprits are poor diet and insufficient physical activity. Together they account for at least 365,000 deaths in the United States each year (Blair, 2005). Only tobacco use contributes to a greater number of preventable deaths (440,000) (Centers for Disease Control and Prevention, 2005).

According to the Centers for Disease Control and Prevention (2006), an estimated 30 percent of U.S. Adults aged 20 or older—more than 60 million people—are obese, and 16 percent of U.S. children and adolescents (ages 6-19) are overweight, triple the 1980 percentage. The sidebar below highlights some interesting facts related to the obesity epidemic and the sobering reality that combating obesity will be a formidable challenge, especially in a technological society that has largely removed physical activity from most Americans' daily lives.

Type 2 diabetes is rapidly becoming a worldwide epidemic. Eighty percent of the cases are related to obesity. The disease usually appears in middle age. However, due to the spiraling rate of childhood obesity in the United States, caused primarily by poor diet and physical inactivity, type

© Human Kinetics

It's important to get students up and moving!

Facts Related to the Obesity Epidemic in the United States

- In 1969, 80 percent of children played sports every day; today only 20 percent do.
- By age 17 a child has spent 38 percent more time in front of the TV than in school.
- In most gym classes, kids are aerobically active for only three minutes.
- Nearly all high schools have vending machines; on average, teens get 10 to 15 percent of their daily calories from soda.
- 25 percent of U.S. vegetable consumption is of french fries.
- In 1957 a typical hamburger weighed 1 ounce and contained 210 calories. Today it weighs 6 ounces and contains 618 calories.

Lemonick, 2004.

2 diabetes is now showing up in children. Just 15 years ago medical schools were teaching students that the disease was rarely found in people younger than 40; physicians now are seeing the disease in children younger than 10.

The problems associated with poor diet and inactivity are well documented. The solution lies in motivating millions of adults to change their lifestyle and in helping millions of schoolchildren to establish healthy habits at an early age. A good place to start is to establish quality PE programs in schools.

A School's Mission

We believe that schools, especially PE classes, can do much more to improve young people's chances for positive development and success.

Many schools limit their mission statements to academic goals. "The overwhelming concern of all educators is to ensure that every student demonstrates good performance to challenging academic standards," one such statement notes (Bogden, 2003, p. 8). Academic achievement is only one part of successful human development. Success in school is closely tied to school environment and includes all dimensions of health. According to research conducted and published by Search Institute in Minneapolis, Minnesota, in order to help children develop intellectually, emotionally, socially, and physically, schools must provide an environment in which students feel safe, secure, cared for, and valued, a place where they feel they belong and can make a contribution (Starkman, Scales, & Roberts, 1999). The research confirms a fact that the educational community often overlooks: "Children who feel better about school do better in school" (p. 2).

Rethinking the Mission of a School

The importance of a school's environment in reducing unhealthy behaviors in adolescents and increasing their chances of succeeding in school is well documented. The National Longitudinal Study of Adolescent Health states the following: "When adolescents feel cared for by people at their school and feel like a part of the school, they are less likely to use substances, engage in violence, or initiate sexual activity at an earlier age" (McNeely, Nonnemaker, & Blum, 2002, p. 138).

Many educators believe that school health programs (such as physical education and classroom health education) not only help to prevent social problems and improve a school's environment but also help to develop important assets such as responsibility, resilience, and cultural competence (feeling comfortable around people of different cultural or racial backgrounds) (Kolbe, 2002).

Taking account of the research just cited, a revised mission statement might read, "The mission of a school is to educate students and assist in their intellectual, emotional, physical, and social development by providing a safe, secure, and caring school environment within which learning and student success can best occur" (Starkman et al. p.3).

Rethinking the Mission of Physical Education

Just as schools can increase students' chances for success by rethinking their mission, PE instructors can provide opportunities and experiences that contribute more fully to an improved school environment and student development by rethinking the mission of physical education.

Traditional physical education is based on an outdated model centered on team sports, athletics, an excessive emphasis on physical fitness, and inappropriate teaching strategies (Fleming, 2001). It meets the needs of only the athletically gifted. Other students simply accumulate unpleasant experiences. Today many schools are moving toward more-inclusive approaches to PE that meet the needs of all students. The mission statements of many PE programs include the health benefits of a physically active lifestyle, a student-centered orientation that provides opportunities for each student to succeed, and activity programs based on the characteristics of quality physical education.

Successful Physical Education Instruction

This book is about health and physical education activities, increased health literacy, enhanced physical fitness, elevated skill levels, and improved social competence. However, it's also about helping young people to succeed in a broader sense.

To help students succeed, we must implement broader instructional strategies. *PE Connections: Helping Kids Succeed Through Physical Activity* is about providing PE teachers with instructional choices that can improve students' chances for success. The instructional choices presented in this book require new levels of commitment by teachers, schools, and communities. Each instructional choice has criteria that determine if a student is successful.

Choice 1: Teaching Quality Physical Education Activities

Choice 1 emphasizes student outcomes consistent with contemporary physical education objectives such as fitness, skill development, and socializa-

KEY POINTS
Instructional Choices for the Teacher

Instructional Choice	Instructional content	Chapter
1	Quality PE activities	2
2	Quality PE activities and developmental assets	3
3	Quality PE activities, developmental assets, and health content	4

tion. Instruction is based on the characteristics of a quality PE program (see chapter 2). Teachers can use the quality PE activities in this book in their daily lesson plans.

We've found that teachers and students succeed in this model if students do the following:

1. Participate in and enjoy a variety of physical activities.

2. Exhibit characteristics of a physically educated person. For example, they understand that physical activity provides opportunities for enjoyment, challenge, self-expression, and social interaction; demonstrate understanding of and respect for differences among people in physical activity settings; and demonstrate competence in many movement forms and proficiency in a few movement forms (Texas Essential Knowledge and Skills, 1997).

Choice 2: Quality Physical Education Activities Plus Developmental Assets

Choice 2 explains that physical education teachers should use activities to go beyond traditional PE objectives and focus on building positive characteristics in young people not generally associated with PE (see chapter 3). Focusing on building developmental assets is a proven, research-driven approach designed to help young people develop the skills and tools they need to succeed. Introduced by Search Institute in 1989,

© Human Kinetics

Choice 1 emphasizes physical activity for everyone and addresses mental, emotional, and social growth as well as physical growth.

the developmental assets framework has been adopted by more than 1,400 communities and can be initiated in YMCAs, religious communities, schools, homes, and other settings, including PE classes.

Search Institute has identified 40 developmental assets, or "building blocks of human development that help children grow up healthy, caring, and responsible" (Welch, 2004, p. 9). These 40 assets help children make good decisions and grow up less likely to engage in problem behaviors (Benson et al., 1998). Instructional choice 2 encourages PE teachers to build or reinforce developmental assets in the physical activity setting. For example, it is easy to help students build the asset of cultural competence (asset 34) simply by having them work together. Children build cultural competence when they are comfortable with their own cultural identity and with people of different racial, ethnic, and cultural backgrounds (Benson et al., 1998).

In this model students are successful if they meet the following criteria:

- Engage in behaviors that promote cooperation, fair play, and responsible participation.
- Demonstrate resiliency in the face of challenge and are willing to try new experiences (Scales, Sesma, & Bolstrom, 2004).
- Engage in positive actions—such as regularly helping others and valuing racial and ethnic diversity—that suggest optimal development, or thriving (Scales et al.).

Choice 3: Quality PE Activities Plus Health Content and Developmental Assets

The role of many PE teachers now includes health teacher. This role results from a number of developments:

- Research has demonstrated that regular physical activity confers health benefits (U.S. Department of Health and Human Services, 1996). Choice 3 allows a teacher to integrate various health topics into quality PE activities and perhaps champion a coordinated health program within a school or district (see chapter 4).
- An emphasis on core subjects (math, reading, science, social studies) has changed the PE teacher's instructional responsibility in some elementary schools and requires that many PE teachers also teach health. Although PE teachers have integrated some health instruction into their classes for years, they're doing this to a greater extent now that elementary classroom teachers are devoting more instructional time to academic, state-tested subjects such as math and reading.

An increased need to teach health has prompted some PE teachers to add the goal of health literacy to their classes. Defined as the "capacity of an individual to obtain, interpret, and understand basic health information and services and the

A PE setting is ideal for building and reinforcing developmental assets.

© Human Kinetics

competence to use such information and services in ways that are health-enhancing" (Curriculum Development and Supplemental Materials Commission, 2003), health literacy is an important goal in any health-promotion setting, including physical education. The concept is embedded in many state health frameworks and coordinated school health programs and reflects a shift from an emphasis on imparting information to an emphasis on developing skills that will help students use health information effectively.

California has developed a health curriculum framework for grades K-12 that connects curriculum standards, school health programs, and health literacy in a way designed to improve young people's health and well-being (Curriculum Development and Supplemental Materials Commission, 2003). The framework's four criteria for health literacy in grade-schoolers are excellent measures of student success. Utilizing instructional choice 3 will help students acquire these qualities:

- Acceptance of personal responsibility for lifelong health
- Respect for and promotion of others' health

- An understanding of the process of growth and development
- Informed use of health-related information, products, and services

Connections and Instructional Choices

In an ideal world we might have written a book only about instructional choice 3, Quality PE Activities Plus Health Content and Developmental Assets. Such a book would have extolled the virtues of a coordinated school health program, and there would have been no need to discuss other instructional approaches. A coordinated school health program would include quality physical education, classroom instruction, nutrition/cafeteria services, parental involvement, and build students' developmental assets. However, because relatively few U.S. school districts have coordinated school health programs and intentionally build assets in students, we recommend using physical education as a way of introducing coordinated school health and developmental assets to a school community.

© Human Kinetics

A program that emphasizes overall health can help students learn to make healthy food choices, a lesson that can last far beyond a student's school days.

As the title *PE Connections: Helping Kids Succeed Through Physical Activity* indicates, starting with separate but connected components can move schools toward an ideal health model. As you read this book, keep in mind that physical education, asset building, and coordinated school health programs improve your students' chances of success. Imagine the possibilities for success if the three choices were combined into one coordinated school health program in each U.S. school.

Summary

Although this book provides more than 100 quality health and physical education activities, the teacher's instructional focus and intent are key to moving the PE experience beyond those outcomes commonly associated with physical education.

A PE class can be much more than physical fitness. It should teach movement skills and provide enjoyable activities. Even if your teaching style is contemporary, you provide quality activities, and your students love your class, we hope that you'll consider trying instructional choice 2 or 3. Your students will greatly benefit as your concept of what constitutes student success within a PE class expands.

Teaching Quality Physical Education

© Human Kinetics

Physical activity has been, and will continue to be, the backbone of physical education.

Today's PE teacher faces multiple challenges when planning and delivering instruction.

Research on health and physical activity affects a teacher's instructional decisions.

Contemporary PE instruction helps all students to succeed.

13

Quality physical education is a matter of philosophy as well as curriculum. It focuses on physical activity goals rather than physical fitness and athletic-driven outcomes; it provides all students an opportunity to succeed. Teachers of quality PE may emphasize different aspects of physical education, but they share the same basic vision of physical education as a way to help people enjoy physical activity now and for the rest of their lives. The sidebar below lists the characteristics on which all of the activities presented in this book are based.

Old and New Physical Education Models

A good way to grasp the difference between traditional (old) PE and quality (new) PE is to compare these instructional approaches. It's easy to see from table 2.1 why the old model didn't work for most students and why new PE is much more attractive to them: the new model meets the needs of all students.

What a Teacher Can Do

A successful PE program can't be built overnight. It takes motivation, sound planning, and good class management. It requires that PE teachers implement new instructional strategies and evaluate their teaching by reflecting on the results of lessons taught. The volume of information related to quality programming can overwhelm a PE teacher. The key points below offer guidelines that can be gradually implemented in any teaching situation.

KEY POINTS

Building a Successful Physical Education Program

- Embrace new techniques of PE instruction; stay abreast of current ideas about quality physical education.
- Use positive instructional strategies.
- Use effective class management techniques.

Characteristics of Quality Physical Education

- Emphasizes knowledge and skills for a lifetime of physical activity
- Is based on national standards that define what students should know and be able to do
- Keeps students active for most of the class time
- Provides many physical activity choices
- Meets the needs of all students, including those who are not athletic
- Features cooperative as well as competitive games
- Develops student self-confidence and eliminates practices that humiliate students (e.g., having team captains choose team members or playing dodgeball or other elimination games)
- Assesses students based on their progress in reaching goals, not their achievement in terms of some absolute standard
- Promotes physical activity outside of school
- Teaches self-management skills such as goal-setting and self-monitoring
- Actively teaches cooperation, fair play, and responsible participation in physical activity
- Is an enjoyable experience for students
- Improves overall school climate
- Positively influences students' lives by providing positive experiences and encouraging positive relationships and personal qualities (see chapter 3)
- Integrates and coordinates health and physical education instruction while establishing the framework for a coordinated school health program (see chapter 4)

*The first twelve characteristics are derived from the Texas Education Agency, 2002.
Copyright © Texas Education Agency. All rights reserved.

Table 2.1   Contrasting PE Instructional Styles

Traditional approach	Contemporary approach
Curriculum is based on an outdated perception of varsity sports, an athletic model, and sport-specific activities.	Curriculum is based on developmentally appropriate physical education. Lessons fit individuals' needs, developmental status, previous experience, fitness and skill levels, and body size and shape.
Students play in large groups.	Students play individually, in pairs, or in small groups.
Activities are teacher-directed, with little student choice.	Activities are teacher-facilitated, with student input.
Students share a few pieces of equipment.	Each student has equipment.
Focus is on keeping score and winning or losing.	Competition is a choice; cooperation is encouraged.
Inappropriate practices predominate.	Quality instructional practices are in place.
A team-line approach is used; everyone in a large group does the same thing.	Individualized work stations are used; the approach is child-oriented for interest and high participation.
Students play lead-up games and activities that look like (and with rules like) the real thing.	Activities include choices that help students meet expectations.
Few or no activities focus on health topics other than physical activity.	Some activities teach nontraditional physical education topics such as nutrition, conflict resolution, and resistance skills.

Embrace New Instructional Techniques

PE instructors should embrace the concepts behind a quality PE program and stay abreast of current ideas regarding instructional strategies.

- Plan lessons and activities so that students experience a variety of activities, experience success, and have fun. Many PE teachers use a four-part lesson format that includes the following (see appendix A on page 212 for the complete lesson):
  - Introductory or warm-up activity
  - Fitness activity
  - Lesson or skill focus
  - Closing
- Stay current in the field. In today's world of Internet access, a wealth of information on quality physical education is readily available. For example, you can instantly obtain detailed information about national standards in physical education from Web sites such as those of the American Association for Health, Physical Education, Recreation and Dance (AAHPERD) and the National Association for Sport and Physical Education (NASPE). You also can get the latest information about developmentally appropriate PE programs for children and youth at the PE Central Web site. (This book's References and Resources lists include health and PE Web sites.) Here, we translate the array of information about quality PE programs into a workable summary that includes effective activities.
- To get started, look at what other schools, districts, and states are doing. Conferences, in-services, and the Internet can provide valuable information on quality PE programs. For example, take a quick trip to the Seattle Public Schools Web site and see how Seattle's new PE contrasts with the old athletic model. Seattle Public Schools used the acronym PHYSICAL to promote quality physical education (see table 2.2).

Table 2.2 The "New" Physical Education in Seattle

Is educational	Rather than merely recreational
P = planned and purposeful	Just rolling out the ball
H = health-related	Game-oriented
Y = youth-centered	Teacher-directed
S = success-oriented	Winners and losers
I = inclusive	Eliminates the less skilled
C = cooperative	Competitive
A = all active	Waiting for turns
L = lifetime focus	Only traditional sports

From *Ready-to-Use Pre-Sport Skills Activities Program* by L.F. "Bud" Turner and Susan L. Turner, © 2001 by Pearson Education, Inc., publishing as Parker Publishing. Used by permission.

Use Positive Instructional Strategies

Most converts to a contemporary PE model agree that the greatest curriculum in the world, if taught with a traditional approach, will probably fall short of helping all students to enjoy physical activity now and for the rest of their lives. Without instructional strategies grounded in the philosophy of quality PE and energized by teachers with a student-oriented focus, physical education is likely to fail at a time when it should be one of the most important components of the school day (Weir, 2000).

We think that the following instructional strategies are indispensable for quality PE.

Instructional Strategies

- Eliminate activities that are purposeless, dangerous, or likely to embarrass or humiliate students (as line basketball and dodgeball often do).
- Provide choices for students. Just knowing that they were given a choice can encourage students to participate and help students and teachers meet their goals. During a lesson's fitness portion, you might give student a choice of jogging, walking fast, or jumping rope for a designated time.
- Have students work in small groups or pairs as often as possible to maximize participation and practice time. This strategy contrasts sharply with the traditional PE emphasis on large groups of students, all of whom are doing the same thing.

- Begin class with an introductory activity that provides a transition from a classroom environment to a physical activity setting and prepares the body for physical activity.
- Try to have half of the class time devoted to moderate to vigorous physical activity. Reportedly, in most U.S. gym classes students are aerobically active, on average, for only 3 minutes (Lemonick, 2004).
- Integrate fitness into most lessons in such a way that the activity reflects a student's personal best effort and goal setting rather than strict adherence to a predetermined standard (such as a set time in which the student must run a mile). Focus on activities that are fun, encourage improvement (e.g., personal records), and place emphasis on using time instead of repetitions.
- Provide a variety of activities. Allow students to select activities and equipment suited to their interests and abilities.

For additional ideas and details, see the Web links in References and Resources.

Use Effective Class Management Techniques

Physical education classes are dynamic environments with different types of equipment and many students of varied abilities. A successful PE class requires preparation. Good management is necessary for creating a safe, secure, productive environment conducive to learning.

© Human Kinetics

Simple changes in instructional strategy, such as allowing students to work in small groups, can help students enjoy physical activity.

Effective PE teachers plan and direct the lesson. They choose appropriate lessons and equipment, give instructions, keep students on task, and move students in and out of activities. Teachers who carefully consider their instructional and management strategies will accomplish their lesson objectives and improve the chances that students will be safe, have fun, and succeed (Fleming, 2006).

Making MOVES in the Gym

To better manage their PE program, teachers can use the acronym MOVES:

M   Moderate to vigorous activity during class

O   Opportunity to be active outside of a PE class

V   Variety of and within activities

E   Enjoyment of physical activity

S   Success in applying physical activity, health, and asset-building concepts

The MOVES acronym provides teachers with a simple checklist that they can use to evaluate the activities and whether activity goals and student needs are being met within the lesson.

Managing Physical Activity Sessions

Although quality instructional activities are important because they allow teachers to meet objectives and standards, class management and its accompanying strategies bring order and success to any physical activity session or PE classroom. Because of physical education's dynamic environment, students' varied ability levels, safety issues, the large number of participants, and the demands of hands-on teaching and learning, the teacher or physical activity director faces many challenges. Class management includes establishing rules and routines, implementing them, and reviewing them often. By following the tips in the sidebar on page 18, PE teachers can increase the chances that their students will have fun, learn, be safe, and succeed. Learning time will increase, and distractions will decrease. Combined with traditional classroom methods, acting on these tips will enhance students' learning experience and allow teachers to focus on teaching instead of on micromanagement of classes.

© Human Kinetics

A physical education program should allow students to engage in some moderate to vigorous activity in class.

Activity Management Tips

Tip 1

Create a positive learning environment that includes rules, boundaries, and expectations.

Tip 2

Establish classroom routines and teach them to students.

Just as classroom teachers have classroom protocols, PE teachers must establish routines at the beginning of the year. These routines should be taught and practiced during the first few weeks of the school year in order to establish class structure and expectations. The goal is for the routines to become automatic. They allow for safe movement, traveling, transitions, and action during lessons.

Teachers should create their own routines to meet their students' needs. The routines for physical activity may include how to

- enter and exit the gym,
- stop on signals,
- get equipment,
- listen,
- form groups, and
- get a drink of water.

All routines should be posted in three or four simple steps for students to see. Once students have learned the routines, revisit them often to remind students of the expectations for movement in class. A sign describing the routine for stopping play when signaled might read as follows:

How to Stop on the Signal When Playing

1. Freeze.
2. Put any equipment on the floor between your feet.
3. Put your hands on your hips.
4. Look at the teacher.

Tip 3

Prepare for the lesson beforehand.

Prepare the lesson, room, and equipment. Know the needs and abilities of the students in each class. Consider potential pitfalls and devise appropriate solutions. Have alternative activities ready.

Tip 4

Give clear, concise instructions.

Students are most likely to remember instructions when they're brief (e.g., three or four sentences). Give the directions and then briefly repeat them. Always begin the directions with "When I say, 'Go'" in order to cue the students to begin activity. For example, you might say, "When I say, 'Go,' walk, get one beanbag, go to your own space, and put the beanbag on your head." Stop the activity if a student isn't following the directions. Repeat the directions to big groups as necessary.

Tip 5

Plan for transitions during class.

Check out traffic patterns and equipment placement so that students can move quickly and safely. Tell students ahead of time that the class will be changing activities in a certain amount of time. For example, you might say, "Students, in five minutes you'll be putting your beanbags away. When I say, 'Go,' find a new partner and continue to toss and catch underhand until I say, 'Stop.'"

Tip 6

Keep students in view at all times.

Keep your back to the wall. Teach from the perimeter of the area from a variety of spots.

Tip 7

Use music to motivate students and encourage participation.

Tip 8

Link students' reactions in class to developmental assets.

Praise students who are working responsibly. Give them points for responsible behaviors. Have them add up their points during class to see how many points they can get for the day. Give points for caring, encouraging, sharing, listening, stopping on the signal, coming to class dressed for movement, and so on.

Tip 9

Guide students to a conflict corner to resolve relationship problems.

Establish a conflict corner. Cut out a paper table and hang it on the wall. Students can sit in front of the paper table to work out their problems. See the References and Resources section for Web sites on conflict resolution.

Tip 10

After lessons, reflect on them and, if necessary, redesign them.

As necessary, make notes on plans to redesign or reteach routines. (See "Four-Part Lesson Format" in appendix A.)

Conflict Resolution Strategies

A major goal of this book is to help students succeed in school and in life. Physical education teachers can help their students develop the skills and strategies necessary for success. One of the most important skills for anyone to learn is how to get along with other people. Social, or interpersonal, skills are important because we all must interact with others throughout our lives. A major component of interpersonal skills is the ability to resolve conflicts as they arise. Conflicts are inevitable among children of elementary and middle-school age. The authors have successfully applied the following tips for many years:

Tips

1. Remind students that bullying, fighting, pushing, or any other kind of harming is not allowed in class. That includes hurtful speech.

2. Teach conflict resolution skills. Sit down with the class and discuss potential conflicts. Also, discuss minor conflicts before they escalate. For example, if two students want to use the same ball, you might tell the students to play Rock, Paper, Scissors to determine which student gets to use the ball this time. Alternatively, the students could decide which of them will use the ball this time and which will use it next time.

3. Teach students to use "I" messages. Search Institute suggests the following formula for an "I" message: "I feel _____ when _____ because _____. I want you to_____." (Benson et al., 1998, p.185). Instead of saying, "You make me so mad when you kick the ball I'm using," a student could use an "I" message: "I feel *angry* when *you kick the ball away* because *then I have to chase after it and I lose playing time.* I want you to *wait for your turn.*" The "I" message is less confrontational.

4. Choose a corner, and label it either "Conflict Corner" or, as Search Institute suggests, "Peace Place" (Benson et al., 1998, p.186). Cut out a paper table and put it on the floor or wall in a place where students can pretend to sit at the table. The corner can serve two purposes: More than one student can go there to quietly resolve a conflict by talking and negotiating a solution, or a student can go there alone to relax, calm down, or diffuse anger. Post the following rules for resolving conflicts (Benson et al., 1998):

- If someone asks you to go to the corner, go.
- Be respectful.
- Take turns speaking and listening.
- Use "I" messages.
- Stay calm.
- Ask for a teacher's help if you can't negotiate a solution.

How to Solve a Problem

You can post the following message on the classroom or gym wall.

- Invite the other people involved in the conflict to the Conflict Corner or Peace Place.
- Go to the Conflict Corner or Peace Place if someone asks you to.
- Listen to the others involved.
- Allow everyone involved to talk.
- Don't blame others. Use "I" messages such as, "I feel bad when you won't share the equipment with me because then I don't get to practice. I want you to share so I can have a turn."
- Use respectful words.
- Get help if things don't work out.

Summary

The basic instructional choice presented in this book (choice 1) is to teach a physical education class using contemporary PE philosophy and characteristics that are incorporated into the activities found in part II. Teachers can apply these activities, and the concepts explained in this chapter, in either a PE class or an after-school program. To help young people succeed in the broadest sense, a teacher can select instructional choice 2 (see chapter 3), which incorporates developmental assets into activity lessons. Choice 2 allows physical education teachers to use their particular PE environment and the activities in this book to build and reinforce students' developmental assets. Building developmental assets in a PE or other physical activity setting is the subject of chapter 3.

Building Developmental Assets

© Human Kinetics

Developmental assets strongly influence young people's lives.

Schools can directly affect many developmental assets.

Developmental assets increase a person's chances of succeeding in school and in life.

Quality physical education programs build students' assets.

This chapter focuses on instructional choice 2, quality physical education activities plus developmental assets. PE teachers can use the activities in this book to provide instruction that builds developmental assets. A short story will illustrate the general concept of developmental assets. Please read the story of Eddie Chavez in the shaded box.

Eddie has experienced the power of developmental assets simply through being recognized and greeted by name by his teachers. Calling each student by name helps students to feel cared for and supported. Adult support helps young people develop into caring, competent adults. Ms. Perkins' use of developmental assets in her PE class contributed to Peach Tree Elementary's being an asset-rich environment.

An asset-rich environment is a place where students feel valued, safe, and secure, a place where students sense that adults care about them and their success. A physical activity setting has the potential to become a powerful, asset-rich environment.

What Are Developmental Assets?

Search Institute (Starkman, Scales, and Roberts, 1999) has identified 40 developmental assets that strongly influence young people's lives (see table 3.1). Assets are developmental building blocks—positive experiences, opportunities, relationships, values, and qualities that guide individuals, give them direction, and enable them to succeed in school and in life.

Starkman, Scales, and Roberts (1999) divide developmental assets into external and internal assets. External assets are the positive experiences and relationships that are made available to young people, especially by the adults in their lives.

Eddie Chavez held his sister's hand as they crossed a busy intersection on their way to school. Until three years ago, Eddie's family had lived in a small Mexican town. Now they lived in a sprawling city on the Texas Gulf Coast. The early August heat reminded Eddie of his previous home. He was a fifth-grader and his sister, Aida, a fourth-grader at Peach Tree Elementary. Turning the corner on Elm Street, Eddie and Aida spotted the yellow school buses and the children near the school. They began to run and laugh. Eddie remembered being scared at the start of the second grade. Learning a new language had been hard, making new friends in a strange place even harder. He had cried every day. He had wanted to go back to Mexico, where people knew who he was and where he felt he belonged. This year he couldn't wait to go back to school.

As Eddie walked Aida to her classroom, greetings from classmates came from all directions. Mr. Sanchez, a third-grade teacher, smiled and welcomed them back to school. Ms. Hobbs, the cafeteria manager, stopped and hugged both of them. As Eddie said good-bye to Aida, he thought, *The teachers all seem to care about me. They tell me that I'm a hard worker. I have many friends at school, which is a place where everyone feels important. My friends and I agree that the school is like another home since Ms. Perkins, the new PE teacher, came to our school.*

As she had done for three years, Ms. Perkins stood at the entrance to the old gym and greeted each of the first-period students by name, all 52 of them! Eddie didn't remember any other teacher ever doing that. Ms. Perkins loved the children, and they loved her. She made each student feel important. Eddie liked the different activities in her class, especially when they were accompanied by music because he loved to dance. Ms. Perkins displayed colorful posters around the gym. These posters and the PE activities taught lessons such as the need to care about other people and to be honest, fair, and responsible. Ms. Perkins was Eddie's favorite teacher, and physical education was his favorite class.

As Eddie hurried to his homeroom after physical education, he noticed that his teacher, Mr. Lacy, wasn't sitting at his desk as he had done on the previous year's first day of class. Instead he was standing at the door and greeting each student as they entered the room, just as Ms. Perkins did.

"Hello, Eddie! How was your summer?"

As Mr. Lacy continued to greet each student at the door, Eddie knew it was going to be a very good year.

Table 3.1 Developmental Assets

Asset type		Asset name and definition
External assets	Support	1. Family support—Family life provides high levels of love and support. 2. Positive family communication—Young person and her or his parent(s) communicate positively, and young person is willing to seek advice and counsel from parent(s). 3. Other adult relationships—Young person receives support from three or more nonparent adults. 4. Caring neighborhood—Young person experiences caring neighbors. 5. Caring school climate—School provides a caring, encouraging environment. 6. Parent involvement in schooling—Parent(s) are actively involved in helping young person succeed in school.
	Empowerment	7. Community values youth—Young person perceives that adults in the community value youth. 8. Youth as resources—Young people are given useful roles in the community. 9. Service to others—Young person serves in the community one hour or more per week. 10. Safety—Young person feels safe at home, at school, and in the neighborhood.
	Boundaries and expectations	11. Family boundaries—Family has clear rules and consequences and monitors the young person's whereabouts. 12. School boundaries—School provides clear rules and consequences. 13. Neighborhood boundaries—Neighbors take responsibility for monitoring young people's behavior. 14. Adult role models—Parent(s) and other adults model positive, responsible behavior. 15. Positive peer influence—Young person's best friends model responsible behavior. 16. High expectations—Both parent(s) and teachers encourage the young person to do well.
	Constructive use of time	17. Creative activities—Young person spends three or more hours per week in lessons or practice in music, theater, or other arts. 18. Youth programs—Young person spends three or more hours per week in sports, clubs, or organizations at school and/or in the community. 19. Religious community—Young person spends one or more hours per week in activities in a religious institution. 20. Time at home—Young person is out with friends "with nothing special to do" two or fewer nights per week.

(continued)

Table 3.1 *(continued)*

Asset type		Asset name and definition
Internal assets	Commitment to learning	21. Achievement motivation—Young person is motivated to do well in school. 22. School engagement—Young person is actively engaged in learning. 23. Homework—Young person reports doing at least one hour of homework every school day. 24. Bonding to school—Young person cares about her or his school. 25. Reading for pleasure—Young person reads for pleasure three or more hours per week.
	Positive values	26. Caring—Young person places high value on helping other people. 27. Equality and social justice—Young person places high value on promoting equality and reducing hunger and poverty. 28. Integrity—Young person acts on convictions and stands up for her or his beliefs. 29. Honesty—Young person "tells the truth even when it is not easy." 30. Responsibility—Young person accepts and takes personal responsibility. 31. Restraint—Young person believes it is important not to be sexually active or to use alcohol or other drugs.
	Social competencies	32. Planning and decision making—Young person knows how to plan ahead and make choices. 33. Interpersonal competence—Young person has empathy, sensitivity, and friendship skills. 34. Cultural competence—Young person has knowledge of and comfort with people of different cultural/racial/ethnic backgrounds. 35. Resistance skills—Young person can resist negative peer pressure and dangerous situations. 36. Peaceful conflict resolution—Young person seeks to resolve conflict nonviolently.
	Positive identity	37. Personal power—Young person feels he or she has control over "things that happen to me." 38. Self-esteem—Young person reports having a high self-esteem. 39. Sense of purpose—Young person reports that "my life has a purpose." 40. Positive view of personal future—Young person is optimistic about her or his personal future.

External assets fall into four categories: support, empowerment, boundaries and expectations, and constructive use of time. Internal assets are the skills and values that young people need to make good choices in life. The level of support that young people receive from adults influences their internal assets, which fall into four categories: commitment to learning, positive values, social competencies, and positive identity.

Originally Search Institute developed a list of 40 developmental assets intended for use with children in grades 6 to 12. Search Institute then modified the list for use only with younger children (Scales et al., 2004). Two assets that were modified (assets 22 and 31) are used in some of the activities in this book. Originally, asset 22 was called "school engagement." However, with reference only to elementary-aged children, asset

© Human Kinetics

The benefits of addressing developmental assets are easy to see in students' behavior.

22 is called "learning engagement" to emphasize how important it is that younger children develop an interest in learning, whether inside or outside the school environment. Originally, asset 31 was called "restraint" and defined as the young person's belief that "it is important not to be sexually active or to use alcohol or other drugs." Restricted to elementary-age children, asset 31 is referred to as "healthy lifestyle" and described as "good health habits and an understanding of human sexuality." Consistent with younger children's developmental level, the revised assets focus on healthy lifestyle behaviors such as physical activity, sound nutrition, and interpersonal skills.

The Power of Assets

Developmental assets are powerful because they work. Search Institute has surveyed more than two million young people across the United States and Canada since 1989 (Search, May 2006). Results consistently show that the more developmental assets young people have, the more successful they are in both school and life. For example, they get better grades and are less inclined to engage in risky behavior. Search research shows that 61% of the students surveyed who reported only having 0 to 10 assets engaged in violent behavior. Only 7% of students who reported having 31 to 40 assets engaged in violent behavior. Differences were also shown in a student's tendency to maintain good health. Only 26% of the students who reported having 0 to 10 said they took good care of their bodies by eating healthy foods or exercising regularly. 89% of students who reported having 31 to 40 assets said they maintained good health habits. Assets help young people grow up to be more caring, responsible, and resilient (Benson, 1997).

According to a 1998 survey (Benson et al.), on average a young person in the United States achieves only about 18 of the 40 assets. Search Institute (March 2005) maintains that a young person must possess approximately 30 of the 40 assets in order to thrive and succeed in today's world. According to Search Institute, the more assets young people have, the more positive behaviors they exhibit, such as avoiding dangerous behavior, helping other people, succeeding in school, and paying attention to healthy nutrition and physical activity (Benson, Galbraith, & Espeland, 1998).

Although asset building can occur anywhere, schools are an important setting. A Search Institute report states, "Schools can have a direct impact on more than half the developmental assets, including 13 assets that research suggests are important in promoting academic success" (Starkman et al., 1999, p.45). Based on Search Institute research, teachers have tremendous asset-building potential, second only to parents. (For more information about developmental assets, visit the Search Institute Web site at www.search-institute.org.)

What a Teacher Can Do

Using the physical education setting to help students develop assets involves creating an environment, opportunities, and relationships through which all students can experience success. Teachers need to include asset building in their daily plans. Just as quality PE programs increase the likelihood that students will incorporate physical activity into their lives beyond their school years, PE classes that incorporate asset building increase the likelihood that students will experience emotional, social, intellectual, and physical success.

Quality PE programs have asset-building potential for these reasons:

- In many schools PE teachers and coaches are considered role models; they're in a position to build supportive relationships with students (see asset 14).

- Asset building is facilitated by such characteristics of quality PE programs as meeting the needs of all students, emphasizing cooperative games, teaching fair play and responsible participation in physical activity, and providing enjoyable physical activity.

- Class management techniques for large groups, and established rules and routines,

create a safe, supportive environment conducive to learning and productive activity.

- Movement, interactive games, and sports can enhance social skills such as supportiveness, honesty, and caring. National content standards in physical education state that students should be able to demonstrate responsible personal and social behavior in physical activity (National Association for Sport and Physical Education, 2004).

- Because of the unique environment of physical education and the constant interaction that occurs when students are involved in movement skills, games, and sports, PE classes may be especially suited to developing social skills.

On Your Mark . . . Get Set . . . Go!

The following sections offer guidelines for integrating developmental assets into a physical education class.

On Your Mark

To help young people build assets through physical education, the PE teacher must become aware of asset-building principles. Search Institute developed all of the principles listed in the sidebar except for 4, 5, and 6, which the authors added (www.search-institute.org/assets).

KEY POINTS

Principles of Asset Building in Physical Education

1. All young people need assets.*
2. Anyone can build assets.*
3. Relationships and environment are key.*
4. Quality PE is essential for asset building.
5. Asset building is a natural extension of social skills development in physical education.
6. Many assets can be developed through physical education.
7. Intentional, consistent, and repetitive messages are important.*
8. Asset building is an ongoing process.*

*Based on principles by Search Institute

All Young People Need Assets

Surveys such as the Youth Risk Behavior Survey developed by the Centers for Disease Control and Prevention suggest that a majority of U.S. young people are involved in high-risk behaviors that compromise their health. Search Institute research indicates that students with fewer assets are more likely to engage in high-risk behaviors such as problematic alcohol use, illicit drug use, sexual activity, and violence (Scales et al., 2004). However, the benefits of asset building are not limited to at-risk young people. In all young people assets promote positive behaviors, attitudes, and outcomes such as academic success, maintenance of good health (e.g., through exercise and good nutrition), and positive interactions with people of other racial and ethnic groups.

Anyone Can Build Assets

Anyone willing to encourage and help young people can build assets. Adults need to help young people become responsible individuals. All school personnel can contribute to asset building, including PE teachers, school nurses, after school care providers, classroom teachers, counselors, and cafeteria workers.

Relationships and Environment Are Vital

When their school environment makes them feel supported and valued, young people feel better about school and do better in school (Search Institute, 2005). Establishing a nurturing environment for young people starts with relationships. The vital relationships in a school include teacher to student, other school personnel to student, student to student, and adult to adult. For asset building to occur, students must interact in a positive way with friends, teachers, and other adults at school.

Quality Physical Education Aids Asset Building

For young people to build assets through physical education, the PE environment must be safe and caring. A student is more likely to feel valued and empowered if a PE class provides many opportunities for success. Meeting the needs of all students is a major characteristic of quality physical education.

© Human Kinetics

Parents should help build assets, too. Your physical education program should encourage parental involvement—for example, in helping students to remain active outside of school.

Asset Building Is an Extension of Social Skills Development in Physical Education

Even in quality PE programs, some teachers emphasize movement and physical fitness rather than social skills. Because of the interaction that occurs when students engage in movement, games, and sports, PE settings are especially conducive to developing social skills such as supportiveness, honesty, courtesy, caring, and tolerance of personal differences. Those social skills are similar to some of the developmental assets listed earlier in this chapter and allow a teacher to connect asset building to instructional practice that is already in place (Starkman et al., 1999). PE teachers who already are teaching social skills should find it easy to incorporate more asset building into their instruction.

Many Assets Can Be Developed Through Physical Education

Assets that can be developed through physical education are both external (adults give them to young people, such as support) and internal (skills and values that are developed inside a young person, such as honesty) and may include but are not limited to:

External

- 5. Caring school climate (school provides a caring, encouraging environment)
- 8. Youth as resources (young people are given useful roles)
- 10. Safety (young person feels safe at school)
- 12. School boundaries (school provides clear rules and consequences)
- 14. Adult role models (parents and other adults model positive, responsible behavior)

Internal

- 24. Bonding to school (young person cares about the school)
- 26. Caring (young person places high value on helping others)
- 29. Honesty (young person tells the truth even when it is not easy)
- 30. Responsibility (young person accepts and takes responsibility)

- 32. Planning and decision making (young person knows how to plan ahead and make choices)
- 33. Interpersonal competence (young person has empathy, sensitivity, and friendship skills)
- 34. Cultural competence (young person has knowledge of and comfort with people of different cultural/racial/ethnic backgrounds)

The actual number of assets will depend on many factors related to local situations, including the capabilities and motivation of the family, teacher, school, and community. All sorts of settings and events provide opportunities for asset building, such as after-school programs and community-sponsored health fairs. Adults who stop and talk with the students in such settings help build "other adult relationships" (Starkman et al., 1999). Along with quality PE programs, such spontaneous opportunities can build assets.

Intentional, Consistent, and Repetitive Messages

Teachers should make a conscious effort to build students' assets. The positive messages that build assets should be intentional (Starkman et al., 1999.), consistent, and repeated over time and in different settings, such as family and community settings.

Asset Building Is an Ongoing Process

Asset building begins at birth and continues throughout life. The process can be as simple as getting to know the children in a neighborhood and greeting them by name. Physical education teachers should make a conscious effort to build assets in class. They also can encourage their entire school, district, or community to help young people develop assets. Asset building is maximized when a variety of adults care about young people's development.

In his book *All Kids Are Our Kids* (1997), Search Institute president Peter Benson states that "the widespread and growing belief that kids are the responsibility of family" impedes young people's development (p. 55). Young people benefit when neighbors, friends, and others outside their family actively contribute to their care. The less community support there is for young people, and the less time parents spend with their children, the greater the need for school-based asset building.

Get Set

A teacher needs to create an asset-rich environment: An environment that is warm and caring, conveys positive expectations about the students, and gives students a sense of connection to the entire school but also recognizes students' limits and boundaries. In an asset-rich environment students feel safe, secure, and empowered.

To provide an asset-rich environment in a PE class,

- create a caring, supportive environment and
- use asset-building activities in class.

Create a Caring, Supportive Environment

Teachers can use the following tips to create a PE environment that will build assets.

- Create and maintain a positive atmosphere. Two top reasons that young people participate in sports and physical activities are to have fun and to spend time with friends. Winning is not one of their top reasons.
- Find ways for every child to participate in your class, even if some children aren't skilled in a particular sport. Inclusive PE teaching provides many different physical activity choices and opportunities for success.
- Work with students to set rules and boundaries. Post a written set of your rules in the classroom and the gym. Make copies, and have students and parents sign an agreement indicating their understanding of the rules.
- Post a list of developmental assets in your classroom and the gym.
- Develop a bulletin board in your classroom and the gym with asset-building messages such as "Did you help someone in class today?"
- Display asset-building posters in your classroom and the gym. You can obtain asset posters from Search Institute.

- Display a list of shared values and social competences such as encouragement, helping, kindness, courtesy, caring, complimenting, active listening, and accepting personal differences.
- Provide opportunities for students to contribute to charities—for example, by participating in Jump Rope for Heart or School Walk for Diabetes.
- Connect asset building to social skills building already in place in your school. For example, if your school has a "word of the week," use that word often in your PE class.
- Learn the names of all of your students and use their names any time that you see them.
- Remember that highly competitive class situations can cause stress. Help students improve their personal skills instead of comparing them to students with more skills.
- Develop leadership skills in your students by giving them opportunities to lead practice drills and develop a team code of conduct.
- Congratulate successes with verbal praise, a written note, or a phone call home. Praise should be more specific than "good job" or "way to go." Such general phrases soon lose their effect.
- Encourage student self-management, such as goal setting and self-monitoring. Students can establish fitness goals for themselves and follow their progress toward those goals.
- Provide many activity choices. Choice increases a student's chances for success and builds self-confidence.
- Teach conflict resolution strategies. Establish a place in the classroom where conflicts can be negotiated. (See chapter 2 for conflict resolution strategies.)

Use Asset-Building Activities in Class

Physical activities provide opportunities to build and reinforce assets. Teachers can use the activities provided in part 2 of this book or develop their own.

Go!

PE teachers cannot build social skills or developmental assets unless they intentionally make them part of a lesson. Already familiar to physical educators, social skills such as caring, honesty, and encouragement are similar to some developmental assets. In general, building an asset in a PE class entails the same process as building a social skill. The three primary steps to teaching social skills are introducing the skill, practicing it, and reviewing the practice (Kirby, 1997).

- *Introduce* an asset or a social skill such as caring. You can ask students questions such as:
  - "What does it mean to be caring?"
  - "Can you describe a situation in which someone showed caring behavior"?
  - Encourage students to say what caring looks and sounds like. You might want to put aspects of the students' descriptions on a "T" chart (see table 3.2).
- *Practice* the skill by having students play games in which they exchange partners. For example, they can play Partner Jump and Jive (page 50).
- *Review* the experience. When students line up at the end of a class, remind them about the social skill that you've been developing. For example, you can ask if anyone saw or heard an example of caring in class that day. You can ask questions such as "How did it make you feel when you witnessed caring?" and "Where can *you* show caring today?"

Table 3.2   Sample "T" Chart

What would you notice?	What would you hear?
Smiling	"Come play with me."
Helping by teaching	"I can help you."
Working together	"Would you like me to show you?"
Taking turns	"You can go again." "You can be first in line."
Kind words	"Thank you for helping." "I'm glad you were my partner."
Compliments	"Cool shoes." "You're a good runner."

Summary

It's easy to build assets in a physical education class. For teachers accustomed to teaching social skills, it's even easier. Begin by building an asset-rich environment using the principles and tips discussed in this chapter. After establishing a supportive, caring class environment, consciously build and reinforce specific assets through physical activity lesson plans.

Establishing Coordinated School Health

© Human Kinetics

Coordinated school health improves student health and learning through the joint efforts of families, schools, and communities.

Integrating health messages into a physical education class is a great start toward coordinated school health.

ealth and physical education are separate but closely related curriculum areas. Each discipline has its own goals and teacher certification guidelines. Classroom teachers, with support from PE teachers, school nurses, counselors, and community organizations, have been responsible for much of the health instruction in schools. Considering the enormous health challenges facing adolescents today (e.g., obesity and type 2 diabetes), other health instruction models should be considered.

In addition to national health issues such as the obesity epidemic, educational reform initiatives (testing and accountability) have prompted schools to find ways to meet student health needs. One way to advance student health is to integrate selected health topics into PE instruction. Another way is to teach students about health through schoolwide efforts such as "5-a-Day Week" or family exercise days and wellness nights at school. Perhaps the best way is for many people in a school community to work together to address health issues. This approach is called coordinated school health.

Like asset-building messages, coordinated school health requires that families, schools, and the community work together to improve young people's well-being. Combining asset building with coordinated school health strengthens both. This chapter examines the need to integrate health topics into physical education.

KEY POINTS

Factors Influencing the Need to Integrate Health Topics Into Physical Education

- The changing role of physical education teachers
- Widespread obesity and type 2 diabetes
- More effective instructional models

The Changing Role of Physical Education Teachers

Integrating health topics into other subjects, including physical education, is not a new concept. However, in recent years new information regarding how adolescents learn has prompted educators in all subject areas to consider thematic integration across content areas (Caine & Caine, 1991). In elementary schools the primary responsibility for school health education traditionally has fallen to classroom teachers (Lohrmann & Wooley, 1998). However, elementary schools' current focus on testing and accountability has transferred some of this responsibility from classroom teachers to PE teachers (Poag, 2000).

Improved U.S. curriculum standards have been central to the educational reform movement

© Human Kinetics

As you work toward coordinated school health, keep the focus on physical activity.

since the mid-1980s. Schools have worked hard to align curriculum, instruction, and assessment. However, one result of standards-based reform has been an overemphasis in some schools on core subjects (reading, writing, science, and math) in which students are tested and a corresponding underemphasis on untested subjects such as fine arts, health, and physical education. This shift away from a well-balanced curriculum has changed the school day and PE teachers' instructional responsibility. Although many PE teachers have an increased responsibility to teach health, it is important that physical activity remain the major focus of physical education classes.

The information and activities in this book will help teachers incorporate health instruction into physical education without compromising physical activity.

The Obesity Epidemic

The main causes of the obesity epidemic are poor diet and inadequate physical activity. In general, Americans eat too many high-calorie foods and don't burn enough calories through physical activity (Lemonick, 2004). The illness and mortality associated with obesity and related health problems such as type 2 diabetes are largely preventable. Reducing the risk of these health problems requires lifestyle changes, especially changes in diet and level of physical activity.

Physical education programs are increasingly important in combating obesity. Health-related

habits acquired in childhood tend to continue in adulthood (Kolbe, 2002). As discussed in chapter 2, numerous studies have confirmed the strong connection between physical activity and health (Blair, 1995). Given that classroom health instruction has recently decreased rather than increased, it is especially important for physical education teachers to integrate selected health topics such as nutrition into their PE classes.

Throughout the United States, efforts to improve cafeteria meals and limit student access to vending-machine junk food, such as high-calorie snacks and unhealthy soft drinks, are on the rise. Coupled with such efforts, integrating nutrition, physical activity, and health-related fitness information into PE lessons is a great start to combating poor eating habits and inactive lifestyles. It also moves schools toward a more efficient instructional model: coordinated school health.

More-Effective Instructional Models

Choice 3 integrates health instruction into PE classes and provides a foundation from which a PE teacher can become a school or district champion of a coordinated school health program (Hoelscher et al., 2001). It helps create the basis for more effective health instruction.

In some U.S. school districts, school health has been limited to fragmented and inconsistent curricular interventions. School nurses, some

© Getty Royalty Free Images

A coordinated approach to health assures that messages regarding healthy eating come from a variety of sources.

classroom teachers, and some PE teachers have delivered health messages, but there has been little effort to coordinate physical education, health education, cafeteria services, school health services, and family and community initiatives. The obesity epidemic has issued a wake-up call to schools and communities.

Communities in many U.S. states are beginning to realize that a coordinated approach to school health improves student health and learning (Fleming, 2006). The momentum for change continues to grow as the public becomes aware of the staggering health-care costs of preventable illnesses. Tobacco-related health problems and the current obesity epidemic alone show the need for coordinated school health programs.

Components of Coordinated School Health

The Division of Adolescent and School Health (DASH) within the Centers for Disease Control and Prevention (CDC) has promoted an eight-component model since the early 1980s (figure 4.1).

However, coordinated school health can be effective with fewer components. The Texas legislature recently mandated that all elementary schools in the state implement a four-component model that includes the following:

- health education,
- physical education,
- nutrition and cafeteria services, and
- family and community involvement (Texas Congress, 2002).

One of the four programs approved by the Texas Education Agency for use in Texas elementary schools is the Coordinated Approach to Child Health (CATCH), which is designed to help children and their families adopt healthy eating and physical activity behaviors. To date, CATCH is the largest school-based school health promotion program ever conducted in the United States. More than 1,550 Texas elementary schools have adopted CATCH. For more information, visit the CATCH Web site at www.catchtexas.org.

Nygard, Green, and Koonce (2005) have created another popular program for coordinating school health elements. Designed for K-5, the World of Wellness (WOW) program includes nutrition education, physical education, and parent involvement. For additional information about this comprehensive wellness program, visit www.wowhealth.org.

Whatever the number of its components, a coordinated school health model enables communities and schools to collaborate in improving the school environment and advance students' physical, mental, and social well-being.

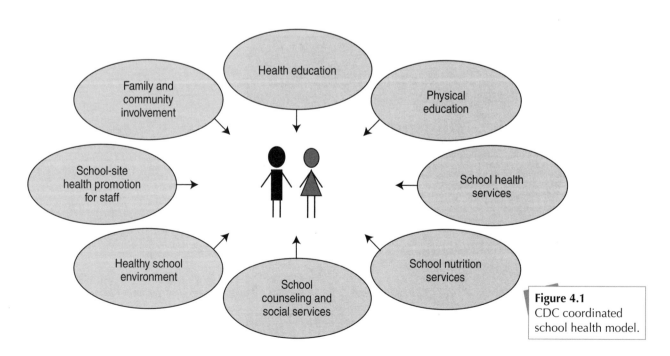

Figure 4.1
CDC coordinated school health model.

What a Teacher Can Do

Physical education classes can better meet students' health needs by integrating health information into daily lessons. Integration

- provides important health information and
- assists in the creation of coordinated health models.

How can physical education teachers integrate health information into their classes? And how does integration pave the way for coordinating the efforts of many people within a school and community?

Ideas for Integrating Health into a PE Class

- Integrate the health activities in this book into PE activity lessons (see chapters 5 to 16).
- Create visual bulletin boards that provide health information (see Appendix A, page 211).
- Develop "Your Health Minute" morning announcements. The announcements can include nutrition facts and a minute of physical activity in the classroom. A principal, teacher, student, or other member of the school community can be the announcer. Here's a sample principal's announcement: "Good morning, girls and boys. As I visited your classrooms yesterday, I noticed that many of you brought food to school for snack time. I know that many of you also snack at home after school. Snacks give you energy to work and play. A healthy snack is better for you than a sugary or salty snack, because it can give you the nutrients that

your body needs to function well. Some great snack choices are fruit, raw carrots, and whole-wheat bread. I'll be asking your teachers to check out your snacks. Remember: A healthy snack is good for you."

- Participate in Jump Rope for Heart and School Walk for Diabetes and use their educational kits to send health messages to students, faculty, and parents.
- Create a "Health Question of the Week," and post it around the school.

Ideas for Integration and Coordination Outside of the Physical Education Class

- Establish a school health team to plan coordinated school health activities.
- Create all-school celebrations associated with national health observances, and invite parents to participate. (See appendix A for examples.)

Ideas for Implementing a Coordinated School Health Model

- Investigate programs that work (such as CATCH) through DASH (www.cdc.gov/nccdphp/dash).
- Physical education teachers become leaders in promoting a program such as CATCH.

Summary

Integrating health instruction into a physical education class is a first step toward coordinated school health, a model based on the premise that student success is more likely when families, communities, and schools work together to enrich children's lives. Wide cooperation improves student learning and health.

Activities

The activities presented in part II allow a teacher to implement activity lesson plans that are connected to the instructional choices discussed in part I, thereby helping young people to achieve more success through physical education. The activities can be used effectively to promote traditional PE outcomes such as physical fitness and movement skills or, in the case of activities that include developmental assets or coordinated school health features, as a basis for student growth and well-being in a broader sense.

The activities in chapter 5, "Superstarters," require little or no equipment and can be used as warm-ups or expanded into other parts of a lesson. Chapters 6 through 16 present activities grouped by type of equipment or other teaching aid: Let's Get Physical cards, playing cards, balls, hoops, jump ropes, beanbags, dice, task cards or sheets, spinners, polyspots, and food labels or pictures. Each chapter addresses activities in alphabetical order and includes clear instructions, detailed descriptions, and suggested ways of modifying the activities to accommodate different student needs and developmental levels. Each chapter also suggests ways to connect the activities to developmental assets and coordinated school health, or provides teaching tips to develop these concepts generally.

Each activity is organized as follows:

- **Content Connections**—the content area that details the skills and information that will be covered.

- **Ready for Action**—the equipment and setup needed for the activity.

- **Let's Play**—the directions for the activity itself.

- **Crank It Up**—challenges for advanced students or for extending lessons.

- **Gear It Down**—simplified instruction appropriate for younger or less advanced students.

- **Asset Action**—asset-building tools. Many of the activities in this book reinforce or build a particular asset or deliver general, asset-building tips for teachers. As explained elsewhere in this book, the physical activity setting is rich in asset-building opportunities, both in and out of school. Physical educators, teachers, and after-school providers are perhaps in the best position to build assets in young people because assets can be built through the activity itself and the caring environment where the activity occurs.

- **Coordinated School Health Links**—ideas that link or bridge physical education activities and games to health concepts. Including health concepts in PE activities, especially if linked to classroom instruction in health, is a first step toward coordinated school health (see chpater 4). Some of the activities in Part II are *directly* connected to coordinated school health components such as family and community involvement, healthy school environment, and classroom health education. Other activities are *indirectly* connected to coordinated school health in that they link the activity with a health concept. For example, some activities relate to aspects of physical health such as fitness, nutrition, flexibility, strength, or cardiovascular fitness. Other activities relate to emotional and social aspects of health, and stress characteristics such as acceptance of others and friendship skills. Intellectual health is also a feature of some of the more than 100 activities that reinforce academic skills (e.g., reading and math) as well as critical-thinking skills such as goal setting and problem solving.

The activities use the following concepts typically taught in PE and health courses:

- **Direction**—one's bearing within space; up, down, forward, backward, right, or left
- **General space**—the space available within boundaries for movement
- **Health-related fitness**—fitness focused on optimal health; prevents diseases associated with insufficient physical activity and generally includes the following:
  - **Aerobic health**—health brought about by a variety of exercises that moderately increase oxygen uptake and stimulate heart and lung activity for a long enough period to produce beneficial changes in the body
  - **Flexibility**—the range of motion in a joint
  - **Muscular endurance**—the ability to repeat an activity many times, such as a pull-up
  - **Muscular strength**—the force that a single muscular contraction can exert

- **Levels**—low, medium, or high body positions or relationships to objects
- **Locomotor skills**—the ability to move from one place to another (e.g., walk, jog, hop, jump, skip, slide, gallop, leap, or run)
- **Nonlocomotor skills**—the ability to move in place (e.g., swing, twist, bend, or stretch)
- **Pathways**—movements linked to lines in space such as straight, curved, or zigzag
- **Personal space**—the space the body occupies or can naturally extend to
- **Relationships**—the positions of the body and its parts relative to people, places, and things (e.g., close, far, in, out, above, below, beside, in front)

There is no single format for conducting the activities; several adaptations are possible, including the following:

- Combining several activities, such as a warm-up, a fitness, and a skill-development activity, to develop a unique PE lesson (see the four-part lesson plan in appendix A)
- Using the activity strategies in chapter 2 together with the strategies in chapter 3, "Developmental Assets," to expose students to additional ways to succeed
- Using the "Coordinated School Health" tips and chapter 4 strategies to begin the process of coordinated school health in your class
- Setting the stage for asset building through physical activity by creating a safe and supportive environment for students

However you use the activities, the overall goal of enriching young people's lives through a variety of PE opportunities and experiences will help them succeed in your class and beyond.

Superstarters

5

© Human Kinetics

Great activities! Class warm-ups included.

Little or no equipment required.

Is your class environment safe and caring? Do you know your students' names and interests?

Go beyond the basics.

1, 2, 3, Go

CONTENT CONNECTIONS
Warm-up, aerobic health, muscular endurance, flexibility, basketball dribbling, volleying

READY FOR ACTION
- Use table 5.1 as an example to create a poster.
- Place a colored cone in each of three corners of the gym.
- Have groups of three students spread out around the playing area.

Table 5.1   Sample Actions for 1, 2, 3, Go

All numbers match.	Jog around blue cone	5 curl-ups	3 push-ups
Two numbers match.	Jog around orange cone	8 curl-ups	5 push-ups
No numbers match.	Jog around red cone	3 curl-ups	8 push-ups

LET'S PLAY   Students play a game similar to rock, paper, and scissors, except they will use numbers instead of signs. All members of a group of three students simultaneously tap their fists on their open palms three times. On the third tap, each student displays 1, 2, or 3 fingers from their fisted hand. Students use the poster to identify the exercise action for their group. For example, if two students displayed the number 2, then they do exercise listed by action 2 and jog together around the orange cone, perform eight curl-ups, and do five push-ups. The action sequence should be repeated several times.

CRANK IT UP   Change the number of repetitions of the exercise or the length of the jog. Change teams every 5 minutes. Change the entire chart to reflect jump rope tricks. Add chart columns for additional skills such as dribbling a basketball or volleying a beach ball.

GEAR IT DOWN   Keep the same students working together, and have them do only the jogging activity. When students understand the game, add the other two activities (curl-ups and push-ups).

ASSET ACTION
- **Caring (asset 26)**—Remind students that they show caring when they are courteous and wait for everyone to finish the game before beginning the activities on the poster. Ask them to encourage one another as they perform the activities.
- **Honesty (asset 29)**—Remind students about the value of telling the truth. For example, they should be truthful about the number of times that they've repeated an activity.

COORDINATED SCHOOL HEALTH LINKS
Encourage students to use the format in "1, 2, 3, Go!" as the basis for some physical activity with their family. Popular games such as Rock, Paper, Scissors can be a great way to begin involving parents in their child's schooling. Remind students (and their parents) that health isn't limited to physical health but includes emotional and social health, which require a supportive environment.

15-Second Skill Challenge

CONTENT CONNECTIONS   Agility, speed, aerobic health, muscular endurance

READY FOR ACTION   Partners stand by a line on the gym floor or other playing area. If necessary, you can use hula hoops instead of lines, with students standing outside the hoops.

LET'S PLAY   Partner 1 counts while partner 2 performs the skill. After 15 seconds, partner 1 reports to partner 2 the total number of skills (such as jumps) performed; then they switch.

Challenges

- Skier jump—with two feet together, jump sideways over the line and back.
- Front jump—with two feet together, jump forward and backward over the line.
- Crossover jump—straddle the line with your feet; then cross your right foot over your left and return to straddling.
- Scissor jump—face the line, and jump into the air. Land with your right foot in front and your left foot behind. Continue to jump, switching your feet while in the air.
- Handwalker—get into a push-up position. Alternately move your right and left hands back and forth over the line.

CRANK IT UP   Students challenge another student to a jump-off. Students choose one of the challenges and compete against each other to see who can perform the most repetitions during the time interval. After each jump-off, they move to a different partner.

GEAR IT DOWN

Stress proper technique rather than the number of skills attempted. Allow all students to practice the skills to the beat of the music without keeping score.

ASSET ACTION

- **Parent involvement in schooling (asset 6)**—To help get parents involved in their child's schooling, ask students to play 15-Second Skill Challenge at home with a parent as their partner.
- **Honesty (asset 29)**—Remind students to be honest in their counting. If they're fair and play by the rules, their partners will trust them and everyone can have a good time.

COORDINATED SCHOOL HEALTH LINKS

Arrange a meeting with some classroom teachers to discuss connecting what you're doing in PE class to the classroom. Cooperation between PE teachers and classroom teachers leads to an improved school environment and, in turn, improved student health. For example, in 15-Second Skill Challenge students do a lot of jumping. Classroom teachers can create a lesson based on which muscles are used in jumping or how jumping changes heart rate.

Body Shape Bonanza

CONTENT CONNECTIONS   Warm-up, flexibility, body shapes, balance

READY FOR ACTION

- Students scattered in general space
- Stick-figure pictures reproduced on colorful medium to heavyweight paper (see the worksheet in appendix B, page 220)
- Music

LET'S PLAY   The teacher holds up a stick-figure picture for the class to see. When the music starts, the students adopt the body shape shown in the picture. When the music stops, they freeze and wait for a new picture.

CRANK IT UP   After a brief warm-up, the students perform stick-figure postures that are more difficult. Students are then challenged to create their own shapes while the music is playing. When the music stops, students find a partner and copy their partners' stick-figure shape. Repeat for several rounds with students choosing a new partner each time.

GEAR IT DOWN   Ask students to create various shapes at their own spot: wide, twisted, curved, small, and narrow. As the students create their shapes, select one student to come to the front and show his or her shape to the class. Ask the other students to match that shape.

ASSET ACTION

Self-esteem (asset 38)—Body Shape Bonanza exemplifies inclusiveness. All of the children are successful as they assume stick-figure postures. The teacher can boost student self-esteem and confidence, and demonstrate caring, by complimenting students on their postures.

COORDINATED SCHOOL HEALTH LINKS

Students can practice the stick-figure postures with family members, thereby linking Body Shape Bonanza to assets such as family support, bonding to school, and high expectations (if family members join the teacher in encouraging students to do their best). Including family members in a child's schooling is an important component of a coordinated school health program.

Countdown

CONTENT CONNECTIONS   Warm-up, aerobic health, muscular endurance, rhythms, jumping

READY FOR ACTION

- Students scattered in general space
- Music with a strong, quick beat such as 120 to 128 beats per minute

LET'S PLAY   Students perform basic jumping patterns to counts of 8, 4, 2, and 1, finishing with fast feet (moving their feet as quickly as possible.)

Hop Combo

1. Eight hops on right foot, eight on left foot
2. Four hops on right foot, four on left foot
3. Two hops on right foot, two on left foot
4. One hop on right foot, one on left foot
5. Fast feet

Jumping Jack Combo

1. Eight jumps with feet apart, eight jumps with feet together
2. Four jumps with feet apart, four jumps with feet together
3. Two jumps with feet apart, two jumps with feet together
4. One jump with feet apart, one jump with feet together
5. Fast feet

© Human Kinetics

More options for teachers are the scissor feet combo (right foot in front and left foot back, then vice versa) and marching feet in and out (in a straddle position).

CRANK IT UP   Have students jog around the area after each jumping or marching sequence. Have them perform a new sequence after each jog. Add an arm or abdominal exercise between sequences.

GEAR IT DOWN   Until all students are comfortable with the jumping rhythms, use clapping or drumbeats to emphasize the beat, and use with basic marching, walking, jumping, and changing of speeds during the sequences. Young children enjoy alternating slow and fast marching, as well as slow and fast jumping.

ASSET ACTION

Other adult relationships (asset 3) and caring school climate (asset 5)—Showing young people that adults are concerned about their welfare and success is a vital part of building social skills and assets. Adapting activities (as in the "Gear It Down" section) to accommodate the varying skill and talent levels within a class demonstrates to students that they are supported. As discussed in part I, kids tend to do better and feel better about themselves in supportive environments.

COORDINATED SCHOOL HEALTH LINKS

Coordinating health messages throughout a student's school experience is an important part of a coordinated health program. Countdown promotes coordination between PE and classroom teachers when adapted for use at recess or in a classroom on a rainy day.

In and Out

CONTENT CONNECTIONS   Warm-up, aerobic health, muscular endurance

READY FOR ACTION

- A rectangle delineated by placing a cone in each of four corners
- Stretch bands, basketballs, beanbags
- Let's Get Physical cards (see Appendix B)

LET'S PLAY   Divide the class into two groups. Group 1 will begin inside the rectangle and perform one of three fitness exercises designated by the teacher: a curl-up, a push-up, or a straddle stretch (seated with legs apart). Group 2 will begin outside the rectangle and, moving clockwise around group 1, perform a predetermined locomotor task. For example, group 1 might do curl-ups while group 2 does race-walking. Every 2 minutes, switch which group is on the inside. When both groups have completed a particular activity, switch to a new activity.

CRANK IT UP   Add equipment to the middle of the activity area. Students can engage in activities such as exercising with stretch bands, dribbling a basketball, or tossing beanbags.

GEAR IT DOWN   The teacher holds up pictures of exercises for the inside group, or a student leads the group. The group outside the rectangle walks behind a leader; no passing is allowed.

ASSET ACTION

- **Interpersonal competence (asset 33)**—Because group PE activities involve lots of interaction, In and Out provides a great opportunity for students to build friendship skills. Remind students to respect others' feelings and accept differences among people. Friendship promotes tolerance.
- **Cultural competence (asset 34)**—As a group-based activity, In and Out allows students to feel comfortable with people of different cultural, racial, and ethnic backgrounds.

COORDINATED SCHOOL HEALTH LINKS

An activity such as In and Out provides an opportunity to discuss physical activity and health-related fitness. Remind students that physical activity is important not only because it can result in a longer, healthier life but also because it makes us feel better (that is, improves our mental and emotional health) and provides a great way to make new friends (that is, enhances our social health).

Instant Replay

CONTENT CONNECTIONS   Locomotor skills, aerobic health

READY FOR ACTION

- Students lined up in pairs, facing their partner
- For "Crank It Up": basketballs

LET'S PLAY   The teacher calls out a sequence of actions from the list below. First, partner 1 performs the sequence to the music; then partner 2 does so.

- Jog to partner; high-five your partner; skip back.
- Do three jumping jacks; skip to your partner; patty-cake five times; walk home backwards.
- Jog to your partner; run around your partner once; gallop home.
- Walk to your partner; crawl under your partner's straddled legs; jog home.
- Slide to partner with your right shoulder leading; do three matching push-ups with your partner; slide back with your left shoulder leading.

CRANK IT UP   The teacher can create sequences using basketballs—for example, dribble to your partner with your right hand, pass the ball to your partner twice; dribble back with your left hand. Allow students to create their own patterns and challenge their partner to copy them.

GEAR IT DOWN   Students form two rows on one side of the court, with one partner in front of the other. The teacher calls out a sequence, for example, jog to partner and skip back. First one partner and then the other performs the sequence.

ASSET ACTION

Interpersonal competence (asset 33) and cultural competence (asset 34)—After the partners in Instant Replay complete the first task, each student in one of the two lines moves one place to the right, so that every student now has a new partner. Before the teacher calls out the second activity, the new partners meet in the middle of the play area, shake hands, and exchange greetings. The positive interaction enhances social skills and creates opportunities to develop new friendships.

COORDINATED SCHOOL HEALTH LINKS

Instant Replay and other PE activities that use partnering help students learn to work with, accept, and befriend others. Let parents, teachers, and school personnel know that adult partnering, too, improves a school's environment and students' well-being. Working together to improve the well-being of young people is the foundation of coordinated school health.

Match Play

CONTENT CONNECTIONS Warm-up, aerobic health, throwing, catching, coordination

READY FOR ACTION

- Place equal amounts of equipment of various types around the room, such as balls, beanbags, hoops, and jump ropes.
- See that students are in personal space.

© Human Kinetics

LET'S PLAY Each student chooses a piece of equipment, takes it to his or her personal space, and practices as many different activities as he or she can think of while using that equipment. At the teacher's signal, each student locates a partner who has the same piece of equipment. Partners then work together to create and perform activities using their matching equipment.

CRANK IT UP Increase the group size, and ask students to create a large-group activity using as much of the equipment as they can. For an added challenge, create groups in which every student has a different type of equipment.

GEAR IT DOWN Distribute only two kinds of equipment, such as beanbags and playground balls.

ASSET ACTION

Interpersonal competence (asset 33) and personal power (asset 37)—Partnering promotes interpersonal competence. Allowing students to create their own activities gives them a sense of achievement and control (personal power).

COORDINATED SCHOOL HEALTH LINKS

In today's accountability climate, school administrators want all teachers to participate in students' academic development. Match Play promotes academic achievement by promoting creativity.

Mickey's Mambo

CONTENT CONNECTIONS   Listening, following directions, aerobic health, muscular endurance, coordination

READY FOR ACTION

- Students scattered in general space
- For "Crank It Up": music

LET'S PLAY   Students perform actions in response to words that the teacher calls out:

- Minnie—Jump with your legs straddled and your arms raised to shoulder level and extended out to your sides. That is, do half of a jumping jack.
- Mickey—Jump with your feet and legs together and your arms straight down at your sides.
- Mouse—Jump with your feet together in a pike (jump and bend at the hips, keeping the legs straight) and join your hands over your head.
- Goofy—Stand on one leg, and make a silly face.
- Donald Duck—Walk on your heels in a circle.
- Pluto—Lie on your back with your hands and feet in the air.

CRANK IT UP   Students jog around the room's perimeter while the music is playing. When the music stops, the teacher calls out commands and students perform the tasks until the music resumes.

GEAR IT DOWN   To teach students how to do jumping jacks, use only "Mickey" and "Minnie" commands and gradually increase the speed of the commands until the students are jumping.

ASSET ACTION

Cultural competence (asset 34). Characters such as Mickey, Minnie, and Pluto appeal to children of all cultural, racial, and ethnic backgrounds. By using these characters, Mickey's Mambo helps create an atmosphere that is comfortable for all children. This atmosphere, in turn, helps students to accept and befriend people whose cultural, racial, and ethnic backgrounds differ from their own.

COORDINATED SCHOOL HEALTH LINKS

Listening is an important skill. In Mickey's Mambo students need to listen to the teacher's directions. Such practice in listening will help them with many aspects of their school experience, such as getting better grades.

Mingle and Move

CONTENT CONNECTIONS   Warm-up, throwing, catching, muscular endurance, flexibility

READY FOR ACTION

- Beanbags, balls, and hoops
- Students scattered in general space
- Music
- For "Crank It Up": a beach ball or basketball

LET'S PLAY   Students walk around the play area while music plays. When the music stops, they go to the center of the room. The teacher calls out a number from 2 to 6, and students quickly form groups consisting of that many members. Students high-five each other, and each group then jogs to an open space within the play area. The teacher describes a task for all to perform. See table 5.2 for sample tasks.

Table 5.2   Sample Tasks for Mingle and Move

Group Size	Tasks
2	Follow the leader Beanbag foot tag Matching exercising
3	Triangle beanbag tossing Up, Down, All Around (see page 126)
4	One in the middle leads exercises Sit in circle, do curl-ups, and high-five in the middle
5	Circle straddle stretch (seated circle with adjacent students touching feet), two ball passing (keep two balls going without dropping them)
6	Form a line, and pass a ball over and under

CRANK IT UP   Add sport skills such as beach ball volleying; circle Keep It Up, in which students form a circle and collectively keep a ball from falling to the ground; or shooting a basketball through a hoop a predetermined number of times.

GEAR IT DOWN   Using no equipment, students work in pairs or in groups of three and change partners with each new activity. They might pass a ball back and forth, mirror a partner's movements, or, acting in concert, make the shape of a letter with their bodies.

ASSET ACTION

Interpersonal competence (asset 33) and cultural competence (asset 34)—Encourage students to choose partners from outside their usual circle of friends. Mingle and Move provides an enjoyable opportunity for kids to become more comfortable with people of different cultural, racial, and ethnic backgrounds. Make acceptance of differences a class motto.

COORDINATED SCHOOL HEALTH LINKS

- Challenge older students to name the muscles involved in at least one Mingle and Move activity.
- Respect is important to social health. Remind all students to respect the talent and skill levels of their new partners.

Operation Cooperation

CONTENT CONNECTIONS   Aerobic health, muscular endurance, flexibility, locomotor skills

READY FOR ACTION   Pairs of students spread out in general space

LET'S PLAY   When the teacher says, "Go," partners perform matching or differing actions. If the partners have performed differing actions, they switch actions when the teacher says, "Switch." See table 5.3 for an example.

Table 5.3   Sample Actions for Operation Cooperation

Matching action	Alternate action	
Both partners	Partner 1	Partner 2
Hop five times on right foot. Hop five times on left foot. Do bicep curls. Jump and twist. Do right-leg kick, then left-leg kick. Do jumping jacks.	Stands at attention. Marches in place. Does curl-ups. Jumps up and down. Frog jumps in place. Jogs in place.	Curls up in a ball. Slides around play area. Does push-ups. Walks silly in play area. Gallops. Does straddle stretch (sits on floor with legs apart, reaches for ankles).

CRANK IT UP   Use only fitness exercises. Add jogging around the perimeter, and extend the time of activity.

GEAR IT DOWN   Add animal walks. Students imitate the way an animal moves. Call, "Switch" so that each student experiences different types of activity.

ASSET ACTION

High expectations (asset 16), achievement motivation (asset 21), school/learning engagement (asset 22), personal power (asset 37), and positive view of personal future (asset 40)—Find ways for each child to participate in your class, even if he or she is not particularly skilled in the sport. Quality physical education provides many physical activity choices and opportunities for success. Success builds confidence and self-esteem, and a more positive attitude about school. Operation Cooperation fosters a positive environment that helps students to build developmental assets and social skills. By working with partners, showing respect, and encouraging each other, students learn to be comfortable in an environment that is safe and fun.

COORDINATED SCHOOL HEALTH LINKS

Have students check their heart rate during the various activities in Operation Cooperation so that they can determine which activity caused their heart to beat the fastest. Health, math, or science teachers can help students chart this information over time so that students will better appreciate the importance of frequent aerobic activity while increasing their knowledge of academic subjects.

Partner Jump and Jive

CONTENT CONNECTIONS   Aerobic health, muscular endurance, locomotor skills, jumping patterns

READY FOR ACTION

- Music
- Pairs spread out in general space

LET'S PLAY   The teacher calls out an activity from the list below. Partners perform the activity until the teacher says, "Do the fitness jive." Students then perform the following sequence with their partner: right-hand high-five, high-ten, one full spin, handshake with partner. Next, students find a new partner. When all students have located a new partner, the teacher calls out a new task from the following list below.

Jump Task List

1. Partners ski jump side to side.
2. Partners do jumping jacks in unison.
3. Partners scissor jump in unison (jump into the air, land with their right foot in front and their left foot in back, and switch foot positions while jumping).
4. Partners hop, in unison, on their right foot and then their left foot.
5. The teacher chooses some activity not shown on this list.

CRANK IT UP   Expand the fitness jive sequence. For example, you might use right-hand high-five, left-hand high-five, high-ten, elbow "high-five," knee "high-five," and sole of feet high-five. Ask students to create their own jive sequence. Add a variety of partner exercises for all parts of the body.

GEAR IT DOWN   Students keep their original partner and perform all of the tasks together.

ASSET ACTION

Interpersonal competence (asset 33)—To know how to make and keep friends is an important part of being a responsible, successful person. Friendship promotes emotional and social health. Remind students while they work with their partners in Partner Jump and Jive that friendships are based on treating others with kindness and respect.

COORDINATED SCHOOL HEALTH LINKS

Encourage students to create their own exercise routine. Young children can use Partner Jump and Jive as a start. Student-created exercise routines increase student motivation and creativity and encourage students to develop a personal exercise plan that extends beyond school. Have students discuss the benefits of creating an exercise program with their parents.

Partner Mix-Up

CONTENT CONNECTIONS   Locomotor skills, flexibility, rhythms, aerobic health, muscular endurance

READY FOR ACTION

- Upbeat music
- Students find a partner and spread out in general space

LET'S PLAY   The teacher calls out an action from the list below, and students respond in creative ways. For example, students might respond to "Jump" by facing a partner and jumping up and down in unison.

Partner Action List

- Shake hands
- Stretch
- Jump
- Jog
- Push-up
- High-five
- Curl-up
- Dance

CRANK IT UP   Students begin by walking within the activity area. When the teacher says, "Find a partner," students do so. They then perform a designated task from the list above but in a way that they choose. Next the teacher asks students to find a new partner and announces a new task. As before, students perform the designated task but in their own way. Students must remember which task they performed with which partner. When a teacher calls out a task, students must go to the appropriate partner and perform the task as originally performed with that partner.

GEAR IT DOWN   The teacher tells students how they should respond to particular calls. For example, she or he might tell students to respond to "Stretch" by sitting in a straddle with their feet touching. Younger students can stay with the same partner throughout the session.

ASSET ACTION

Cultural competence (asset 34)—By choosing multiple partners as they do in this activity, especially in a multiethnic class, students learn to work with people from different backgrounds. As in other partner activities, friendships can develop as a result of the interaction.

COORDINATED SCHOOL HEALTH LINKS

Partner Mix-Up can be used indoors on a rainy day. Working with the classroom teacher, decide on an opening activity sequence for each weekday. For example, Monday's opening activity might consist of the following: jog one lap; stretch or hula hoop for 5 minutes. Tuesday's might consist of jumping rope or jumping a line 50 times. On any given day, students can either repeat the opening activity sequence or switch to new activities.

ALL THINGS ARE CONNECTED

Run and Rap

CONTENT CONNECTIONS   Aerobic health

READY FOR ACTION

- A rectangular activity area delineated by four cones
- Music

LET'S PLAY   Students choose a partner when they enter the class. While music is playing, students walk and talk about topics designated by the teacher. For example, the teacher might ask students to discuss their hearts:

- Tell your partner everything you know about keeping your heart healthy.
- Where is your heart and how big is it?
- Describe the heart's action.
- What kinds of foods are heart-healthy?

When the music stops, students perform a stretch of their choice.

CRANK IT UP   For the stretch portion, designate a few suitable exercises for different muscle groups and let students choose an exercise. For example, to exercise the abdominal muscles, students might choose to do curl-ups, back bicycles, crunches, or V sit-ups.

GEAR IT DOWN   The teacher provides a heart fact or mini-lesson to the students during a pause in the music and then holds up pictures of exercises for the group to do during the stretch portion of the activity.

 ASSET ACTION

- **Cultural competence (asset 34) and interpersonal competence (asset 33)**—Within quality PE activities, certain words signal an opportunity to build a social skill or asset. For example, the word *partner* signals a chance to build cultural competence. Parts of Run and Rap are linked to the important social skill of communication, which helps build interpersonal competence.

- **Youth as resources (asset 8), positive peer influence (asset 15), caring (asset 26), healthy lifestyle (asset 31), and sense of purpose (asset 39)**—Look for opportunities in your class to encourage communication between students, especially about health issues. Run and Rap helps to create these communication opportunities by having the students find partners and talk about health issues. Discussing healthy lifestyles is a good way for young people to begin the process of establishing healthy habits.

 COORDINATED SCHOOL HEALTH LINKS

Ask older students to name the muscles involved in the workout or to describe the circulation of blood. Share this idea with classroom teachers. Encourage students to invite their parents to walk with them and discuss lessons learned at school. Such student–parent discussion can help students review for tests. It also provides an opportunity for parents to become more involved in their child's schooling, an important component of asset-building.

Scramble

CONTENT CONNECTIONS   Cooperation, aerobic health

READY FOR ACTION

- Upbeat music
- Students scattered in general space

LET'S PLAY   On the signal "Scramble," students randomly jog or walk around the room to the music while avoiding other students. When the music stops, the teacher calls out a way of forming groups. For example, the teacher might say, "Find students who have the same favorite color as you." Students then communicate with each other to form groups as quickly as possible.

Here are some grouping possibilities:

- Same favorite color
- Same favorite movie
- Same favorite vegetable
- Same shoe size
- Born in the same month
- Have the same kind of pet
- Like the same sport

CRANK IT UP   After students have formed groups, have them line up in some particular order. For example, you might tell them to line up from lightest to darkest hair color, darkest to lightest shirt color, shortest to longest name, or shortest to tallest height.

GEAR IT DOWN   Give students a few minutes, then help those who are having difficulty finding groups.

 ASSET ACTION

Achievement motivation (asset 21), school/learning engagement (asset 22), and bonding to school (asset 24)—Scramble reinforces important social skills such as cooperation, respect, caring, and communication. Such skills help build friendships and other positive relationships, creating an environment conducive to asset building.

COORDINATED SCHOOL HEALTH LINKS

Meet with classroom teachers and discuss the thinking skills that Scramble can reinforce. One such skill is the ability to group similar things together. Scramble can encourage students to group by vegetable, body part, animal, or countless other categories. Administrators expect all teachers to contribute to the academic success of students. Activities such as Scramble provide that opportunity for PE teachers.

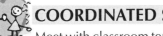

Side by Side

CONTENT CONNECTIONS   Agility, quickness, locomotor skills

READY FOR ACTION

- Students are in pairs, side by side.
- Students can hold hands or wrists, or hold a flag between them if they are squeamish about holding hands.
- All pairs should line up in the middle of the play area, with one pair behind the other and sidelines designated on the right and left.

LET'S PLAY   The teacher calls out, "Ready," waits for everyone to be quiet, and then calls out a number. This number indicates how many times the pairs will slide, side to side, from one sideline to the other and then back to the middle as quickly as they can. To ensure safety, students must slide only, not turn and run. Groups also must be careful to slide together, not out of their line.

CRANK IT UP   To increase cardiovascular endurance, increase the number of sliding trips; have students perform an activity, such as 5 to 10 curl-ups, before sliding; or increase the distance the students cover. Change the group size to include three or four students.

GEAR IT DOWN   Students work with a partner. While one partner slides, the other stretches. After each trip, students switch actions. Ask students to hook elbows and walk, rather than slide, from sideline to sideline.

ASSET ACTION

Planning and decision making (asset 32)—Emphasize that all members of a group should work together to decide the best way to achieve fast, unified movement. Stress that we must work with others throughout our lives. When people make group decisions, some will lead and others will follow. Students must learn to respect other people's opinions.

COORDINATED SCHOOL HEALTH LINKS

Respect is an important social skill, especially as people with different ideas and viewpoints come together. Encourage students to respect the skill levels and ideas of all members of their group by being polite and considerate.

Starting off Right

CONTENT CONNECTIONS
Warm-up, aerobic health, coordination, ball manipulation, beanbag manipulation, jumping rope

READY FOR ACTION
- Upbeat music
- A sign at the entrance to the activity area (see table 5.4)
- For "Crank It Up": jump ropes or other equipment

Table 5.4   Starter Tasks

Sign	Student task
Seeds	Find personal space. Warm up using previously learned exercises. Teacher leads, or students work independently. (For ideas, see Let's Get Physical cards from chapter 6.)
Balls	Retrieve a ball. Find personal space. Practice ball-handling tricks: dribbling, catching, or bouncing.
Hoops	Find personal space. Practice hula hoop tricks, jump in and out of the hoop, or stretch inside the hoop.
Chalk talk	Walk around the area's perimeter with a friend. Read the questions on the chalkboard and discuss them. (Teacher should write questions appropriate to the day's lesson, such as questions on nutrition or a sport skill taught in class.)
Ropes	Retrieve a jump rope. Find personal space. Practice previously learned tricks, or shape the rope into a circle or line and practice a variety of age-appropriate jumping techniques.
Beanbag bash	Retrieve a beanbag. Create new beanbag tricks.

LET'S PLAY   Students enter the class, read the sign, and perform the activity indicated. Pictures on signs help younger students. Create your own signs based on your students' interests and abilities. The chart shows examples of prelesson activities. As early in the year as possible, clearly communicate to students the expectations and boundaries associated with the activities.

CRANK IT UP   Have students create a warm-up routine that uses a particular type of equipment. For example, one sign might read, "You are trying out for the after-school jump rope team. Get a jump rope, go to personal space, and create your rope routine."

GEAR IT DOWN   Younger students can benefit from repeatedly reading and following the directions on one sign. Later on, the teacher can vary the tasks and movements.

ASSET ACTION
- **Empowerment (assets 7-10)**—Allowing students to warm up on their own helps them to feel valued and in control.
- **Responsibility (asset 30)**—Independent warming up fosters personal responsibility.

COORDINATED SCHOOL HEALTH LINKS
Let parents and school administrators know that you're using written words and pictures on signs to communicate directions and instructions to students. Establishing contact with other groups leads to cooperation that improves students' well-being.

Trading Places

CONTENT CONNECTIONS   Locomotor skills, directions, pathways, levels

READY FOR ACTION

- A set of action cards (each card specifies one locomotor movement and one pathway; for example, a card might state, "Skip in a curved pathway" or "Gallop straight ahead")
- Students scattered in general space
- Music

LET'S PLAY   Each student draws an action card. When the music starts, she or he performs the activity on the card, moving safely in the general space. When the music stops, she or he quickly assumes a back-to-back position with a nearby student. When the music resumes, students swap cards and perform the new action until the music stops.

CRANK IT UP   Add a modifier to the movement specified on the action card. For example, the card might say, "Walk *quietly* in a curved path" or "Jog *slowly* in a zigzag pattern."

© Human Kinetics

GEAR IT DOWN   The teacher reads one card for the entire class, and the students perform the action while the music plays.

ASSET ACTION

Cultural competence (asset 34) and interpersonal competence (asset 33)—Trading Places makes a game of finding partners quickly and dealing with them politely. Encourage the students to go to a different partner each time, so that they don't just go to their closest friends each time.

COORDINATED SCHOOL HEALTH LINKS

Teacher Tip—Asset building requires consistent messages. As discussed in chapter 4, a coordinated school health program ensures that parents and teachers can work together to let children know that they are valued and supported. Whether your school has a coordinated health program or not, a good way to get parents involved in the PE program and asset building is to send parents a letter about asset building and then use assets as springboards for discussions in conferences with parents and students.

Tri-Color Action

CONTENT CONNECTIONS   Warm-up

READY FOR ACTION   Using a red cone, blue cone, and yellow cone, divide the playing area into three zones (red, blue, and yellow).

LET'S PLAY   Use this activity when students first enter the gym and have been sitting in class. As a warm-up, students hurriedly move from zone to zone.

Students play Rock, Paper, Scissors to move from zone to zone. Partners begin in the red zone. The winner moves into the yellow zone; the loser stays in the red zone and plays again. If a student in the yellow zone loses, she or he moves back to the red zone; if she or he wins, she or he moves into the blue zone. If a student in the blue zone loses, he or she returns to the yellow zone; if he or she wins, he or she gets one point and may start again.

CRANK IT UP   After winning or losing in a zone, the student must perform a simple exercise—such as 10 jumping jacks—at the entry line before moving back into the zone to play.

GEAR IT DOWN   Place cones in a circle. When students win, they move to the next cone. When they lose, they stay at their current cone and continue to play until they win.

ASSET ACTION

Teacher tip—In a physical education setting, giving students exercise and activity choices has many benefits. Children love activity, especially when they're allowed to select activities that match their abilities and interests. Choice results in greater participation and enjoyment. It also helps to build assets.

COORDINATED SCHOOL HEALTH LINKS

Tri-Color Action, which promotes cooperation, can easily be adapted for use at recess or in a classroom on a rainy day. Teachers can also use this activity to study different nations by changing the colors given on the cones to the flag colors of the nation the class is studying.

Whistle While You Work Out

CONTENT CONNECTIONS   Aerobic health, muscular endurance, flexibility

READY FOR ACTION
- A whistle or drum
- Students scattered in general space
- Let's Get Physical cards (see chapter 6)

LET'S PLAY   Students walk around the room and perform the exercise associated with the number of times the whistle is blown. See table 5.5 for an example.

Table 5.5   Actions for Whistles or Drumbeats

Number of whistles or drumbeats	Action
1	Walking
2	Jumping jack
3	Jogging
4	Push-up

CRANK IT UP   Ask students to create exercises for 5 and 6 whistles and then perform the exercises they created. Add these exercises to the routine described under "Let's Play." Make the walking interval shorter. Reproduce and place all of the Let's Get Physical cards from appendix B in a box. Draw out four cards and assign each card a number. Play as indicated in the "Let's Play" section.

GEAR IT DOWN   Use two actions:
- Blow the whistle one time to signal "Walk."
- Blow the whistle twice to signal "Sit and stretch."

ASSET ACTION

School boundaries (asset 12)—Listening to the teacher's directions is an important communication skill. Following those directions is equally important and is linked to social skills and assets such as responsibility, and school boundaries. Class management techniques are discussed in chapter 2.

COORDINATED SCHOOL HEALTH LINKS

Asset building and coordinated school health share an important principle: It is important for many people in a school or community to be concerned with all aspects of a child's development. Adults need to have positive expectations for children but also set boundaries, both at home and at school. To help parents and students understand your class rules and regulations, make copies of the rules and have students and parents sign a form indicating their willingness to stay within the boundaries. Whistle While You Work Out helps students get used to rules and regulations because they have to follow a whistle code to do the activity properly.

Let's Get Physical Cards

© Human Kinetics

Reproduce and laminate the Let's Get Physical cards from appendix B for the activities.

Use timed intervals instead of required repetitions during fitness activities.

Before using the Let's Get Physical cards, make sure that students are trained in the correct form and safety precautions for each exercise. Under teacher supervision, these exercises can be performed without mats.

Exercise Exchange

CONTENT CONNECTIONS   Aerobic health, muscular endurance, flexibility

READY FOR ACTION

- One Let's Get Physical card per student
- Students scattered in general space
- Music

LET'S PLAY   While music plays, students move around freely in general space and trade their cards with each student they meet. When the music stops, each student performs the exercise on his or her card for 15 seconds. When the music resumes, students continue walking and trading cards.

CRANK IT UP   Increase the time of the exercise interval (say, to 30 seconds). Ask students a question about a muscle that is being exercised. For example, you might say, "Who has a card with an exercise on it that works the triceps?" Students with that card might demonstrate their exercise to the class or lead the class in the exercise.

GEAR IT DOWN   Put 20 to 30 cards (or more for larger classes) on the floor in a circle around the room. While the music plays, students walk around the circumference. When the music stops, students do the exercise on the nearest card. More than one student can be at one card.

ASSET ACTION

Empowerment (assets 7-10) and social competencies (assets 32-36)—Let's Get Physical cards provide opportunities for students to make choices and lead exercises. Such opportunities help students feel valuable and in control—empowered—and build social competence.

COORDINATED SCHOOL HEALTH LINKS

- Any health-related fitness activity can easily be connected to health information. Remind students that regular physical activity and good eating habits are essential for a healthy heart.
- Play the Food ID game. Put food cards on the floor in a circle. When the music stops, the students freeze, identify the food on the card, and then perform a teacher-designated exercise.

Exercise Excitement

CONTENT CONNECTIONS   Health-related fitness

READY FOR ACTION

- Have several sets of Let's Get Physical cards on hand.
- Give each younger student a sheet of paper that you've divided into six square sections by folding or by marking and then photocopying. (The paper will have a windowpane appearance.) Give each older student a blank sheet of paper, and have them fold it into six square sections.
- For "Crank It Up," use basketballs.

LET'S PLAY   Have each student place their sheet of paper, unfolded, on the floor. Direct the students to choose one Let's Get Physical card and place it in one of the six squares, direct them to select and place a second card into a square, and so on. When the students have placed six cards on the sheet of paper, have them practice each depicted exercise. Next, start the music and call out any number from 1 to 6. Ask the students to perform the exercise under the corresponding number, or ask them to perform each exercise in number sequence and, at your signal, change to the next number.

CRANK IT UP   Extend the intervals so that students perform more repetitions. Use basketball tricks instead of exercise cards. Allow students to do the exercises depicted in the pictures on another student's paper grid.

GEAR IT DOWN   As students enter the room, give each of them three cards. Ask them to hold the cards and jog or briskly walk around the room's perimeter. When the music stops, they should lay their cards down in any order. By calling out, "One," "Two," or "Three," direct students the exercise depicted on one of their three cards.

ASSET ACTION

Caring (asset 26) and responsibility (asset 30)—In addition to respecting other people, students should treat objects (such as exercise cards) and their environment (such as the gym) responsibly. Ask the class to leave things as neat and clean as they found them.

COORDINATED SCHOOL HEALTH LINKS

Invite other teachers to borrow your Let's Get Physical cards for use outside of the PE period. By having students play Exercise Excitement, classroom teachers reinforce the importance of physical activity. They also can use the game as a lead-in to discussions about health topics such as nutrition.

Exercise Parade

CONTENT CONNECTIONS

Aerobic health, muscular strength, flexibility

READY FOR ACTION

- Have 8 to 10 Let's Get Physical cards on hand.
- Students stand around the perimeter of the area, safely spaced and waiting to join in the parade.
- Choose six students to lead the exercise parade, and give each of them an exercise card.
- For "Crank It Up," use basketballs.
- For "Gear It Down," use music.

© Human Kinetics

LET'S PLAY   One exercise leader at a time begins by slowly walking counterclockwise inside the entire student perimeter, displaying a card that shows the exercise to be performed. As the leader passes by, the other students continuously perform the depicted exercise. After 10 to 15 seconds, another leader starts to make the circuit with a different exercise card. The process continues: Leaders complete their circuit, return their exercise card to the teacher, and join other students exercising at the periphery; other leaders take over. At any given time some students are performing different exercises than other students. Students must wait until a card passes by before they begin a new exercise. Use a variety of exercises so that students receive a total-body workout.

CRANK IT UP   Extend the intervals so that students perform more repetitions. Use basketball tricks (see chapter 8) instead of exercise cards.

GEAR IT DOWN   Ask one leader to go all the way around the perimeter before the next leader starts. Another option is to put on music, and have all of the students exercise together as the teacher holds up the picture, walks around, and discusses proper form for each exercise.

ASSET ACTION

Positive view of personal future (asset 40)—Help students feel optimistic about their future. When they have trouble with a particular Exercise Parade activity, encourage them with messages such as "I know you'll do better next time."

COORDINATED SCHOOL HEALTH LINKS

Discuss fitness components and the relationship of fitness to health. Ask students to create their own exercises, draw them on a piece of paper, and bring them to class for a future parade. Share your Let's Get Physical cards and the students' cards with the classroom teachers for use in their classes or post them on a bulletin board in the hallway.

Fitness Four Square

CONTENT CONNECTIONS   Throwing, catching, underhand tossing, bounce passing, muscular endurance, flexibility

READY FOR ACTION

- Have foam or soft balls on hand.
- Divide the playing area into four large, adjacent squares numbered 1, 2, 3, and 4.
- Place two Let's Get Physical cards attached to cones at the perimeter of each square.
- For "Crank It Up," use basketballs.

LET'S PLAY   Divide the class into four groups, one group to each square. Give several students in each group a foam ball. These students try to throw their ball into the next number square so that another student can catch it. When a ball is caught, the thrower moves outside their square and performs an exercise (whichever the student chooses) displayed on one of the cards at the square's perimeter. The student then moves into the next square to play. If a thrown ball is not caught, the thrower moves outside the square to exercise but must return to the same square instead of advancing to the next number. The thrower is the only player to exercise and move. When a student catches a ball, they become a thrower and throw to the next square.

CRANK IT UP   Use basketball bounce passes and chest passes.

GEAR IT DOWN   Students form pairs, and each pair is given a ball. Partners must complete 15 throws and catches within a square, exercise together, and then move to the next square for a new ball challenge.

ASSET ACTION

Caring (asset 26), personal power (asset 37), and interpersonal competence (asset 33)—Many PE activities, such as throwing or catching a ball, are easier for naturally athletic students. Have physically skilled students mentor less skilled ones. The process will empower both the highly skilled and the less skilled students. Helping others is another way to show that you care.

COORDINATED SCHOOL HEALTH LINKS

Place nutrition questions at each exercise card. After exercising, a student mentally answers the questions and checks the correct answer written on the back of the card before moving to the next square.

Flexibility Frenzy

CONTENT CONNECTIONS   Flexibility, chasing, dodging

READY FOR ACTION

- Have flexibility Let's Get Physical cards on hand.
- Designate one tagger for every 8 to 10 students.
- Each tagger holds a flexibility card which specifies a particular stretching/flexibility exercise.
- Mark a section outside of the play area for stretching.

LET'S PLAY   Students with a flexibility card try to tag a student who doesn't have a card. When they succeed, they give their card to the student they've tagged. The tagged student performs the stretch indicated on the card for 30 seconds in the stretch area and then reenters the game.

CRANK IT UP   Color-code the flexibility cards. Post two cards of the same color in each corner. When tagged, a student goes to the corner whose cards match the color of the tagger's card. The student chooses between the two flexibility exercises depicted on the cards, performs that exercise, stretches for 20 seconds, and then reenters the game. Add muscular endurance cards for a tougher workout.

GEAR IT DOWN   Students play any simple tag game for 3 minutes. Then the teacher chooses a flexibility card, and the entire class performs the depicted stretch exercise for 20 seconds.

ASSET ACTION

Honesty (asset 29) and responsibility (asset 30)—Remind the students that everyone has more fun when games are played fairly. Students must be honest about whether or not a particular student has been tagged.

COORDINATED SCHOOL HEALTH LINKS

Familiarize students, especially elementary students, with the various health-related fitness components. Ask them which component Flexibility Frenzy builds. Encourage students to discuss health-related fitness with their parents.

Locomotor Interval Training

CONTENT CONNECTIONS   Aerobic health, muscular endurance, flexibility

READY FOR ACTION

- Four cones, placed in a square or rectangle
- Two Let's Get Physical cards, representing the same health-related component, on the back of each cone
- A "Skip" sign at cones 1 and 3 and a "Jog" sign at cones 2 and 4
- Music
- For "Crank It Up," a chart for each cone with *Flexibility, Strength,* and *Endurance* columns

LET'S PLAY   While music plays, students move from sign to sign, performing the designated locomotor movements. When the music stops, the students move to the nearest sign and perform an exercise of choice from the back of the card.

CRANK IT UP   Students stop at each cone and perform their exercise of choice. A chart with *Flexibility, Strength,* and *Endurance* columns is at each cone. Before leaving a station, students place a checkmark by the health-related fitness component on which their exercise focused.

GEAR IT DOWN   Label each cone with a different locomotor skill: Skip, hop, jump, gallop, etc. Students work on these skills while traveling from cone to cone when the music is playing. When the music stops, the teacher draws one exercise card from a pile of cards, and the entire class performs the task.

ASSET ACTION

Responsibility (asset 30)—During Locomotor Interval Training, students must follow written instructions which help them learn to follow rules and regulations. Praise students who act responsibly, and establish clear and fair consequences for irresponsible behavior.

COORDINATED SCHOOL HEALTH LINKS

Discuss fitness components and their relationship to mental, as well as physical, health. Have students create a bulletin board display for their classroom or a school hallway that stresses the importance of health-related fitness components and physical activity in general.

Lots of Lottery

CONTENT CONNECTIONS
Aerobic health, muscular endurance, flexibility

© Human Kinetics

READY FOR ACTION
- A numbered Let's Get Physical card for each student
- Music

LET'S PLAY   While music plays, each student holds their card and walks within the activity area. When the music stops, the teacher calls out three numbers. Students holding the cards with those numbers come to the front of the area. They've won the lottery. They now take a victory jog around a short course and then teach the class their exercise. The entire process is repeated several times. You may want to have students trade cards during walk time.

CRANK IT UP   Students jog while the music is playing. Call out five winning numbers. Have the winning students line up in the order of their numbers. The student with the middle number leads the exercise.

GEAR IT DOWN   Pick six winning numbers. The winners come to the front and perform any exercise of their choosing. All other students perform the exercise on their card.

ASSET ACTION

Self-esteem (asset 38) and personal power (asset 37)—Lots of Lottery develops leadership skills. Students lead their group in an exercise, which they also teach to the entire class. Such leadership opportunities build self-esteem and make students feel valued and empowered.

COORDINATED SCHOOL HEALTH LINKS

Remind students that mental and physical health require an ability to resolve conflicts peacefully. Ask students to discuss the concept of conflict resolution in their homes and list ways to peacefully resolve disagreements that might arise in the course of playing Lots of Lottery.

Partner Pathways

CONTENT CONNECTIONS   Locomotor skills, pathways

READY FOR ACTION

- Let's Get Physical cards randomly placed in the front of the activity area
- Pairs of students scattered in general space
- Music

LET'S PLAY   The teacher calls out a particular movement and pathway, such as "Walk in a zigzag," "Skip on a curve," or "Jog in a straight line." While music plays, one partner leads the other in performing the designated movement. When the music stops, the leader goes to the front of the activity area to choose a card while the follower stretches. The leader returns with the card and leads the follower, for 30 seconds, in the exercise shown on the card. Partners then switch places.

CRANK IT UP   The teacher tells the leaders of each pair to perform an exercise that will increase flexibility, and the partners then perform the exercise together. This activity helps the teacher to assess students' understanding of the components of health-related fitness.

GEAR IT DOWN   Students play Follow the Leader. When the music stops, all leaders report to the teacher. The teacher shows the students an exercise card and provides some information about the exercise, such as "This is a great exercise for your legs" or "This exercise helps your heart." The students then return to their partners, repeat the information, and lead their partner in the exercise.

ASSET ACTION

Teacher tip—This activity is rich in possibilities for building social skills and reinforcing assets. There are opportunities for students to develop leadership skills, be creative, and teach other students. Changing partners in a group setting requires students to interact with many other students and develop friendship and caring skills. Ask the class to find out special interests of their new partners.

COORDINATED SCHOOL HEALTH LINKS

Partner Pathways is an easy activity for teachers to supervise and a fun activity for kids. Teach classroom teachers about Partner Pathways, and ask them to have students play it at recess before moving to unstructured play.

Rectangle Romp

CONTENT CONNECTIONS   Aerobic health, muscular endurance, flexibility

READY FOR ACTION

- Around the perimeter of the activity area, form a rectangle out of 6 to 8 equally spaced cones.
- Each cone should have a Let's Get Physical card on the back and, on the front, a sign specifying a type of locomotor movement (e.g., jump, hop, skip, slide, gallop, walk). The cones are placed with the fronts of the cards (locomotor side) facing the approaching students so they can easily see the movements.
- For "Crank It Up," use signs with the names of muscles.

LET'S PLAY   Students start at different cones and perform the locomotor action listed as they move clockwise around the perimeter. At each cone, the students stop and perform the exercise from the back of the cone.

CRANK IT UP   To increase student interest and choice, put two or more exercise cards on the back of each cone. Here's another possibility: Place the names of muscles, rather than exercise cards, on some of the cones, and have students perform exercises that work those muscles.

GEAR IT DOWN   Don't use exercise cards. Simply have students simply move from cone to cone performing the locomotor movement indicated on the front of each cone.

ASSET ACTION

Responsibility (asset 30)—One of the most important skills or assets a student develops is the habit of acting responsibly. PE classes help students to develop responsibility. For example, they encourage students to make responsible decisions with regard to class rules and their own health. Ask the students to describe responsible behavior that they witnessed during Rectangle Romp. Praise students for acting responsibly.

COORDINATED SCHOOL HEALTH LINKS

Teach classroom teachers the locomotor portion of Rectangle Romp, and ask them to have students perform that portion at recess before engaging in unstructured play. Students can check their heart rates after performing the romp two times. In cooperation with classroom teachers, PE teachers can lead students to a healthier lifestyle.

Tag Team Fitness

CONTENT CONNECTIONS   Aerobic health, muscular endurance, flexibility

READY FOR ACTION

- Create a circle of 10 to 12 equally spaced cones in the center of the activity area to create a jogging area.
- Place an exercise card on each cone so that the card faces the circle's center.
- Students form pairs.
- For "Crank It Up," use jump ropes or signs with the names of muscles.

LET'S PLAY   One student in each pair remains inside the circle and performs any exercise while the partner jogs once around the circumference. The jogger then enters the circle and tags their partner's hand, and the partners switch places. After each partner has jogged and exercised, the pair chooses a new exercise and repeats the process.

CRANK IT UP   Increase the lap time, or mix the exercises with jump rope tricks. You also can place muscle names, rather than exercise cards, on some cones. Students then will perform exercises that they believe focus on the specified muscles.

GEAR IT DOWN   Don't place cards on cones. Instead, call out a new exercise every 5 minutes. All students inside the circle will do the same exercise.

ASSET ACTION

Positive values (assets 26-31) and social competencies (assets 32-36)—Partner activities such as Tag Team Fitness develop social skills. When students work with a partner and offer physical or verbal assistance, they are showing that they care. Ask students to give reasons why working with a partner might be especially conducive to improving fitness and skill levels.

COORDINATED SCHOOL HEALTH LINKS

The ability to get along with people, as in Tag Team Fitness, is an important part of social health, and social health builds assets. With your school's classroom teachers, discuss the possibility of making asset-building activities part of the curriculum.

Tag Training

CONTENT CONNECTIONS   Aerobic health, muscular endurance, chasing, dodging, fleeing

READY FOR ACTION

- Divide the activity area in half with cones.
- Place Let's Get Physical cards on several cones on side 2 (see figure 6.1).
- Have half of the students go to side 1 and half to side 2.

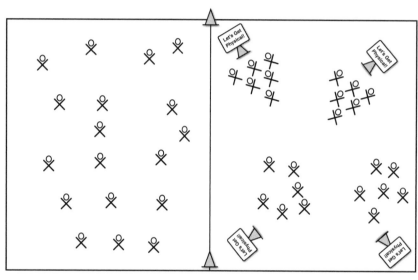

Side 1 (tag)   Side 2 (exercise)

Figure 6.1 Tag Training diagram.

LET'S PLAY   The students on side 1 play tag games while the students on side 2 exercise at one of the stations. Every 2 minutes the students switch sides. Instead of regular tag, you might have students play tag while moving like an animal such as a crab or bear. Animal movements develop strength and balance. Use regular tag rules, including a prohibition on tagging back and forth between two students. Designate a reentry task area for tagged students to do a teacher-designated task before reentering the game.

CRANK IT UP   Move outside so that students have a large area in which to jog, run, and dodge.

GEAR IT DOWN   Enlarge the play area, and have all students play a game of walk tag for 2 minutes. Next have the entire group perform an exercise depicted on a Let's Get Physical card for 1 minute. Either designate the exercise, or allow students to choose.

ASSET ACTION

Planning and decision making (asset 32) and achievement motivation (asset 21)— Provide a process in the gym or classroom that involves students in setting goals for themselves and evaluating their own performance. Such a process empowers students and actively engages them in learning. For example, in Tag Training, the students on side 2 can set goals for how many exercises they will be able to perform before resting, and then work to increase that number. Students can self-evaluate their form as they do the exercises.

COORDINATED SCHOOL HEALTH LINKS

Tag Training provides an especially enjoyable activity for kids because they enjoy animals so much and for teachers because they can see an improvement in physical, emotional, and social health while reinforcing a positive attitude toward school. Ask yourself the following questions: "Did I provide an inviting learning environment? Did students have a chance to participate at their own level? Were students successful? What are my criteria for determining student success?" Refer to chapter 1 and criteria for success in a contemporary, quality PE model.

Team Card Combo

CONTENT CONNECTIONS

Aerobic health, muscular endurance, flexibility, rhythm, cooperation

READY FOR ACTION

- Mix several sets of Let's Get Physical cards, and place the cards in the middle of the play area.
- Use upbeat music.
- Form groups of three or four, scattered in general space.
- For "Crank It Up," create a few cards that specify dance or locomotor steps, one move per card.

LET'S PLAY   One student from each group jogs to the middle of the play area, draws an exercise card, and returns to their group. The card is placed face up for all group members to see. While music plays, all group members perform the exercise. They stop when the music stops. A second group member now jogs to the middle of the play area and picks an exercise card. The card is placed face up next to the first card, and the group performs the exercise on the second card while the music plays. The activity continues until all students have drawn a card. The teacher then calls out the numbers 1 to 4 in sequence during 15-second intervals. Each number represents the order of the exercises. Each time a number is called, the students perform the exercise associated with the number. This creates an exercise routine as the students perform in unison. The teacher can help keep the students together by counting the beats of music.

CRANK IT UP   Create a few cards that specify dance or locomotor steps, one move per card, such as step touch, grapevine, heel tap, walk forward three steps and clap on the fourth beat, snake, wiggle, march, skip in place, jazzy jumps, attitude walk, freestyle, or even more stylized movements such as the cabbage patch, the hammer, running man, and "get jiggy." Use movements that you are familiar with and that the kids will easily pick up. Ask students to name and demonstrate currently popular steps. Include these steps in the cards to be drawn. Have students create an exercise dance, perhaps one that includes steps familiar to them.

GEAR IT DOWN   Have students work with a partner and alternately draw cards and exercise. Include locomotor and animal moves.

ASSET ACTION

Interpersonal competence (asset 33), cultural competence (asset 34), and creative activities (asset 17)—Physical education activities that are fun include music and give students a chance to interact with many other students develop social skills such as tolerance and friendliness. Especially when students create dance and fitness routines, PE activities like this also can motivate students to pursue creative activities—such as music, drama, and dance—outside of school.

COORDINATED SCHOOL HEALTH LINKS

Encourage students to create their own exercise program. This fosters a supportive environment and motivates students to stay interested in physical activity. In addition to encouraging creativity, Team Card Caper teaches a wide range of physical and social skills. It's an ideal activity to use when parents or school personnel observe your class.

Terrific 10s

CONTENT CONNECTIONS   Warm-up, aerobic health

READY FOR ACTION

- Clip three or four Let's Get Physical cards to each of six posters.
- Place the posters, in a line, across the front of the activity area. Cards can be grouped by fitness component or mixed.
- Divide the students into six groups.

LET'S PLAY   Send each group to a different poster. Students perform the first exercise on their poster 10 times and then move to the next poster. Once again they perform the first exercise on the poster and then move on. When they've completed every first exercise on each poster, students perform the second exercise on each poster. Students are encouraged to perform with good form, so they will move at different rates depending on their strength and ability.

CRANK IT UP   After each poster exercise, students jog one lap before moving to the next poster.

GEAR IT DOWN   Students stay in assigned spots while the teacher moves from poster to poster and announces each exercise. They pretend they are moving to the next poster by jogging in place. Students may repeat the entire exercise sequence several times.

ASSET ACTION

School/learning engagement (asset 22)—Building this asset requires an environment in which the child feels comfortable. To help children feel comfortable within a PE setting, address their developmental activity level. This book's alternative activity sections (*Let's Play, Crank It Up,* and *Gear it Down*) ensure that all students can perform activities commensurate with their ability level. Developmentally appropriate activities and exercises foster active student engagement. Encouraging each student to work at their own pace as they work on form during this activity ensures higher levels of success. Success in activities engages children in the activities.

COORDINATED SCHOOL HEALTH LINKS

Discuss the exercises on the posters with the students. Ask students if anyone can name the health-related fitness category that the poster exercises represent.

You Make the Call

CONTENT CONNECTIONS   Flexibility, aerobic health, muscular endurance

READY FOR ACTION

- Hoops
- Jump ropes
- Let's Get Physical cards
- Music

LET'S PLAY   Divide the floor into three aerobic exercise areas: a hula hoop area, jump rope area, and jogging area. Students exercise in the area of their choice for 3 minutes while music plays. Then the teacher stops the music and holds up two flexibility cards. Students choose one of the exercises depicted on the cards and perform it for 1 minute. The whole sequence then is repeated except that students do a different type of aerobic exercise followed by a strength-card exercise. The activity concludes with a third type of aerobic exercise followed by an endurance-card exercise.

CRANK IT UP   During the 1-minute exercise, the teacher calls out a fitness component and the students perform an exercise, of their own choosing, that focuses on that component. The teacher uses this activity to assess students' knowledge of health-related fitness components.

GEAR IT DOWN   The teacher reduces the exercise time; chooses an aerobic exercise, such as jogging, fast walking, or jumping, that requires no equipment; and has students choose an exercise from the Let's Get Physical cards.

ASSET ACTION

- **Responsibility (asset 30) and interpersonal competence (asset 33)**—Your PE instruction will be more effective and you'll be better able to help students succeed if your classroom management is well planned. Stressing responsible behavior and respect for others is indispensable to effective teaching. Students show responsibility in PE by always trying to do their best. They show respect for others by being polite and considerate.

- **High expectations (asset 16), achievement motivation (asset 21), and personal power (asset 37)**—When You Make the Call is over, ask each student to evaluate how she or he did. Tell students to give themselves a thumbs-up, thumbs-sideways, or thumbs-down for the following: trying hard, doing exercises with perfect form, helping others, encouraging those who were having difficulty.

COORDINATED SCHOOL HEALTH LINKS

Discuss health-related fitness components. Describe various exercises or hold up pictures of activities and ask students which fitness components those activities focus on. (For example, jogging focuses on cardiovascular fitness.) Show students the U.S. Department of Agriculture food pyramid and stress the connection between good eating habits and physical activity. Explain the connection between good eating habits and physical activity: that nutritious food is like high-quality fuel for the body, and we need nutrients from food in order to perform well in physical activity. Also, eating nutritious food is one component of health, just as getting regular physical activity is a component and avoiding unhealthy habits (smoking, taking street drugs, drinking) is a component.

Deck of Cards

7

Kindness, acceptance, caring, and encourage- ment are required.

Is there a place in your class- room to post a list of social competencies?

Deal some health and fitness tips today!

75

Bank Tag

CONTENT CONNECTIONS
Aerobic health, chasing, dodging

READY FOR ACTION

- Each player has three playing cards.
- Students are scattered in general space.
- A hoop or box representing a bank is placed at the front of the room.

LET'S PLAY   Select three or four students to be taggers. The taggers are the bankers. If a banker tags someone, the tagged student must freeze. The banker then guesses a suit: hearts, diamonds, spades, or clubs. If the tagged player has one or more cards of that suit, she or he must pay the banker by giving him or her that particular card. The banker puts the money (card) in the bank. When a player is out of cards, she or he must see the loan officer (teacher) and request a loan (card or cards). After receiving the loan, the player may return to the game.

CRANK IT UP   Before a player returns to the game, she or he must perform a reentry task.

GEAR IT DOWN   Play a simple tag game. Give each student one card. When the student is tagged, he or he goes to the banker (teacher), turns in his or her card, performs an exercise, and gets another card from the teacher (a loan) that he or she returns.

 ## ASSET ACTION
Caring (asset 26)—Ask the students to encourage one another during activities. Encouragement is a sign of caring and friendship. Bank Tag is good for developing caring because the students interact so much.

 ## COORDINATED SCHOOL HEALTH LINKS
Bank Tag nurtures social health in young people by stressing the importance of kindness. Some students may see other students' incorrect guesses as an opportunity to tease. You can help by encouraging students to be supportive of one another.

Card Collection

CONTENT CONNECTIONS   Aerobic health, flexibility

READY FOR ACTION

- Have several decks of cards on hand.
- Use cones, domes, or poly spots as markers.
- Hide the cards under a cone, poly spot, or dome. All cards should be completely covered.
- Use exercise bands for the "Crank It Up" section.

LET'S PLAY   Divide the students into small groups (if possible, groups of three). Assign each group a playing card to locate—for example, group 1 = aces, group 2 = 2s, and so on. Students try to collect as many cards as possible within a designated amount of time. The members of each group stretch together around the perimeter. One student at a time goes and looks under a marker. If the card matches the assigned card of his or her group, the player takes that card back to his or her team and jogs once around the perimeter. If the card doesn't match the group's assigned card, the students replaces the card, returns to her or his team, performs the same number of line jumps as the incorrect card's value, and tags the player next in line. That player repeats the process. Groups who have found a matching card should continue to stretch until the middle contains no more cards and play ends. Students should play in rounds and trade assigned cards.

CRANK IT UP   Change the jogging and jumping to meet students' needs. Include exercises with bands, bench step-ups, and push-ups.

GEAR IT DOWN   Allow students to collect any card they find, take it back to their team, and jog one lap. If a student looks under a marker and finds no card, she or he returns to her or his team and leads the team in 5 push-ups or 5 curl-ups. Teams can add up their points, and the winning team may jog a victory lap.

ASSET ACTION

Caring school climate (asset 5)—Do you have a bulletin board in your classroom or gym that lists assets? If not, devote a bulletin board to asset-building messages. For example, focus on honesty. Playing fair is a part of playing honest. Ask students what the word "honest" means. Then ask if they saw students playing honestly/fairly. What did they see when someone was honest?

COORDINATED SCHOOL HEALTH LINKS

Place pictures of food under the markers. Each team will be assigned a type of food, such as fruits, vegetables, meat, or grains. Follow with a discussion about the benefits of eating a variety of healthy foods. Ask each group to pick one food from their assigned type and write a short sentence on the importance of eating or limiting that food. Post all of the student statements in the cafeteria by the lunch lines.

Card Run 21

CONTENT CONNECTIONS   Aerobic health, game skill development

READY FOR ACTION

- Place four cones in the activity area so that they form a large rectangle.
- Remove the face cards from two decks of cards. Put one box of cards each at opposite ends of the rectangle.
- Designate safe activity areas for rope jumping, hula hoop, beach ball volleying, and basketball dribbling. (See figure 7.1.)
- For "Crank it Up," use 4-6 posters, each with the name of a different health-related fitness component.
- For "Gear it Down," use music.

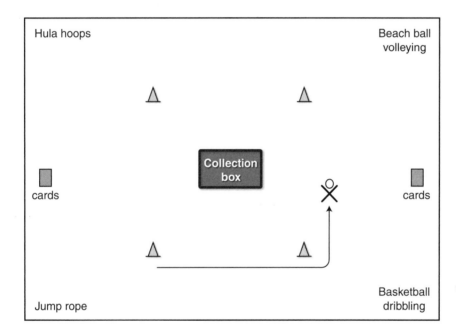

Figure 7.1   Card Run 21 diagram.

LET'S PLAY   Students jog or walk laps around the activity area. Each time they pass a box of cards, they take one card. When a student has collected cards totaling 21 or more in number value (an ace = 1), she or he shows the teacher and puts her or his cards in the collection box in the middle of the room. Then the student chooses any activity in the play area. Each time a student accumulates at least 21 points, he or she selects a new activity to perform. Allow play time. Call students by activity groups (the jump rope group, the hula hoop group, etc.) back to jog or walk and repeat the game.

CRANK IT UP   Change the winning score to a larger number. Change the activity areas to represent different health-related fitness components. Write the name of each component on a poster, and ask students to do a favorite exercise that matches the health-related component. For example, for arm endurance and strength, a student might perform chin-ups at a bar or push-ups.

GEAR IT DOWN Reduce the number of stations to two. While music plays, students jog and pick up cards. When the music stops, each student adds up his or her number of card points. Group the students by points, and send each group to a different station. For example, students with fewer than 21 points might go to the jump rope station, and students with more than 21 points might go to the hula hoop station.

ASSET ACTION

- **Other adult relationships (asset 3)**—When students show you that their cards add up to 21 or more, speak to them personally, addressing them by name and perhaps complimenting them on following the rules of the game or always being interested in the class.

- **Personal power (asset 37)**—As this asset develops, young people begin to feel that they have control over their lives. In giving students a choice, Card Run 21 builds the asset of personal power.

COORDINATED SCHOOL HEALTH LINKS

Discuss health-related fitness components. Ask students to discuss aerobic health at home. Tell them to ask their parents or guardians two questions:

- Why is aerobic health important?
- What are the two most important things a person can do to prevent heart disease?

Card Suit Fitness

CONTENT CONNECTIONS

Health-related fitness, aerobic health, muscular endurance, flexibility, jumping rope

READY FOR ACTION

- Prepare four posters: a heart, a diamond, a club, and a spade. Each suit will represent a health-related fitness component (e.g., heart = aerobic health; diamond = flexibility; club = abdominal or muscular endurance; spade = arm strength).

- Place two exercise instructions or two Let's Get Physical exercise cards under each poster. For example, you could place the instructions "Jump rope" and "Jog in place" or two cards under the heart poster.

- Place each poster in a corner of the room.

- Put several decks of playing cards in the middle of the area.

- For "Crank It Up," add jump ropes.

LET'S PLAY   Each student draws a card from the card pile and goes to the matching suit poster to choose an exercise to perform. The student stays at the station and perform her or his chosen exercise for an amount of time specified by the teacher, based on the student's ability and fitness level as well as the goals of the lesson. When time is up, the student chooses a new card and play continues. At each exercise area the student focuses on form, not number of repetitions, while exercising.

CRANK IT UP   For an increased cardiorespiratory workout, students can jog one or two laps before getting their next card. Older students can benefit from choosing sport skills or jump rope tricks under each poster.

GEAR IT DOWN   Do this activity in teams. Allow each student a turn as leader. The leader draws the card, directs the team to the poster that shows the same suit, and leads the group in the exercise that he or she chooses. Alternatively, the teacher can draw a card and let the entire class perform one of the listed exercises in order to acquaint younger students with the exercises and game format.

ASSET ACTION

- **Youth as resources (asset 8)**—Card Suit Fitness cultivates leadership skills. It provides a friendly, supportive environment in which students develop their capacity to be of service to others. Teachers can give students the opportunity to lead an activity. This process happens best when a student feels safe and comfortable like in a physical education setting that is friendly and supportive.

- **High expectations (asset 16)**—Card Suit Fitness encourages students to do their personal best and set goals. Ask them to use their best form and to perform each repetition correctly. Students should focus on improving, not on being better than other students.

- **Parental involvement in schooling (asset #6)**—This asset is an important component of asset building because the child's home has great influence in building assets and values. The connection to home is also an important component of a coordinated school health program.

COORDINATED SCHOOL HEALTH LINKS

Ask students to get their classroom teachers and parents involved in developing at least two posters representing health-related fitness components. Students might practice poster exercises under adult supervision at home or at recess. This is an excellent rainy-day recess activity to share with a classroom teacher.

Dealer's Choice

CONTENT CONNECTIONS   Aerobic health, cooperation, muscular strength, muscular endurance

READY FOR ACTION

- Have several decks of cards, as determined by the size of the class.
- Each student is given one playing card as she or he enters the room.
- Have music on hand.

LET'S PLAY   The teacher calls out a particular locomotor movement that the students perform to music. As the students move throughout the area, the teacher tells students how to form groups based on the cards that they're holding. For example, the teacher might call out any of the following:

- Group by card suit.
- Form a same-suit group of six.
- Find two of a kind (cards with the same number).
- Form a group whose card numbers total more than 25.
- Form a group of four whose card numbers are in sequence.
- Group by card number or face.
- Find a partner with the exact same card.
- Find three who have the same color.

CRANK IT UP   Have students perform (create) a designated exercise for a certain amount of time after forming their groups. Add balls for students to work on sport skills.

GEAR IT DOWN   Play without cards. When you call out a number, students find that many partners and form a circle. Partners then shake hands with one another and say, "Hi. My name is…" Next select a playing card and an exercise, and ask students to do an exercise like jumping jacks equal in number to the card's number.

ASSET ACTION

- **Planning and decision making (asset 32) and interpersonal competence (asset 33)**—Dealer's Choice helps students build social competence as well as the ability to plan and make decisions (such as food choices). Ask them to be kind and welcoming toward their group members and to help students who are having trouble finding their group. Close this activity by asking students to describe how one or more students showed friendliness.
- **Caring (asset 26)**—Have students give someone in each of their groups a compliment. The teacher can join in a group and recall the names of all children in that group, mentally or verbally.

COORDINATED SCHOOL HEALTH LINKS

Each student holds a picture or model of a food. Students form groups based on categories such as food color or type—for example, green foods, fruits, high-fat foods, breakfast foods. Group members share their food pictures (or models) and the names of their foods. They also discuss why certain foods are good for them. The group then performs an exercise designated by the teacher.

Digit Draw

CONTENT CONNECTIONS   Aerobic health, muscular endurance, flexibility

READY FOR ACTION

- Shuffled decks of cards in the middle of the room
- Poster board or chalkboard in the front of the room
- Students seated in small teams scattered around the perimeter of the area

LET'S PLAY   The teacher displays a number series, such as 2,4,5,7, on the poster or chalkboard. One player at a time draws a card from the pile of cards. If the card doesn't match any number in the series, the player leaves the card in the middle of the floor and the group performs three push-ups. If the card does match a number in the series, the player returns to the group with the card and places it on the floor. The player then jogs once around the perimeter before rejoining his or her group. The first group to hold the displayed number series selects an exercise for the entire class to do, but the winning group does two exercises fewer than the rest of the class.

CRANK IT UP   Give the students a math problem to solve. Ask all students to jog when the correct number is drawn.

GEAR IT DOWN   Limit each series to two numbers. Or display three simple math problems (such as 1 + 2, 3 + 3, or 4 − 2) and ask the students to find the answers.

ASSET ACTION

School/learning engagement (asset 22)—Cooperation between PE teachers and other teachers in a school helps students succeed academically. It is also important to actively engage students with a variety of teaching methods. Digit Draw reinforces numbers in a new way and helps students recognize that PE is more than exercise.

COORDINATED SCHOOL HEALTH LINKS

Meet with classroom teachers and discuss the thinking skills that Digit Draw reinforces. Communicating with other teachers can be a first step in establishing a coordinated school health program.

Flash Card Fitness

CONTENT CONNECTIONS   Aerobic health, muscular endurance, flexibility

READY FOR ACTION

- Write three numbers and one exercise on each of seven posters.
- Place the posters around the perimeter of the play area (see figure 7.2).
- Place mixed decks of cards in the center of the play area.

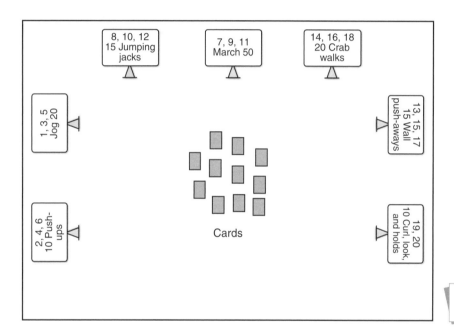

Figure 7.2 Flash Card Fitness diagram.

LET'S PLAY   Each student draws two cards from the pile and finds the sum of the numbers on the cards. (A face card = 10; an ace = 1; a joker = 0.) The student then puts the card, facedown, back into the pile; locates the sum on one of the posters around the perimeter; and performs the exercise associated with that number. (The posters could be standing against or hung on the wall or cone.)

CRANK IT UP   Have older students subtract, multiply, and divide, as well as add, card numbers. Change the number cards (used for answers) on the walls accordingly. Ask students to jog or jump rope between draws.

GEAR IT DOWN   Use only one mathematical operation (addition, subtraction, multiplication, or division). Allow students to work with a partner or form them into groups with a volunteer student choosing a card. The teacher calls out the math question, one student points to the answer, and the class exercises together.

 ASSET ACTION

School/learning engagement (asset 22)—Flash Card Fitness promotes asset 22 by incorporating math skills in a fun way.

 COORDINATED SCHOOL HEALTH LINKS

Ask other teachers to play Flash Card Fitness with students. The child also can play this game at home with family members or alone.

Lottery Tag

CONTENT CONNECTIONS   Aerobic health

READY FOR ACTION

- One playing card per student
- Students scattered in general space
- For "Crank It Up": beanbags

LET'S PLAY   At the signal, students jog around the room with their cards concealed. When the teacher calls, "The winning lottery numbers are," all students move to an open spot and continue to jog there while the teacher announces the numbers. If a student's number is called, the student goes to the middle of the room and becomes a tagger. After all winners are in the middle, they attempt to tag as many students as possible within a teacher-designated time (about 2 minutes.) During this time, tagged students go to the sidelines and balance on one foot or perform an exercise until the 2-minute interval is up. After each round, students trade playing cards, and the teacher calls out new winning numbers.

CRANK IT UP   Play the game as described in "Let's Play," but give students a beanbag as well as a card. A student whose number is called slides her or his beanbag on the floor, attempting to tag others on their feet with the beanbag.

GEAR IT DOWN   Instead of playing tag, lottery winners come to the front and stretch while the other students perform an exercise that the teacher assigns.

ASSET ACTION

Healthy Lifestyle (asset 31)—Remind students that being active for a lifetime improves the health of your heart and increases the chances of living longer. More importantly, incorporating enjoyable activity into your life can also improve the quality of your life. Ask the students to name some fun activities that they could do with their parents.

COORDINATED SCHOOL HEALTH LINKS

Lottery Tag is a fun game that students can share with their parents at home or at a school open house. Including parents in children's schooling helps the children by giving them coordinated adult support and coordinated health messages.

Stock Exchange Tag

CONTENT CONNECTIONS

Chasing, dodging, locomotor skills

READY FOR ACTION

- One card per student from a deck of playing cards
- A whistle, bell, or drum
- A card pile for the teacher
- Music

LET'S PLAY   While music plays, students hold their cards, which represent stocks, and jog freely in space. On the bell signal all students are "it" and try to tag others. All students who are tagged must trade cards until the closing bell sounds. No tagging back and forth is allowed. The teacher then draws three cards, which represent the day's highest-trading stocks. Students with those cards are the winning traders for that round.

CRANK IT UP   Assign exercises to the winning traders; they do an exercise, stretch, and then rest after a hard day at the market. Losing traders get ready for the next day's trading by jogging during the winners' rest period.

GEAR IT DOWN   Eliminate tagging. Have students do a different locomotor skill before each opening bell. At the opening bell, ask students to trade cards. Conclude with the winning stocks as done earlier in "Let's Play".

ASSET ACTION

Teacher Tip—Get to know your students personally. Ask them about their interests, hobbies, goals, and dreams. Showing personal interest in your students signals that you support them and helps to create an asset-rich environment, which provides more opportunities for students to succeed.

COORDINATED SCHOOL HEALTH LINKS

Teacher tip—Talk to classroom teachers about asset building and how it is being incorporated into the PE program. This is a good way to begin the process of establishing a coordinated school health program.

Two for the Road

CONTENT CONNECTIONS   Aerobic health

READY FOR ACTION

- Playing cards spread facedown in the middle of the play area
- Four cones forming a rectangle around the perimeter of the play area
- Balls

LET'S PLAY   Each student draws a card from the card pile and then moves around the middle of the room trying to locate someone who has a card of the same number. When a match is found, the students with matching cards walk or jog around the coned perimeter and return their cards to the teacher. Play continues as students draw a new card. The teacher replaces the cards in the middle of the play area as needed. Change the locomotor patterns the students perform with their partner. For example: Skip, jump, or gallop side by side around the perimeter.

CRANK IT UP   Change the designated exercise task to an exercise or a ball skill such as chest passing with a partner followed by jogging one lap around the room.

GEAR IT DOWN   Students follow the same procedure to locate a partner; however, they remain with the same partner for three activities before drawing a new card.

ASSET ACTION

Teacher tip—In group activities or partners, mix students in a way that reflects the diversity of your school. Kids who form diverse friendships are less likely to develop prejudices. One of the important elements of social competency skills is building healthy relationships and making friends. The more developmental assets and social skills a child develops, the more likely it is that he or she will grow up healthy and successful.

COORDINATED SCHOOL HEALTH LINKS

Use food pictures instead of playing cards. Ask students to find a partner who has a food in the same group as theirs. When students finish walking or jogging, have them place their food pictures in the appropriate food group box at the front of the room. This activity helps students develop a healthy lifestyle that includes being physically active and having good eating habits.

Balls

8

© Human Kinetics

Ball games should meet the needs of all students, not just the athletically gifted.

Don't forget to have fun!

Use a selection of balls with a variety of weights and sizes to ensure success.

10-Minute Ball Fitness Workout

CONTENT CONNEC-TIONS Ball handling, fitness, muscular endurance, muscular flexibility

READY FOR ACTION
- Each student has a ball.
- Students are scattered in general space, and use their personal space to perform skills.

© Human Kinetics

LET'S PLAY Call out each skill for students to perform. If necessary, demonstrate the skill. Mix the calls up as the students become competent in performing the skills.

Action Calls

1. Wrap it—Move the ball around your waist.
2. Knees—Move the ball around your knees.
3. Around the world—Move the ball around your head.
4. Push and pass—While in push-up position, use one hand to push the ball from your right side to your left side. Alternate hands.
5. Right hand—Dribble with your right hand.
6. Left hand—Dribble with your left hand.
7. Curl and touch—Lie down with your back on the floor in sit-up position. Tap the ball above your head, curl up, tap the floor in front of the toes, and tap again behind your head.
8. Jog it—Jog while moving the ball away from and to your chest.
9. Spider stand—With your feet shoulder-width apart, roll the ball on the floor in a figure eight.
10. Fingertip drill—Holding the ball away from your body, use your fingertips to move the ball from hand to hand.

CRANK IT UP Add advanced ball-handling tricks such as "Pass the ball under your legs while walking" or "Kneel on one knee and dribble the ball by pushing it under the other knee," Have students dribble around the room while avoiding others, stop when the teacher signals, and then perform a trick that the teacher calls out. Have students perform ball tricks with a partner. (See Partner Ab Fitness, page 108.)

GEAR IT DOWN Add a straddle stretch with the ball on the floor in front of the student. Use the action calls for numbers 1, 2, and 3 exclusively. Allow students to bounce and catch the balls between calls.

ASSET ACTION

Teacher tip—Students become more engaged in the school and class when they develop confidence in school-related activities. Encourage students as they attempt to improve their skills in your class. Provide lessons at an appropriate developmental level. Remember that when students become more engaged in school and feel more connected to the school, their chances of success improve. To boost the confidence of less-skilled students, encourage them with comments such as "I know you can do this" or "I know you'll do your best."

COORDINATED SCHOOL HEALTH LINKS

Share 10-Minute Ball Fitness Workout with classroom teachers. Students can do this activity at recess or during a special play break. If the classroom doesn't have enough balls for the students, suggest using paper balls (crush paper from the recycling bin) and perform all skills except 5 and 6.

Asteroids

CONTENT CONNECTIONS   Overhand throwing

READY FOR ACTION

- Divide the playing area in half.
- In the middle of each half of the playing area, form a circle (crater) of upright gymnastics mats (see figure 8.1).
- Have plenty of foam balls on hand.
- Divide the students into two teams.
- For "Crank It Up," add pool noodles.

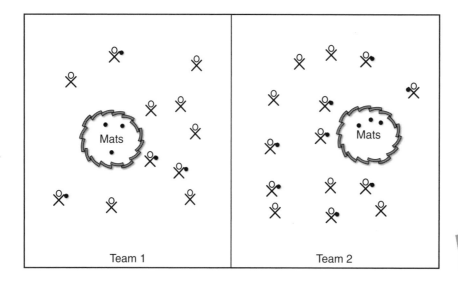

| Team 1 | Team 2 |

Figure 8.1
Asteroids diagram.

LET'S PLAY   Students practice overhand throwing by attempting to throw foam balls (asteroids) across the center line and into the opposing team's circle (crater). Students may guard their team's crater and knock away or catch balls. Have the students play in timed rounds. After each round, count the number of asteroids in each crater. Students can help by throwing balls out of the crater as the class counts.

CRANK IT UP   For more action, place two or three students inside each crater and allow them to throw the balls out to their team members. Give each guard (Jedi knights) a pool noodle and allow them to bat away asteroids.

GEAR IT DOWN   Instead of placing the mats on the floor in a circle, place them across the middle of the gym in a line. For several minutes students catch and throw, underhand and overhand, into the other team's space. Count to see which team has fewer asteroids. That team has saved their planet.

ASSET ACTION

Teacher tip—Have an open-door policy for students who want to talk. Be available as often as you can before and after school. A good opportunity to talk to students is during lunch or recess.

COORDINATED SCHOOL HEALTH LINKS

During Asteroids, refer to the crater as the stomach or heart and to the balls as fatty foods. Players try to knock the fatty foods away from their team's stomach so that their heart won't be damaged by an unhealthy diet. Ask students to share this nutrition information with family members.

Ball Bombardment

CONTENT CONNECTIONS   Overhand throwing, throwing accuracy

READY FOR ACTION
- Place cage balls, beach balls, and foam balls in the center of the playing area to act as targets.
- Divide the students into two groups.
- Give each student two balls or objects to throw such as bean bags, foam softballs, and whiffle balls.

LET'S PLAY   Group 1 stands at the starting line. At the signal, all members of group 1 throw their balls, attempting to hit the target balls in the middle of the playing area to move them away from the starting line. Group 1 retrieves the balls and returns to the starting line behind group 2. Group 2 moves into position on the starting line and throws on the signal. Challenge students to move the target balls in the middle of the gym farther away each round, or time how long it takes for them to move across the end line.

CRANK IT UP   Divide the play area into four equal squares and the students into four teams. Have the members of each team position themselves along the outside boundaries of one square. Place balls in the middle of the play area. On your signal, students throw balls at the balls in the middle, attempting to move them into another team's square. After each round, stop and award points to teams who have balls resting inside their square. The team who has no balls inside their square wins. For safety, students may not enter the playing area to retrieve a ball. They may throw only the balls that they can reach from the sidelines. (A teacher may enter the playing area to knock thrown balls out to the boundary players.) (See figure 8.2.)

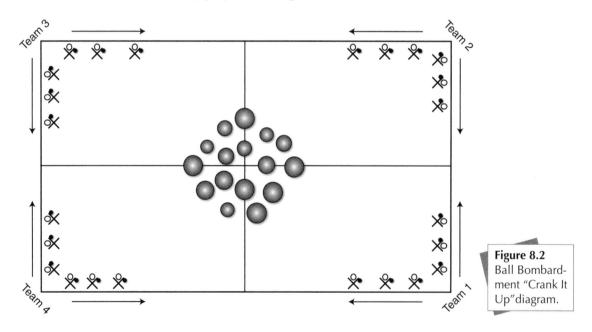

Figure 8.2
Ball Bombardment "Crank It Up" diagram.

GEAR IT DOWN   Working in pairs, students alternate throwing and rolling balls in an attempt to move a ball placed midway between them. When many students are present, place the balls on a boundary line around the gym so that errant balls will hit a wall rather than a student.

ASSET ACTION

Honesty (asset 29)—Before beginning Ball Bombardment, ask the students why honesty is important during a game. Being honest includes playing fair and playing by the rules. After the game, ask the students to consider whether or not they were honest.

COORDINATED SCHOOL HEALTH LINKS

Modify Ball Bombardment so that it teaches a health lesson. Tell students that they are fat eliminators trying to remove fatty foods from their diet. Label each ball in the middle of the play area with the name of a high-fat food. Discuss with students how hard it is to reduce body fat and how important it is to eat low-fat foods.

Ball Bonanza

CONTENT CONNECTIONS   Ball manipulation, dribbling, passing, catching

READY FOR ACTION

- One ball
- Five lines of equally spaced poly spots, one spot per student (see figure 8.3)
- Cones to mark lines
- Music
- Signs with the following skills:
    - Line 1—Tricks from Globetrotter Games (page 103)
    - Line 2—Dribble drills: In place, students practice dribbling while kneeling, sitting, and lying down.
    - Line 3—Throw-and-catch tricks such as throw to self, jump to catch (rebound), and toss, clap, catch
    - Line 4—Ball stretches. Students use the ball to stretch all around their body. For example, they might sit in a straddle position and push the ball forward with both hands.
    - Line 5—Ball camouflage. See Beanbag Fitness Challenges, page 144.

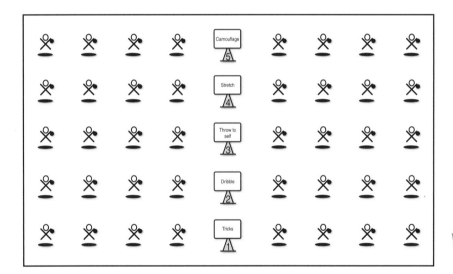

Figure 8.3   Ball Bonanza diagram.

LET'S PLAY   Each student has a ball and stands on a poly spot. Students perform the assigned task while the music is playing. When the music stops, students keep their ball and move to the next line. Row 5 jogs once around the entire play area and stops at line 1.

CRANK IT UP   Add advanced skills for older students. Add a shooting station. Use all available baskets for free throws.

GEAR IT DOWN   Change the task to the following:

Line 1—Bounce and catch.

Line 2—Do two-handed dribbles.

Line 3—Toss and catch to self.

Line 4—Sit-and-reach ball stretch (push ball down legs to toes).

Line 5—Curl up and down with the ball in your hands.

ASSET ACTION

Teacher tip—Develop a bulletin board in your class and in the gym with asset-building messages such as, "Did you help someone in class today?" Remind students to encourage other students who may need help with the skills in Ball Bonanza.

COORDINATED SCHOOL HEALTH LINKS

Ask the students to practice line 1, 2, and 3 tricks at home. Encourage students to ask family members to join them in Ball Bonanza exercises. Parental involvement in a child's schooling is an important component of a coordinated school health program and is a first step toward making sure that the child receives coordinated health messages. It also provides a child with adult support and role modeling.

Bazooka Ball

CONTENT CONNECTIONS   Throwing, fitness

READY FOR ACTION

- Provide 100 or more tennis balls or assorted balls. Balls will need to be marked with a number from 1 through 10.
- Place 10 hoops (one for each team) at the starting line.
- Students form 10 teams and stand behind the starting line.
- Assign each team a number from 1 to 10.
- Place 10 balls inside each team's hoop. Mix the numbers so that students don't throw their own balls.

LET'S PLAY   On the teacher's signal, one student at a time from each team throws a ball out into the playing field and then goes to the end of their team line. One student at a time throws from each team until all balls are thrown. Reverse the action: On the signal, one student at a time from each team retrieves their team's numbered ball. Play continues until all balls are found. Have students play in rounds, changing teams after each round.

CRANK IT UP   When a student finds a ball with another team's number on it, she or he may hike the ball (throw it backward between the legs) to another place in the play area to confuse that team. Students awaiting their turn can play throw-and-catch with one another or practice ball tricks.

GEAR IT DOWN   Eliminate team numbers, and tell students to quickly pick any ball to return to their team.

ASSET ACTION

Caring school climate (asset 5)—Connect asset building to existing social skill building currently in place at your school. For example, if your school has a "word of the week" program, use the word of the week (e.g., *respect*) often in your PE class. In Bazooka Ball, you can integrate the word of the week by making it the signal to throw. With older students, you can use the word in a sentence.

COORDINATED SCHOOL HEALTH LINKS

Discuss Bazooka Ball with the students. Ask them what muscles were used to throw the balls. Classroom teachers of older students might use Bazooka Ball to demonstrate mathematical concepts such as fractions.

Beach Ball Blast

CONTENT CONNECTIONS   Volleying

READY FOR ACTION

- 12 to 18 beach balls
- Students scattered in general space
- For "Crank It Up": volleyballs (or other balls other than beach balls)
- For "Gear It Down": balloons and foam paddles

LET'S PLAY   Use basic volleying cues (e.g., flat arm surface contact and quick feet) as a basis for instruction. In Beach Ball Blast, students attempt to volley a beach ball to themselves. The teacher calls out a cue, and students toss a ball up into the air and volley to themselves. After the volley ends, students must exit the play area, perform a preassigned fitness move or skill task (e.g., five jumping jacks), and then return to an open space to retrieve a ball. Continue play for several minutes.

CRANK IT UP   Have students use their forearms to pass the ball two or three times before they leave. Increase the number of forearm passes as students succeed. To increase the challenge, change the type of ball. For example, have students use volleyballs rather than beach balls.

GEAR IT DOWN   Have students play in pairs. One partner volleys while the other exercises on the sideline. Replace balls with balloons. Add foam paddles.

ASSET ACTION

Integrity (asset 28)—Beach Ball Blast presents excellent opportunities for students to demonstrate fairness, a component of integrity. As students reenter the game to retrieve a ball, they should make sure that everyone has had a turn to volley the beach ball. If they realize that a particular student has not had a turn, they should yield the ball to that student.

COORDINATED SCHOOL HEALTH LINKS

Remember that health encompasses mental, as well as physical, well-being. Success in Beach Ball Blast requires a fair amount of skill. You can help a student with weak volleying skills feel comfortable by modifying the task and having a well-skilled student work with a student with less skill. Such helpful gestures establish friendship and social skills, an important component of health.

Come and Get It

CONTENT CONNECTIONS   Skill-related fitness, quickness, changing direction, agility

READY FOR ACTION

- Place a cone in front of the play area.
- Scatter hoops in the play area. Place one ball in each hoop and have one student behind each hoop.
- For "Gear It Down," use beanbags.

LET'S PLAY   Each student tries to collect three balls and place them inside his or her hoop. Students may go to any hoop and get one ball at a time. When a student has three balls inside her or his hoop, she or he runs to the front of the play area to form a line next to the cone. The round ends when there is a student behind each cone.

CRANK IT UP   Spread the hoops out, and have the students dribble the balls they collect back to their hoops.

GEAR IT DOWN   Practice the traditional shuttle run using beanbags. Place two beanbags on a line 20 feet (6 meters) from a starting point. Students run and pick up one beanbag at a time and place it on the starting line.

ASSET ACTION

Peaceful conflict resolution (asset 36)—Come and Get It is a fun game, but one that can lead to squabbles over who gets to take or leave a ball in a hoop. Remind students that there are class rules related to conflict resolution. Briefly discuss the rules. Discuss the Conflict Corner or Peace Place where students can go to resolve conflicts.

COORDINATED SCHOOL HEALTH LINKS

A healthy social environment requires caring, respect, cooperation, and peaceful conflict resolution. Come and Get It affords an excellent opportunity to develop students' social skills because they can easily become frustrated if they continually return to their hoops to find fewer balls than they left there.

Dribble Mania 1

CONTENT CONNECTIONS
Coordination, ball manipulation, dribbling skills

© Human Kinetics

READY FOR ACTION
- One ball per student
- The song "Wipeout" by the Safaris

LET'S PLAY Under the teacher's direction, students perform the following actions:

- Follow the leader—A student without a ball leads another student (the follower) in different directions while the follower dribbles.
- Switch—Students "follow the leader," but both members of a pair have a ball. When the teacher says, "Switch," the pair changes direction and the leader becomes the follower.
- Copycat—Students "follow the leader," but both members of a pair have a ball. The leader walks or switches hands while bouncing and catching the ball. The follower copies the leader's pathway and ball movements.
- Wipe out—"Wipeout" plays. During the verses, the students dribble freely around the area. During the drum solo, students perform ball-handling movements.

CRANK IT UP The following activities increase the challenge:

- Rotate—Students "follow the leader," but both members of a pair have a ball. When the teacher says, "Rotate," the follower becomes the leader.
- Change and rotate—In the course of "follow the leader," teams change directions on the word "change" and rotate whenever the teacher directs them to.

GEAR IT DOWN Dribbling in one spot, students practice switching hands and bouncing the ball with two hands. They may count how many times they dribble the ball within one minute. Add dribbling while walking; let the students choose whether to dribble with one hand or two hands. Walking, bouncing, and catching is also appropriate for some students.

ASSET ACTION

- **School boundaries (asset 12)**—Dribble Mania 1 is an excellent activity to get students listening and following rules. Work with students to set boundaries and rules. Post a written set of your rules in the classroom and the gym. Photocopy the rules, and have students and their parents sign a form indicating their willingness to stay within the boundaries.
- **Planning and decision making (asset 32)**—Good planning and decision making rely on a habit of setting goals. Dribble Mania 1 helps students to form this habit because students plan ahead, evaluate their progress, and try to improve. Encourage students to set dribbling goals for themselves, such as "I'll dribble 50 times with each hand without losing control of the ball."

COORDINATED SCHOOL HEALTH LINKS
Ask teachers to consider having students play Dribble Mania 1 during recess, and to create and name their actions. Cooperation among teachers fosters coordinated school health.

Dribble Mania 2

CONTENT CONNECTIONS   Ball handling, manipulation, dribbling

READY FOR ACTION

- One basketball per student
- Varied formations per activity
- For "Gear It Down": hoops

LET'S PLAY   Under the teacher's direction, students perform the following activities:

1. Dribbling math—Students dribble throughout the play area. When they meet a new student, they stop moving and dribble in place. Both students count out loud to three and then flash a certain number of fingers with their free hand. Each student tries to be the first to say the sum of the numbers shown.

2. Continuous dribble tag—Mark off two play areas. All students have a ball and dribble freely in one of the two areas. Students try to tap away other students' balls. When a student's ball is tapped away or the student otherwise loses control of his or her ball, that student must move to the other play area and begin a new game with other players. Players move back and forth between the two areas.

3. Dribble and go—Put numbers on poly spots and cones and place the poly spots and cones around the play area. Starting at different numbers, students pause in front of a poly spot or cone and dribble the number of times that it indicates. They then look for the poly spot or cone with the next number in the sequence and dribble as before.

4. Line dribbling—Students form lines of three or four students. At the whistle, the last student in each line dribbles to the front of the other students.

5. Countdown dribble—Kneeling at the 12th of 12 lines on the floor, students do 12 dribbles. Then, kneeling at the 11th line, they do 11 dribbles. They continue in this way until they've dribbled once while kneeling at line 1.

CRANK IT UP   The students do countdown dribble with this addition: after each period of dribbling, they take one shot at the basket from the free throw line.

GEAR IT DOWN   Place 10 to 15 hoops throughout the play area. Have one student stand inside each of the hoops. Other students try to cross the play area by bouncing and catching, or by dribbling, the ball through the maze of hoops while the students inside the hoops try to tap balls away from students to get too close.

ASSET ACTION

- **Caring school climate (asset 5)**—During Dribble Mania 2, the teacher can talk to one or two students who aren't socializing with other students. A simple gesture of support helps students feel that they belong.

- **Youth as resources (asset 8)**—Have the more skilled dribblers help the less skilled. When one student helps another, both benefit. The mentor has the opportunity to be of service, and the positive interaction foster friendships.

- **School/learning engagement (asset 22)**—By combining an academic ability (counting) with physical activity, Dribble Mania 2 promotes school engagement, bridges different subject areas, and encourages cooperation among teachers.

COORDINATED SCHOOL HEALTH LINKS

Meet with classroom teachers, and discuss the thinking skills that Dribble Mania 2 reinforces.

Globetrotter Games

CONTENT CONNECTIONS   Ball manipulation, rhythm, dribbling

READY FOR ACTION
- One ball per student
- Students scattered in general space
- Johnny Mercer's song "Sweet Georgia Brown" (or any upbeat music)
- For "Gear It Down": paper balls or fluff balls

LET'S PLAY   Under the teacher's direction, students perform the following skills to the music of "Sweet Georgia Brown":
- Slaps—One hand at a time, slap the basketball on its side in a rhythmical pattern.
- Fingertip drill—Move the ball from low to high and high to low by using the fingertips to push the ball side to side.
- Around the world—Move the basketball in circles around the neck to the waist, knees, and ankles, and back up.
- One leg—While standing with your legs straddled, circle the ball around one of your legs.
- Figure eight—Weave the basketball in a figure eight around your right leg and then your left leg.
- Hike—Hold the ball between your knees. Drop the ball, and move your hands from the front of your legs to the back of your legs without letting the ball touch the ground.
- Cross hike—Hold the ball between your knees. With one hand in the front and one in the back, switch hands without letting the ball touch the ground.
- Walking scissors—Pass the ball between the legs while walking with wide strides.
- Knee dribble—Dribble the ball while kneeling on one knee, then while lying down, and then while kneeling on one knee again.
- Computer—Sit on the floor, and pretend to type on top of the ball.
- Floor rhythm drill—Play the basketball like a drum, attempting to make it leave the floor in order to continue dribbling.

CRANK IT UP   Have students perform the drills faster. Encourage them not to look at the ball. Use the activities in a line circuit or stations. Ask students to create their own activities and show them to the class. Have pairs of students do matching activities for 16 counts and then bounce-pass the ball to each other.

GEAR IT DOWN   Ask students to move the ball along the ground instead of manipulating it. Use paper balls or fluff balls for drills without bouncing.

ASSET ACTION

Caring (asset 26) and youth as resources (asset 8)—Ask the students if they helped anyone during Globetrotter Games. Ask students who are skilled at the drills to teach a small group each drill. Peer teaching provides a foundation for future service to the broader community.

COORDINATED SCHOOL HEALTH LINKS

Ball handling, such as what is done in Globetrotter Games, can increase flexibility. Have a discussion about this concept with the students. Ask them, "What is flexibility? What stretches have you seen a basketball player do before a game? What muscles have to be strong to support the body during basketball handling drills? Why is flexibility important?"

Healthy Kid Tag

CONTENT CONNECTIONS

Chasing, dodging, fleeing

READY FOR ACTION

- Red foam balls, green foam balls
- Students scattered in general space

© Human Kinetics

LET'S PLAY   Explain to students that everyday decisions affect their health. Discuss unhealthy choices such as eating fatty or sugary foods, not exercising enough, or smoking cigarettes as well as healthy alternatives. Encourage students to make healthy decisions.

Show the students a red foam ball and a green foam ball. Tell them that a red ball represents an unhealthy behavior and a green ball represents a healthy one. Give a red ball to each of four students. These "health stoppers" will try to tag other students by using a red ball. Being tagged by a red ball represents being involved in an unhealthy behavior. Give a green ball to each of four students, the "health savers." Students without a ball will walk around the room, trying to avoid the health stoppers. Students tagged by a health stopper must freeze until a health saver unfreezes them by touching them with a green ball, symbolically changing their behavior from unhealthy to healthy.

CRANK IT UP   A "frozen" student tagged by a "health saver" doesn't become unfrozen until she or he declares a health resolution, such as "I'll eat more vegetables each day." The student then jogs one lap and reenters the game.

GEAR IT DOWN   When a student is stopped from being healthy, he or she must immediately jog one lap to reenter the game.

ASSET ACTION

Healthy lifestyle/restraint (asset 31) and planning and decision making (asset 32)—A major goal of physical education is to help young people make healthy choices. Ask students lifestyle questions such as "What if you reduced the amount of fat in your daily diet?" and "Why should you avoid smoking?" These kinds of questions are good to discuss both before and after the game. Discuss what the students learned about choice and consequences after playing Healthy Kid Tag.

COORDINATED SCHOOL HEALTH LINKS

In Healthy Kid Tag, the students are asked to discuss healthy choices. One healthy choice that they can make every day is over their choice of snack food. Ask students to write down their snack choices for two days. Also have them consider whether their lunch foods are healthy or unhealthy. Are they eating low-fat, high-fiber, zero-cholesterol foods such as fruits, vegetables, and whole-grain rice? Or are they eating fatty, high-cholesterol processed foods such as bologna and American cheese? List the students' choices on paper. Invite the cafeteria manager to your class to discuss healthy food choices.

Hoop Shoot

CONTENT CONNECTIONS   Basketball shooting

READY FOR ACTION

- Basketballs
- Basketball hoops
- Poly spots
- A designated "knockout" shooting practice area
- For "Crank It Up": balls other than basketballs

LET'S PLAY

- Knock out—Students line up single-file at the free throw line. Each of the first two players in line has a basketball. Both players shoot at the same time. The first player is "knocked out" if the second player is first to make a basket. If the first player makes a basket before the second player, the first player remains in the game and passes the ball to the next player in line. The new player immediately enters the game and tries to knock out the player in front. Any player who survives goes to the back of the line. Knocked-out players move to an open goal to practice shots of their choice. Students who prefer not to compete may practice at varying height goals or work on other skills.

- 1, 2, 3—Students begin in the center of the play area. On signal, students dribble to an assigned basket and shoot for 30 seconds. (Two students may be assigned to each basket.) They receive points as follows:
  - 1 point: short shot directly in front of the basket, or a lay-up.
  - 2 points: a shot made 3 feet (1 meter) from the basket
  - 3 points: a shot made from the free-throw line

- Hot corner—Place two chairs by each basket near the corner of the play area. Number the chairs 1 and 2. Students form lines at each basket. Each student has a ball. A student who makes the shot goes to the end of the line. A student who misses goes to the hot corner and sits on chair 1. When another student misses, she or he replaces the previous student at chair 1, and the previous student moves to chair 2. When another student misses, the student that was sitting at chair 2 rejoins the game.

CRANK IT UP   Increase the length of the shooting intervals, change the type of ball that is used, and increase the distance from which shots are attempted.

GEAR IT DOWN   For younger students, hang a hula hoop over a basket and count points.

ASSET ACTION

Caring (asset 26)—Tell the students to encourage each other during activities because encouragement is a sign of caring and friendship. For elementary students with limited basketball shooting skills, making a basket is an exciting accomplishment! The fun is even better when a student hears other students cheering when a shot is made in Hoop Shoot.

COORDINATED SCHOOL HEALTH LINKS

Cooperation between PE instructors and classroom teachers is essential to coordinated school health. Offer to train classroom teachers in managing physical activity so that students can play games learned in PE at recess.

Movin' on Up

CONTENT CONNECTIONS   Passing, catching, throwing, teamwork

READY FOR ACTION

- 10 to 12 cones, each with a ball on top
- A grade-appropriate throw line
- Students, in groups of six to eight, lined up single-file opposite a target (see figure 8.4)
- One beanbag per group

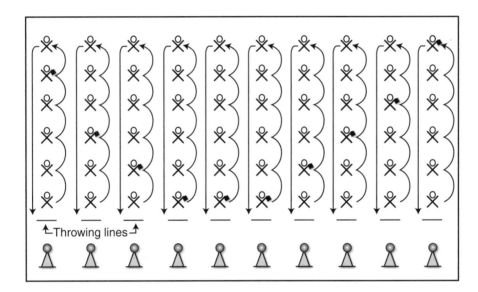

Throwing lines

Figure 8.4   Movin' on Up diagram.

LET'S PLAY   Within each group, students pass the beanbag down the line to the last student. The last student runs, stops at the throw line, and throws the beanbag, attempting to knock the ball off the cone. The student then retrieves the beanbag, resets the target if necessary, goes to the head of his or her team line as team members move back one spot, and starts passing the beanbag down the line. Teams try to score as many points as possible in the time allotted. Play continues for several 5-minute rounds. Announce team scores after each round.

CRANK IT UP   Have students pass three beanbags down the line. Change the targets. Award points to teams who finish first and bonus points for targets hit.

GEAR IT DOWN   Use larger targets. Don't keep score. Eliminate the beanbag passing.

ASSET ACTION

- **High expectations (asset 16)**—Remind students to focus on doing their best. This is especially important for students who aren't athletically gifted.

- **Caring school climate (asset 5), caring (asset 26), and self-esteem (asset 38)**—It has been said that "all things are connected." In building assets and social skills in young people, this is especially true. Ask students to encourage their teammates while they play the game in this lesson. Encouragement helps students, especially less skilled students, feel that they belong and are valued.

COORDINATED SCHOOL HEALTH LINKS

Teacher tip—Invite members of the community to speak to your class about various aspects of health. For instance, you might invite a parent who is professionally trained in medicine, psychology, outdoor education, or exercise science. You could also invite community leaders to speak about teamwork and working together. Ask speakers to tie their remarks to the teamwork necessary in partner activities in PE.

Partner Ab Fitness

CONTENT CONNECTIONS   Cooperation, muscular endurance

READY FOR ACTION

- Balls (foam or soft)
- Students paired as partner 1 and partner 2
- Music with a medium or fast tempo

LET'S PLAY   Partner 1 takes a ball from the equipment zone. Partner 2 chooses a workout spot. While the music plays, partner 1 holds the ball and jogs around the room. Partner 2 stretches in her or his workout spot. When the music stops, partner 1 returns to his or her partner and together they perform one of the following activities. Partner 2 then repeats the action of the partner. After each partner has completed a turn, partner 2 sits and partner 1, taking the ball, finds a new partner.

- Curl and pass—Facing each other, partners alternately pass the ball to each other and do curl-ups.
- Curly pass—Partners curl up and hold the position while passing or handing the ball to each other.
- Pass and push—Partners face each other in push-up position and push the ball back and forth to each other.
- Advance behind-the-back partners—Partners stand back to back but with space between them and hand the ball to each other behind the back.

CRANK IT UP   Change the locomotor movements. Ask students to face their partner, slide and pass the ball as they travel in a group circle. Change the type of balls used. Ask students to dribble, rather than jog, between the intervals.

GEAR IT DOWN   Ask students to throw and catch the ball, or bounce and catch the ball, while the music plays. When the music is off, have them perform a curl-and-pass or pass-and-push as listed under "Let's Play." Students should keep the same partner.

ASSET ACTION

Cultural competence (asset 34)—Encourage students to accept others by choosing new partners. Feeling comfortable with people of different cultural, racial, and ethnic backgrounds is an important asset for anyone. Students will need cultural competence in a world that grows more diverse each day. Make acceptance of differences a motto for your classroom or gym.

COORDINATED SCHOOL HEALTH LINKS

Ask students to explain why it is important to have strong abdominal muscles. Encourage students to work and stretch these muscles on a regular basis.

Score Five

CONTENT CONNECTIONS   Passing, catching, throwing, teamwork

READY FOR ACTION

- Divide the students into teams of four.
- Give each student a number from 1 to 4.
- Assign each team a fluff ball and a starting marker, such as a poly spot or cone.
- Place a cone several yards (several meters) from each team's poly spot.
- For "Crank It Up," use footballs.

LET'S PLAY   Call out a two-digit number whose digits are limited to 1 through 4. The first digit designates the thrower; the second designates the catcher. For example, if you call out, "12," player 1 throws and player 2 catches. The thrower throws from the starting mark, and the catcher catches the ball behind the cone. Each team tries to score five points by making five good catches before their opponents do.

CRANK IT UP   Use footballs, and increase the throwing distance. Or use math problems: instead of calling out a two-digit number, have students calculate the number. For example, instead of calling out, "12," call out, "Six plus six."

GEAR IT DOWN   Eliminate the numbers, and play just for fun. Allow any kind of throw. Students rotate from thrower to catcher and then to the back to the line. Students at the back of the line pretend that they are throwing to the catcher. Use a larger ball and shorter distances when appropriate.

ASSET ACTION

Achievement motivation (asset 21)—Score Five reinforces thinking skills introduced in the classroom. When students are successful in this activity, they may be more motivated to achieve in the classroom or transfer learning from PE to math class.

COORDINATED SCHOOL HEALTH LINKS

Incorporating thinking skills into a PE lesson not only helps the child but also facilitates cooperation among teachers. This cooperation promotes the establishment of a coordinated school health program, which can improve the school climate and the "health of the school." Remember that health addresses children's intellectual and social health as well as physical health.

Star Wars Battle

CONTENT CONNECTIONS   Accuracy, throwing, eye–hand coordination

READY FOR ACTION

- Trash cans or other containers
- Half-pieces of laminated posterboard (shields)
- A circle of poly spots with a trash can in the center for each group (see figure 8.5)
- 5 lightweight balls (such as paper balls) on each poly spot
- Students paired as alien and Jedi Warrior (four pairs at each game station)
- For "Crank It Up": pool noodles

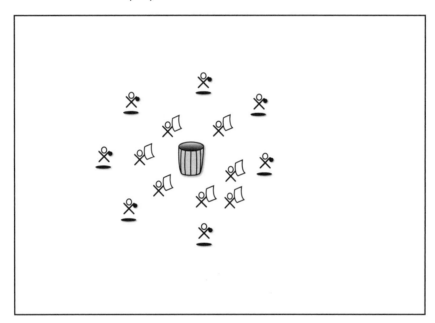

Figure 8.5
Star Wars Battle diagram.

LET'S PLAY   Each alien stands on a poly spot and tries to bombard the planet (trash can) with space balls. Each Jedi uses her or his shield to knock away the space balls. Each alien gets 5 throws before they switch with their partner.

CRANK IT UP   Use pool noodles instead of posterboard.

GEAR IT DOWN   Allow students to throw without any Jedi blocking them. Or reduce the number of guards. Students can throw underhand.

 ASSET ACTION

Teacher tip—As a class, create a list of shared values. See table 3.1 on page 23 for ideas. Talk about what it takes to uphold these values. Set boundaries and expectations based on these values. In this activity, partners are opponents but can still be a caring friend and classmate.

 COORDINATED SCHOOL HEALTH LINKS

Star Wars Battle can be modified to teach a health lesson. Tell students that the balls represent germs that enter our body and cause illness and that the shields represent our immune system, which fights invading germs.

Team Keep-Away

CONTENT CONNECTIONS   Throwing, catching, cooperation

READY FOR ACTION

- Use cones to divide the play area into four or more small squares. The size of the squares will depend on the students' skill level and ability to work in teams. As a start, a good size is one-fourth the size of a basketball court.
- Have students form groups of three, with two groups per square.
- Provide one ball per square. The ball should suit the students' abilities.

LET'S PLAY   To earn one point for their team, students must complete three successive passes. Players move only when they do not have the ball. They try to get open. The defense guards the passing lanes and attempts to intercept passes. If the opposing team intercepts the ball, they immediately take over. Balls that go out of bounds are in-bounded by the opposing team.

CRANK IT UP   Change the type of ball used. Change the size of the court. Increase the number of players. Add a basketball or trashcan goal in a corner to shoot or throw into. After three passes, a team may pass into a corner where a student is standing in a hula hoop. A completed pass to a student in a hoop scores two points for the team.

GEAR IT DOWN   Play two-on-one keep-away with the rules discussed in "Let's Play." Gradually decrease the size of each team's square.

ASSET ACTION

Cultural competence (asset 34)—Group activities such as Team Keep-Away help students to feel comfortable with people of different cultural and racial backgrounds by simply interacting with them on a daily basis.

COORDINATED SCHOOL HEALTH LINKS

As its name indicates, Team Keep-Away requires teamwork. Cooperation is crucial to success. Ask students how the social skill of cooperation can be applied to their family relationships.

Throw and Go

CONTENT CONNECTIONS   Overhand throwing, throwing accuracy

READY FOR ACTION

- Place various pieces of throwing equipment inside hoops in the front of the room (see figure 8.6).
- Place various targets around the perimeter of the room at appropriate distances to accommodate different developmental levels.
- Create starting lines to throw from.

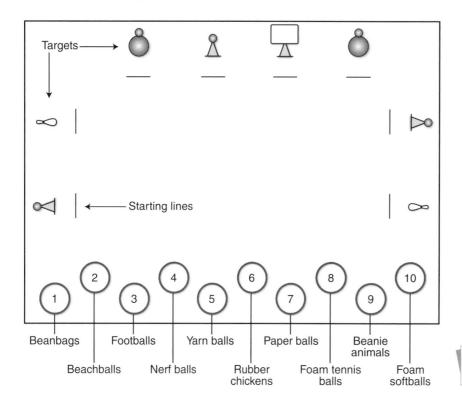

Figure 8.6   Throw and Go diagram.

LET'S PLAY   Students begin at hoop 1 and select an object to throw at any target they choose. After throwing, they retrieve the object and return it to the appropriate hoop. They then move to the next hoop and select an object for their second throw. Continue play for several rounds. Remind students to reset targets that have been knocked down.

CRANK IT UP   Increase the distance to the target. Award points for specific targets. Ask students to keep track of their personal records and points.

GEAR IT DOWN   Give all students the same equipment and the same type of targets. Have them take one step back after hitting a target. Include underhand, as well as overhand, throwing. Alternate between two pieces of equipment inside the hoops—for example, beanbags and fluff balls.

ASSET ACTION

Honesty (asset 29)—Many PE games involve points awarded for hitting a target. It is important that students learn at an early age that one of the most valuable assets a person can have is a reputation for doing the right thing. Being honest means following the rules. Throw and Go fosters honesty by requiring that students award themselves points only when they actually hit the target.

COORDINATED SCHOOL HEALTH LINKS

Remind students that muscles enable us to move. Ask them questions about muscles—for example, "Can you name two muscles that you use when you throw?" Ask the students to name the body system that causes muscles to move our bones.

Throwathon

CONTENT CONNECTIONS   Throwing, catching

READY FOR ACTION

- Poly spots or hoops in two rows of eight
- Beanbags, assorted balls, rubber chickens, or other age-appropriate throw and catch objects at each set of poly spots or hoops (see figure 8.7)
- Music

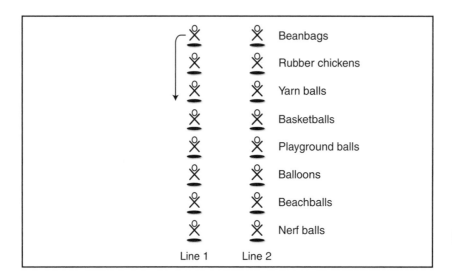

Figure 8.7 Throwathon diagram.

LET'S PLAY   Facing a partner, students stand on a poly spot or inside a hoop. While music plays, students throw and catch their object. When the music stops, they place the object on the poly spot or hoop and move to the next poly spot to throw a different piece of equipment. Continue until students have rotated through all types of throw objects.

CRANK IT UP   Increase the space between markers. For balls that bounce, include basketball passes. Have a contest in which teams try to catch the most balls in a row or partners try to be the first pair to score 50 points by throwing and catching the ball 50 times without missing. Allow students to choose the type of throw they want to make.

GEAR IT DOWN   Give all students the same equipment. Have them move the marker back one step after they make 10 catches.

ASSET ACTION

Teacher tip—You can develop a closer relationship with students by using supportive statements such as, "I know you always do the best that you can." This helps build relationships which can lead to an improved school climate.

COORDINATED SCHOOL HEALTH LINKS

Invite classroom teachers to observe and play Throwathon before students are dismissed back to class. Have students play it during recess.

Hoops

© Human Kinetics

Use the MOVES checklist to evaluate lesson quality.

Hoops are fun for everyone!

Beanbag Tic-Tac-Toe

CONTENT CONNECTIONS   Tossing, throwing accuracy, muscular endurance, body shapes

READY FOR ACTION
- Make several tic-tac-toe boards using nine hoops of 2 or 3 different colors as the grids of each board.
- Place 10 beanbags (five of one color and five of a second color) at a starting line in front of each board.
- Position two groups of three students at each board.
- Assign each group a beanbag color.
- For "Crank It Up," use poly spots.

LET'S PLAY   Within each group, one student at a time throws a beanbag at the tic-tac-toe board. If the beanbag lands mostly or entirely inside a hoop, it counts as having marked that tic-tac-toe grid. If a beanbag lands outside all hoops, the student retrieves it and returns it to his or her team. The first team to complete tic-tac-toe wins one point. Have students play for 10 minutes and then rotate teams. To make Beanbag Tic-Tac-Toe more active, have each hoop color represent a particular fitness activity. For example, if a beanbag lands in an orange hoop, the thrower might have to go to the exercise area and perform 10 jumping jacks before returning to tic-tac-toe. Another option is to have students perform an exercise—such as one push-up—before they throw.

CRANK IT UP   Change the size of the target by using poly spots, or increase the distance from the starting line to the tic-tac-toe hoops.

GEAR IT DOWN   Eliminate the beanbags, and have the students play human tic-tac-toe. Members of one team are Xs; members of the other team are Os. Students choose a hoop to sit in and form either an X (arms crossed over the head) or an O (arms forming a circle).

ASSET ACTION

School/learning engagement (asset 22)—This hoops activity, like so many quality physical education activities, is an enjoyable activity for students. It keeps them attentive and engaged in the learning process. Remind students to find activities outside of school that they find enjoyable. In this way, a quality activity such as this one contributes to an over-arching goal of physical education—lifetime fitness and enjoyment.

COORDINATED SCHOOL HEALTH LINKS

Beanbag Tic-Tac-Toe provides an opportunity to discuss fitness components. Ask students if they know the difference between muscular strength and muscular endurance. Also ask them why muscular endurance and flexibility are important.

Fitness Hoopla

CONTENT CONNECTIONS   Locomotor skills, aerobic health, muscular endurance, flexibility

READY FOR ACTION

- Copy and hang the Fitness Code chart (appendix B, page 240) in a prominent place. The code chart has exercises that match the codes.
- Scatter the hoops (one for each student) within the playing area.
- Mark each hoop with one of the fitness codes or write the codes on index cards. Place the cards on the ground inside the hoops with the codes facing down.
- Have music on hand.

LET'S PLAY   While music plays, students jog around the perimeter to the music. When the music stops, each student finds a hoop to stand in and performs the exercise corresponding to that hoop's fitness code. Repeat the entire sequence several times.

CRANK IT UP   Change the locomotor movements performed around the perimeter. For example, have students skip instead of jog. Add some choice cards, marked "?" to indicate that the students create their own exercises. Change the codes to include other exercises and longer exercising.

GEAR IT DOWN   Remove the codes from the hoops. While the music plays, students move around the area. When the music is off, they find a hoop and perform one teacher-announced fitness code exercise as a group.

ASSET ACTION

Safety (asset 10)—An asset-rich environment is one in which students feel supported, safe, and secure. Provide students with information and training regarding ways to protect their own and others' safety during activities. Ask the students for ways to stay safe while exercising with hoops.

COORDINATED SCHOOL HEALTH LINKS

Have students identify the various health-related fitness components. Ask them which components Fitness Hoopla focuses on.

Hoop Battle

CONTENT CONNECTIONS

Coordination, aerobic health, hula hooping

READY FOR ACTION

- One hoop per student
- Students scattered in general space

© Human Kinetics

LET'S PLAY At the teacher's signal, students hula hoop at the waist while trying to advance toward another student. Continuing to hoop, students try to use their hoop to knock off their opponents' hoops. Students may make contact with the opponent's hoop but not with the opponent's body.

Students must leave the play area if their hand touches their hoop or the hoop touches the ground. While at the sideline, students may practice tricks or practice Hoop Battle with another student. Students remaining in the battle must continually hoop and challenge others.

CRANK IT UP Designate three battle areas. Instead of moving to the sideline after being defeated in a bout, students move to the next battle area and continue the game.

GEAR IT DOWN Students play in pairs rather than a large group. They practice with the same partner. When students lose their hoop, they tell the winner what exercise to do.

ASSET ACTION

- **Peaceful conflict resolution (asset 36)**—Tell students that conflicts may arise in Hoop Battle and that yelling and fighting are poor ways to handle conflicts. Urge them to communicate with one another and to resolve all conflicts peacefully. (See chapter 2 or References and Resources for conflict-resolution suggestions.)
- **Youth as resources (asset 8)**—Ask students who are hoop-proficient to help less skilled students, especially after students leave the "battle" area.

COORDINATED SCHOOL HEALTH LINKS

Have students discuss the concept of conflict resolution and to list ways of peacefully resolving Hoop Battle disagreements. Ask them how they might solve a conflict at home using the strategies suggested in Hoop Battle. Hoop Battle also offers opportunities to discuss character traits such as fairness, honesty, and responsibility.

Hoop It Up

CONTENT CONNECTIONS   Agility, tossing, reaction time, speed

READY FOR ACTION
One hula hoop per student

LET'S PLAY   Have students do the following activities in pairs or small groups:

- Roll and run—Partners stand side by side. Partner 1 has the hoop and remains standing; partner 2 lies down in a tuck position. Partner 1 rolls the hoop while partner 2 rocks back and forth once and then stands up and runs to catch the hoop before it falls.

- Moving target—Partner 1 holds the hoop on the right side of her or his body and moves the hoop up and down. Partner 2 tries to throw a beanbag or ball through the moving hoop.

- Hoop hop—Partner 1 places the hoop flat on the ground and slides it toward partner 2. Partner 2 tries to jump over the hoop or land inside it.

- Partner roll—Partners roll the hoop back and forth to each other.

- Human ring-toss—Partner 1 stands tall with hands clasped overhead. Partner 2 tosses the hoop, attempting to ring Partner 1's clasped hands.

- One member of a group of three holds the hoop in front of his or her body and slowly moves down the activity area. The other two group members stand on either side of the hoop and toss and catch beanbags or balls back and forth through the hoop.

- In a small group of four or more, students place hoops on the ground so that they touch. The various hoop arrangements on the floor create different jumping patterns.

CRANK IT UP   Ask students to create their own Hoop It Up activities to show to the class.

GEAR IT DOWN   Students perform hoop activities that promote spatial skills. For example, they might place a hoop on the ground and then do all of the following: stand outside it, stand inside it, hop around it, and jump inside it. Students can practice rolling the hoop to a partner.

ASSET ACTION

Cultural competence (asset 34)—Having students choose different Hoop It Up partners, especially in multiethnic classes, is a good way to teach students to work together and to accept individual differences.

COORDINATED SCHOOL HEALTH LINKS

Find ways for each child to Hoop It Up, whatever her or his skill level. Encourage other teachers to use Hoop It Up outside of the PE setting.

Hoop Scooting

CONTENT CONNECTIONS   Chasing, dodging, fleeing, cooperation

READY FOR ACTION

- Hoops scattered around the play area
- For "Crank It Up": scarves

LET'S PLAY   This is a walking tag game. Designate several players to be "It." For easy identification, the taggers should wear pinnies, scarves, or flags. Students who are not taggers are safe when they are inside a hoop. Up to two players may be inside a hoop at any given time. A third player may try to enter the hoop, despite the two-player rule, but one player has to leave before he or she can enter. If three players are inside a hoop at the same time, any one of them may be tagged. When tagged, a player performs a reentry task such as jogging once around the perimeter. Frequently change taggers.

CRANK IT UP   Change the reentry task. Students may practice one-on-one knee or toe tag for 1 minute before reentering the game. To play one-on-one tag, partners stand inside an imaginary square 4 feet (1.2 meters) on each side. Staying close to each other, they try to tag each other's knees. Additionally each partner may wear a scarf tucked in at his or her waist and try to pull the scarf from his or her opponent. Have students reenter at your discretion.

GEAR IT DOWN   Have fewer taggers. Allow only one student inside a hoop at a time. When a second student wants to enter a hoop, she or he must say, "Scoot, please," and the other student must exit.

ASSET ACTION

- **Responsibility (asset 30)**—Hoop Scooting reinforces the importance of making responsible decisions, especially when one player has to leave the hoop. How will the students in the hoop decide who leaves? Remind students that a responsible person plays fairly.
- **Peaceful conflict resolution (asset 36)**—Especially among children, decision making can result in conflict. Post a list of conflict resolution strategies in your gym or classroom. Before a game of Hoop Scooting, remind students that conflicts should be resolved peacefully.

COORDINATED SCHOOL HEALTH LINKS

Incorporate a lesson on healthy food choices: in order to enter a hoop already occupied by two people, a player must give them an example of a healthy food. Invite cafeteria staff to see the game played.

Hooping It With Wipeout and YMCA

CONTENT CONNECTIONS   Hula hooping, coordination, fitness

READY FOR ACTION

- One hoop per student
- Students already familiar with a few hoop tricks (see Hula Palooza, page 123)
- The song "Wipeout" by the Safaris
- The song "YMCA" by the Village People

LET'S PLAY   Students perform the following routines:

- YMCA—At each verse the teacher calls out a new hoop trick. During the chorus the students stay in one spot and hoop at the waist while forming the letters Y-M-C-A with their arms. After each "YMCA" sequence, students hula hoop while walking in a small circle in their spot.
- Wipeout—Divide the students into two groups. During the verses all students hoop at the waist. During the chorus or drum solo group 1 performs a teacher-designated hoop trick for the first 16 counts, and group 2 performs the same trick for the next 16 counts.

CRANK IT UP   Increase the complexity of the activity by upping the duration or speed. Ask students to create their own activities and name them. Post the names of the activities for everyone to see.

GEAR IT DOWN   During each routine, students hold the hoop around their waists and walk until the music stops. At each chorus, students either hula hoop or place the hoop on the ground and jump in and out of the hoop.

ASSET ACTION

Self-esteem (asset 38)—Hula hoop activities build students' self-esteem because they can be performed across a wide range of athletic ability. Students feel better about themselves when they perform an activity reasonably well, especially students who aren't athletic.

COORDINATED SCHOOL HEALTH LINKS

Display a list of shared values and social skills such as kindness and helping. To foster positive values and behavior, ask students proficient at hoop tricks to help those who are less proficient.

Hula Hoop Tag

CONTENT CONNECTIONS   Rolling hoops, dodging

READY FOR ACTION

- Hoops
- Pinnies to designate taggers
- A large play area

LET'S PLAY   Designate several students as "It." These students roll their hoops, with which they try to tag other students. A tagged player must leave the play area and perform a task designated by the teacher before returning to the game.

CRANK IT UP   Have the color of a hoop signify a particular instruction to tagged students. For example, a red hoop might represent "Do 10 jumping jacks"; a green hoop might represent "Do five push-ups"; a yellow hoop might represent "Jog in place."

GEAR IT DOWN   Students independently practice rolling hoops. They attempt to roll the hoop in a straight line and for increasingly greater distances. They can also roll the hoops at targets, such as cones.

ASSET ACTION

Caring school climate (asset 5)—Building an asset-rich environment in a PE class can be a first step toward developing a broader caring school climate. Children who feel valued, safe, and secure more readily develop resiliency and other characteristics common to successful people. An important component of building a positive climate within a PE class is to make sure that the activity experience for children not only fulfills educational objectives, but, like Hula Hoop Tag, also satisfies the vital need for children to have fun.

COORDINATED SCHOOL HEALTH LINKS

Remind students to avoid unhealthy habits such as elicit drug use, alcohol consumption, and frequent consumption of fatty foods. Tell students that the hoops used in tagging represent unhealthy habits that they should avoid.

Hula Palooza

CONTENT CONNECTIONS   Coordination, body control, aerobic health, muscular endurance, relationships

READY FOR ACTION

- One hoop per student
- For "Crank It Up": music

LET'S PLAY   Students practice the following activities with their hula-hoop:

- Hoop it up—Continuously hoop around the waist.
- Neck—Continuously hoop around the neck.
- Knees—Continuously hoop around the knees.
- Skip hop—Keep one foot inside the hoop to spin the hoop. Hop on the other foot (either inside or outside the hoop).
- Elevator—While spinning the hoop at your waist, continuously stand up and kneel down.
- Whirlwind—Turn 360 degrees in the same direction that the hoop is spinning.
- Kangaroo—Keep the hoop spinning while you jump up and down.
- Pivot—While hooping, keep one foot in place while turning around.
- Down the Hatch—Hoop at the neck. Then, putting one arm at a time through the hoop, let it slide to your waist, and hoop at the waist. Try waist to knees.

CRANK IT UP   Hoops are placed on the floor. While music plays, students walk around the room, avoiding the hoops. When the music stops, they quickly step inside the nearest hoop. Ask the students to practice one of the skills listed in "Let's Play." Also, ask students to create routines that combine three or four of the skills in sequence. Have students perform their routine for a partner.

GEAR IT DOWN   Instead of calling out the activities, ask the students to practice only Hoop It Up when they are in the hoops. This is also a great time to improve students' listening skills by calling out directions such as "Stand inside the hoop," "Walk around the hoop," "Stand in front of the hoop," and "Stand on the side of the hoop."

ASSET ACTION

- **Personal power (asset 37)**—Physical skills such as hula hooping give students a sense of empowerment. By working at such skills, students see the results of their efforts and are encouraged to work hard in other facets of their life as well.
- **Creative activities (asset 17)**—Hula Palooza provides opportunities for children to develop their creativity when designing their own routines suggested in "Crank it Up."

COORDINATED SCHOOL HEALTH LINKS

Meet with classroom teachers and discuss the thinking skills that PE activities can build. For example, Hula Palooza can lead to a discussion of math and physics concepts such as circumference and centrifugal force.

Musical Hoop Exchange

CONTENT CONNECTIONS   Locomotor skills, basketball dribbling

READY FOR ACTION

- Set up two circles of hoops side by side in a musical chairs formation.
- In each circle the number of hoops should be one fewer than the number of players.
- Place two hoops between the two circles (see figure 9.1).
- Have music on hand.
- For "Crank It Up," use basketballs.

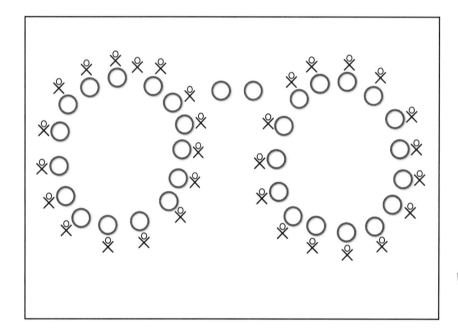

Figure 9.1
Musical Hoop
Exchange diagram.

LET'S PLAY   Play Musical Hoop Exchange in the same way as musical chairs. While music plays, students do a locomotor movement around the circle of hoops. When the music stops, students hurriedly step into a hoop and stretch. Students who find themselves without a hoop meet in the middle of the area between the two circles, exchange greetings, shake hands, and, for the next round, switch circles. For large classes, use poly spots or mix hoops and poly spots.

CRANK IT UP   Change the exercises often. Ask students to dribble a basketball around the circumference and perform a ball-handling skill (see chapter 8) while they freeze within a hoop. Call out a color. All students standing in a hoop of that color must change places with students in another hoop before playing the next round.

GEAR IT DOWN   Students practice locomotor skills around the circle of hoops and nonlocomotor skills while standing inside the hoops. Instead of changing places, students jog once around the circle of hoops before the next round.

ASSET ACTION

Interpersonal competence (asset 33) and cultural competence (asset 34)—Remind students to treat themselves and others with respect. Students can demonstrate respect for their classmates by playing Musical Hoop Exchange fairly and not arguing if another student wins the race to enter a hoop. Meeting and greeting in the exchange area also fosters acceptance of others.

COORDINATED SCHOOL HEALTH LINKS

Play Musical Hoop Exchange with a food picture in each hoop. Students who land on a hoop with a healthy food jump 15 times for joy. Those who land on a hoop with an unhealthy food jog one lap around the hoops.

Up, Down, All Around

CONTENT CONNECTIONS   Flexibility, cooperative warm-up or cool-down

READY FOR ACTION   One hula hoop for each group of three players

LET'S PLAY   Two students in the group hold the hoop, and manipulate it as directed, while the third student performs the sequence called out by the teacher. Sequences are created from the following actions:

- Up—Hoop held high. The third player goes under the hoop.
- Down—Hoop held low to the ground. The third player leaps over the hoop or jumps in and out of it.
- In—Hoop held vertically. The third player goes through the hoop.
- Around—Hoop held waist high. The third player walks around the two players holding the hoop.

The teacher calls out, "Ready," then a sequence (such as "Up, up, down, around"), then "Go." At "Go," the third student performs the designated sequence. After each pattern, a different student becomes the performer.

CRANK IT UP   Students take turns creating their own hoop sequences. Have them share their ideas with the class. Challenge students to perform the sequence while they slowly move down from one end to the other.

GEAR IT DOWN   Each student in a group performs the same sequence before a new sequence is announced. Give one command at a time instead of an entire sequence. Add combinations as the children respond correctly to each command.

ASSET ACTION

Interpersonal competence (asset 33) and cultural competence (asset 34)—Encourage students to show appreciation and respect by praising their partners' hoop skills. Respectful people are considerate of others, including those who come from different cultures and may not be familiar with activities, such as hooping, popular in the United States.

COORDINATED SCHOOL HEALTH LINKS

Encourage groups of students to create a hoops routine. Group initiatives foster friendships and help to keep students motivated. Also, the use of hoops reminds school officials and parents that PE is very different than what they remember. Though today's parents probably played with hula hoops when they were children, they probably were not used in a PE setting in this manner. This understanding is important when promoting coordinated school health and enlisting the support of adults in the school community.

Jump Ropes

© Human Kinetics

Do you have a designated place in your class-room or gym to resolve conflicts?

Jumping to rope in success!

Blast Off

CONTENT CONNECTIONS   Jumping, landing, fitness, aerobic health

READY FOR ACTION

- Mark off a large rectangular area with four cones numbered 1, 2, 3, and 4.
- Provide each student with a jump rope.

LET'S PLAY   Throughout the activity, students keep their own rope. Jumping takes place inside the rectangle, jogging outside it. First, students jump rope 20 times at cone 4, fold up their ropes, jog around the rectangle four times, and stop at cone 3. Next they jump rope 15 times, jog around the rectangle three times, and stop at cone 2. Then they jump rope 10 times, jog around the rectangle twice, and stop at cone 1. Finally they jump rope five times, jog around the rectangle once, and go to cone 4, where they stretch. To avoid congestion in larger classes, start students in groups, use two rectangles, or provide alternative activities. For safety, use poly spots for jumping spots and have students practice jumping without a rope. Add ropes when students are being safe and can find space safely.

CRANK IT UP   Link each cone to a particular jump rope activity, such as bell, skier, twister (see Bump Up, page 129), scissor jump (beginning with one foot in front and one in back and then switching feet), and straddle jump (jumping with the legs spread).

GEAR IT DOWN   Eliminate jump ropes, and have the students do jumping jacks or jump over lines.

ASSET ACTION

Teacher tip—Encourage young people to fulfill their need to be valued by and to contribute to their community. Both empowerment and support assets give young people confidence that adults care about them. You can foster these values in the following ways:

- Have well-skilled students help less-skilled students in class. It is a good start toward being of service to other people in the community.
- Ask students to create pictures or stories depicting a community that values youth.
- Form partnerships with community organizations through which students can volunteer or be mentored by adults. Health-related organizations such as the American Cancer Society, American Diabetes Association, and American Heart Association are interested in promoting health in schools. Ask the students if they would like to participate in these organizations' events.

COORDINATED SCHOOL HEALTH LINKS

Have students check their pulse during Blast Off. Discuss aerobic and muscular health in relation to jumping rope. What kind of muscle care is necessary before and after jumping rope?

Bump Up

CONTENT CONNECTIONS   Jumping rope, aerobic health, muscular endurance

READY FOR ACTION

- On each of 10 cards numbered 1 through 10, write a particular jump rope task. For more examples of jump rope tasks, see Blastoff on page 128 or visit www.americanheart.org, and search under the key words *jump skills*.
- To indicate jumping spots, place poly spots, evenly spaced, in a line behind each cone.
- Provide each student with a jump rope.

© Human Kinetics

LET'S PLAY   Place the jump rope task cards on cones at the front of the room, in order from the simplest to the most complex activity. Have the class form 10 lines, with one line in front of each cone and one student at each poly spot. Students practice the activity written on the cone in front of them. When the teacher says, "Bump up," each line moves to the next cone (students in line 10 move to line 1).

Having students line up alphabetically will help you learn their names.

CRANK IT UP   Use the jump rope cards and cones as described in "Let's Play." Divide the students into 10 equal groups. Members of group 1 line up single file at cone 1. Students try to do each activity 10 times. If they succeed, they may bump up to the next task and move on to any open poly spot in the next line. Students who are waiting can advance to an open poly spot at cone 1. Students who feel uncomfortable with this challenge should be allowed to go to a designated practice area to practice tasks instead of attempting to complete all tasks.

GEAR IT DOWN   Replace the tasks with floor jumping tasks and simple jump rope tasks. Use the same formation as in "Let's Play," but allow students 2 minutes to practice each task before bumping up to the next task.

ASSET ACTION

Teacher tip—Children's ability to build assets is greatly influenced by teachers but even more influenced by parents. The PE teacher can help with this asset building in several ways:

- Personally contact each student's family at least once during the school year.
- Frequently send notes home that tell parents what students are learning and working on in your PE class.
- Consider publishing a class newsletter that students take home to their parents.

COORDINATED SCHOOL HEALTH LINKS

Bump Up is a good activity to share with parents at health fairs. To further involve parents in their child's education, establish parent–student events such as Wellness Wednesdays or Fitness Fridays where parents are invited to school to exercise and play with their children.

High and Low, Here We Go

CONTENT CONNECTIONS   Jumping, landing, aerobic health

READY FOR ACTION

- Give each student one jump rope.
- Divide the play area in half.
- On each side of the play area, hang a sign that lists jump rope tasks such as straddle, scissors, forward jumps, backward jumps, hop on one foot, bell, skier, twister, crisscross, and single side swing. The signs should have a variety of tasks.

LET'S PLAY   Carrying their rope (folded), students walk around the area as instructed by the teacher. For example, the teacher might say, "Walk in a curvy path." When the teacher says, "High and low, here we go," students quickly find a partner and stand back to back. Students determine which partner is taller. The teacher then sends the taller partners to one half of the play area and the shorter partners to the other half. Students on each side spread out to practice one trick from their jump rope card. After 3 minutes of practice, students resume walking. When the teacher says, "High and low, here we go," students find new partners. The teacher can use other ways of dividing the children into two groups—such as larger and smaller shoe size, lighter and darker shirt color, birthday closer to summer break, or Rock, Paper, Scissors.

CRANK IT UP   Students perform, in sequential order, all of the tasks listed on the sign as if they are performing a jump rope routine. Or, ask students to perform each trick eight times before doing the next.

GEAR IT DOWN   Use easier tasks, which you announce—for example, "Place the rope on the floor in the shape of a circle, and jump in and out of the circle," "Place the rope on the floor as a straight line, and jump zigzag from one end to the other," or "Place the rope on the floor as a straight line, and jump forward and then backward over the line."

 ## ASSET ACTION

- **Caring school climate (asset 5)**—To help create a caring school environment, spend extra time with new students or students who are having trouble with some of the jump rope tricks. This display of support and encouragement helps create class and school environments in which students feel welcome and valued.

- **Youth as resources (asset 8)**—To empower students proficient in jump rope tricks, have them help less proficient students. When students act as mentors, they develop leadership skills and the habit of being of service to others.

 ## COORDINATED SCHOOL HEALTH LINKS

Teacher tip—High and Low, Here We Go can be tied to subjects taught in the classroom, such as math. For example, students can be asked to take measurements to determine which partner has longer fingers, smaller feet, and so on.

Jump!

CONTENT CONNECTIONS
Jumping skills, aerobic health, muscular endurance

© Human Kinetics

READY FOR ACTION
- One jump rope per student
- 12 long ropes
- Cones placed in a circle with one jumping skill card on each one. Jumping skills are:

1. Fitness jumping—Do continuous rope jumping.
2. Backward jumping—Jump rope backward, alternately with one foot and both feet.
3. Partner jumping—Practice partner tricks (see Partner Party, page 136).
4. Ladder jumping—Place ropes on the ground so that they form ladder rungs. Students create ways to hop and jump from one end of the ladder to the other.
5. Create a trick—Create and name a jump rope trick.
6. Floor jumping—Form ropes into shapes such as circles, squares, lines, and letters. Jump using a variety of takeoffs and landings through, over, and around the shapes.
7. Jump the river—Place two long ropes in a V. Starting at the closed end, continually jump from one side of the V to the other, advancing to the open end.
8. One claps; one jumps—One student claps while another continually jumps, trying to stay in sync with the claps. The rope can be on the ground or turned by the jumper.
9. Double dutch or single long rope—Proficient students practice double-dutch jumping or turning or single long rope turning and jumping. Younger students jump in place while older students run in and out or create tricks and chants. (For more information on specific jumping skills, see www.americanheart.org and search under the key words *jump skills*.)
10. Jump and count—One partner jumps while the other counts. They switch places after misses. If necessary, limit the number of jumps.

LET'S PLAY   Explain the station activities described in "Ready for Action." Have students rotate, in small groups, from station to station.

CRANK IT UP   Students perform flexibility or strength exercises after every two stations.

GEAR IT DOWN   Use only floor stations: floor jumping, fitness jumping, backward jumping, and ladder line jumping. Use the same rotation format, but have students stretch and rest between rotations. Repeat the circuit twice.

ASSET ACTION
Teacher tip—Children often struggle to develop a sense of control and purpose. Quality PE activities can help build a positive identity. One way is to create life-planning portfolios that follow students from the end of one school year to the beginning of the next school year and include goals, dreams, and hopes. This can be an important tool for the student—and for teachers—to keep track of accomplishments and challenges. Students can use Jump! to set and meet jumping goals.

COORDINATED SCHOOL HEALTH LINKS
Offer to instruct classroom teachers in jump rope activities that can be used during recess.

Jump and Jog

CONTENT CONNECTIONS   Jumping, landing, coordination, aerobic health

READY FOR ACTION

- Scatter jump ropes across the floor. Shape each rope into a circle.
- One student stands inside each rope circle.
- Use upbeat music.

LET'S PLAY   When the music begins, students leave their rope circle and jog around the room, avoiding the ropes. When the music stops, they locate a rope circle and do jumps such as in and out of the circle, forward and backward, or side to side. On the teacher's signal, students pick up a rope and practice basic jump rope skills (such as forward and backward) for several rounds. The teacher can call a different skill to be practiced at each round.

CRANK IT UP   Take away a few ropes, and have students share ropes. When it is time to jump, instruct them to do Partner Party jumping (see page 136).

GEAR IT DOWN   Instead of jumping rope, students change the rope into a variety of shapes and hop or jump along these shapes. For example, students can change the rope into a straight line and hop or jump down and back.

ASSET ACTION

Sense of purpose (asset 39)—Help students to see a purpose in each school activity. You might ask them, "Why jump rope?" and explain the benefits of jumping rope. Goal setting contributes to a sense of purpose. When students play Jump and Jog, you can have them set goals for themselves, such as jumping 20 times in a row.

COORDINATED SCHOOL HEALTH LINKS

Teacher tip—Talk to other teachers about goal-setting activities that they use in their classes. Discussing strategies related to goal-setting activities such as those in Jump and Jog can help to keep young people engaged in school. When young people are engaged, they move toward total health and wellness.

Jumpathon

CONTENT CONNECTIONS   Jumping rope, aerobic health, muscular endurance, teamwork

READY FOR ACTION

- Set up 10 counting stations with cones numbered 1 through 10 (fewer stations for small classes).
- Place two jump ropes at each station.
- Have two students ("counters") sit at each station.
- Use 10 cones to designate on-deck jumpers.
- Use six posters marked, respectively, *1–9, 10–15, 16–25, 26–49, 50–74, 75–99,* and *100-125* (see figure 10.1).
- While waiting to jump, students stretch at numbered cones that match the counting stations.

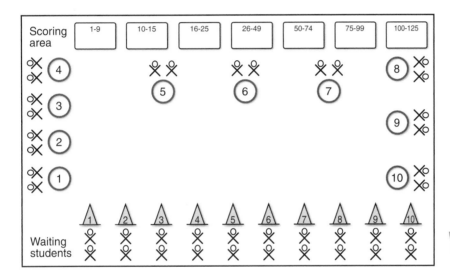

Figure 10.1 Jumpathon diagram

LET'S PLAY   One student at a time goes to a counting station to jump as many times in a row as he or she can. At each station the two counters simultaneously count aloud to obtain the jumper's score. When the jumper misses or stops jumping, the counters tell the jumper her or his score. The jumper then goes to the scoring area to record his or her name and score on the poster for the appropriate score range. (For example, someone who jumps 29 times would write her or his name and score on the 26-49 poster. Hint: If the counters come up with different numbers, tell them to give the average of the two.) The student then goes to another on-deck line and either sits and stretches or does other exercises before jumping again. Establish a line that students join when they've jumped and are waiting to be counters. Intermittently change out counters and jumpers to balance the stretching or counting time with jumping.

CRANK IT UP   Students who record a high jumping score may go to a trick center to practice tricks before they continue with the jump rope challenge. Establish a station or two for advanced jumpers, such as students who can continuously jump for a long time. Monitor this station especially carefully so that students don't overexert themselves. Allow for water breaks.

GEAR IT DOWN   Eliminate the stations. Ask students to work in groups of four. While one student jumps, the other three count. Instead of recording their scores, students should remain in the play area and encourage other jumpers. Ask all jumpers to count together. Students who find it hard to jump rope can place a rope on the ground and jump from one side of the rope to the other without counters.

ASSET ACTION

School/learning engagement (asset 22), honesty (asset 29), and personal power (asset 37)—Jumpathon includes activities that build these assets. For example, counting builds math skills (school engagement), recording the number of jumps requires honesty, and giving students exercise choices helps them to feel empowered.

COORDINATED SCHOOL HEALTH LINKS

Many people don't think of a school's environment in terms of health. However, a health-promoting school environment is crucial for full student development and a key component of coordinated school health. It is important for students and teachers to feel good about their school. Research indicates that kids develop more fully when they feel valued and believe that teachers and other adults care about them. By fostering children's intellectual, social, and emotional development, Jumpathon contributes to a school environment that promotes student health and well-being.

Mouse Tails

CONTENT CONNECTIONS   Chasing, fleeing, dodging, aerobic health

READY FOR ACTION

- Each student tucks one end of a rope into his or her back pocket or waistband so that the rope hangs to the ground like a tail.
- Students are paired, with one partner in the middle of the play area and the other waiting outside the area.

LET'S PLAY   Inside students walk briskly, attempting to step on other students' tails (ropes). When students lose their tail, they pick it up, find their partner, and trade places with her or him. The outside partner stretches or exercises while waiting.

CRANK IT UP   Eliminate partnering. All students play. When students lose their tail, they leave the area, perform a reentry exercise task, and continue with the game.

GEAR IT DOWN   Designate two students as cats. These students try to step on tails while all the other students (mice) move freely around the area. When students lose their tail, they pick it up, go to the tail replacement area, tuck their tail back in, count to 10, and reenter the game.

ASSET ACTION

Teacher tip—Give students useful roles. For example, students proficient in various activities can teach students who are less proficient, and particular students can be in charge of the equipment for a day. For example, getting the jump ropes ready for Mouse Tails helps a student feel useful and increases self-esteem.

COORDINATED SCHOOL HEALTH LINKS

The partnering in Mouse Tails fosters cooperation. Tell students that when they work together as partners or in groups, it is the same as people working together in the community to make things better for everybody. Remind them that social, emotional, and physical health are not just important for improving the health of our own minds and bodies, but that it is also important for schools and communities to be healthy.

Partner Party

CONTENT CONNECTIONS   Jumping tricks, aerobic health, muscular endurance

READY FOR ACTION

- Each student has a jump rope.
- Students are scattered in pairs. (If the total number of students is an odd number, have one group of three so that no one is excluded from the activity. If necessary, show the members of the trio how to take turns.)

LET'S PLAY   Tell students it's time for a partner jumping party. Teach, then allow time to practice the following:

Partners Share a Rope

- Face to face—Facing each other, both partners jump while one turns the rope.
- Front face—Facing the front, both partners jump while one turns the rope.
- Switch—As the rope is turning, the partners try to switch places.
- In and out—One partner holds one handle and stands inside to jump. The other partner holds the other handle and stands outside to help turn.
- Two for the road—Partners stand side by side, each holds one end of the rope with his or her outside hand, and both jump.
- Reverse two for the road—Partners perform "Two for the road" with one facing the front and the other facing the back.
- Giddy up—One partner stands behind the other. While the back partner has her or his hands on the front partner's shoulders, the front partner turns the rope and both jump while moving forward.

Each Partner Has a Rope

- Side by side—Partners stand side by side, trade inside rope handles, and jump forward or backward.
- Front and back—Partners stand side by side, trade inside rope handles, and jump with one facing forward and the other facing backward.
- Mirror, mirror—Partners stand side by side or facing each other. They try to match each others' movements while performing the following tricks:
  - Bell jump—Jump forward and backward.
  - Ski jump—Jump from side to side.
  - Jump and twist—Keeping your hips still, twist from side to side at your waist.
  - Hip hop—Hop on one foot.

CRANK IT UP   Ask students to create and name their own partner tricks. Or have students form groups of three with different numbers of ropes (for example, 3 students with 2 ropes or 3 students with 3 ropes).

GEAR IT DOWN   With one rope on the floor in a straight line, partners practice matching activities. For example, partners might face each other and jump from side to side. Alternatively, select five students proficient in jumping rope. Ask them to work with students who are having trouble with jump rope tricks.

ASSET ACTION

Empowerment (assets 7-10) and positive identity (assets 37-40)—Many skill-building PE activities are easier for naturally athletic students. Ask highly skilled students to help less advanced ones. When one student helps another with jumping rope, both are empowered and both have a more positive sense of self.

COORDINATED SCHOOL HEALTH LINKS

Have each student develop a health-related jumping chant, such as one that lists parts of the body or healthy foods. For example, a student might chant, "F-R-U-I-T. Fruit is good for you and me!" and then call out the name of a fruit every time she or he jumps. The student stops jumping when she or he runs out of ideas.

Wild Over Webs

CONTENT CONNECTIONS   Jumping, landing, rhythms

READY FOR ACTION

- One jump rope per student
- Circles or rings made of plastic or rubber for floor jumping
- Low hurdles or two cones, each with a rope over it
- Music
- For "Crank It Up": equipment such as poly spots, cones, hoops, or jumping rings

LET'S PLAY   Working in pairs, students place their ropes on the ground so that they form a plus sign (+). The students then take turns and:

- hop or jump in each quadrant of the plus sign;
- jump on both feet moving clockwise within each quadrant;
- double jump forward and backward so that they move two squares forward then two squares back;
- scissor jump (one foot in front, one in back) without touching the rope;
- walk like a crab or a bear, placing hands or feet in the quadrants;
- get into a crabwalk position, place their hands behind the +, and move their feet in and out;
- get into a push-up position and hand-walk between quadrants.

Students form groups of three or four. Group members place their ropes on the ground so that they resemble ladder rungs. Then they jump "up" (through) each rung of the ladder to the beat of the music, similar to how a hopscotch game would be used. After some practice time has passed, challenge each group to create its own jumping patterns using the ropes. The patterns can be straight, curved, or zigzag. Start the music and ask the groups to jump their pattern while staying on beat. Then have each group switch to another group's pattern.

CRANK IT UP   Give students four or five other pieces of equipment (e.g., poly spots, cones, hoops, jumping rings). Ask them to create an obstacle course using all of their equipment, including their ropes. Have the students go through the obstacle course.

GEAR IT DOWN   Each student places her or his rope on the ground in the shape of a line, triangle, or circle (the student can choose). The student then leaps back and forth across the line, jumps in and out of the circle, or hops in, out, or around the triangle.

ASSET ACTION

Personal power (asset 37)—Young people with personal power feel that they have control over many things that happen to them. To empower students, give them a choice of activities whenever possible. Their confidence and feeling of control will increase when they can perform activities at their individual skill level. You can also talk to students about circumstances in which they feel powerful or powerless. Ask them what makes them feel powerful. Wild Over Webs gives students the chance to use their personal power when they create their own jumping patterns.

COORDINATED SCHOOL HEALTH LINKS

Place a picture of one or more sugary foods at the starting point of each jumping web. Tell students that they should jump away from food that could keep them from being healthy.

Beanbags

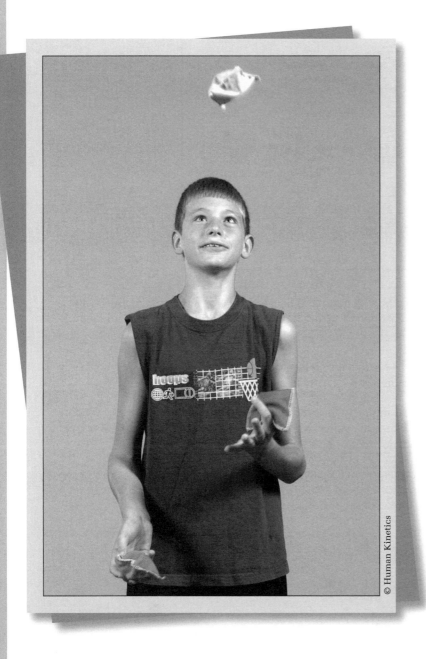

© Human Kinetics

It's beanbag time!

Consider using a personal and social responsibility model to manage class behavior.

Bank the Beanbag

CONTENT CONNECTIONS   Underhand throwing

READY FOR ACTION
- Beanbags of different colors
- Targets (trash cans or buckets) inside the activity area
- Poly spots surrounding each target
- Students divided into teams of three or four in relay style (see figure 11.1)

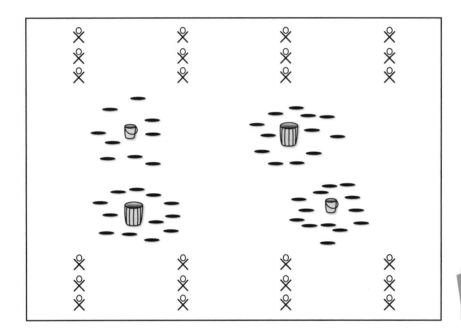

Figure 11.1
Bank the Beanbag
diagram.

LET'S PLAY   Give each team a different color beanbag. One at a time, team members walk to a poly spot and try to toss their beanbag into a target. If they make the shot, they pick up the poly spot and return the beanbag and poly spot to their team. If they miss, they pick up the beanbag and return to their team. The next student in line then takes his or her turn. When no poly spots remain, add up the poly spots accumulated by each team. To keep the game moving, place additional poly spots in the play area when supplies are low.

CRANK IT UP   Challenge one student at a time to throw targets continuously and pick up poly spots after each successful throw. Change the game to include basketballs and basketball shooting. Start with one-minute intervals; continue to add poly spots to prolong the action.

GEAR IT DOWN   Have many targets of varying sizes and shapes. Place the poly spots closer to the targets. Have the students practice without actually playing the game. The students keep their own beanbag, walk to any target, throw, retrieve, and keep their personal score.

ASSET ACTION

Cultural competence (asset 34). Group activities such as Bank the Beanbag allow students to feel comfortable with people of different cultural and racial backgrounds and promote cooperation.

COORDINATED SCHOOL HEALTH LINKS

Share this activity with classroom teachers with suggestions as to how to make it apply to other subject areas. The spots could represent the food groups, and the students have to collect one spot for each food group. Or flashcards with numbers on them could be used instead of spots. Then teams add the numbers they have collected to come up with their score. Or flashcards with letters could be used, and students try to collect letters to spell words on their spelling list.

Beanbag Addition

CONTENT CONNECTIONS   Tossing, throwing accuracy

READY FOR ACTION

- One or two beanbags per student
- Targets (hoops, each with a poly spot in the middle, or posterboard floor targets)
- Students divided into groups consisting of two pairs
- Partners lined up, facing each other, behind the target starting lines (see figure 11.2).
- Additional beanbags for "Crank It Up"

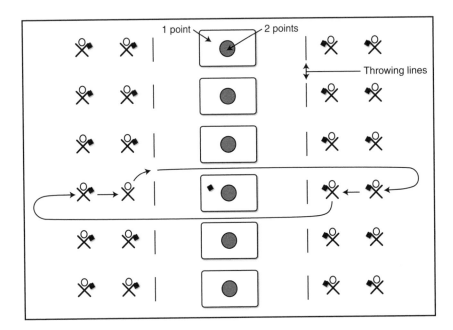

Figure 11.2
Beanbag Addition diagram.

LET'S PLAY   Assign each target area a point value. Partners toss their beanbags at the targets, retrieve their beanbags, and add their points together. For more activity, each partner can quickly walk to and touch an end line opposite the throwing line before getting back in line to play the opposite side of the target. Students play in timed rounds.

CRANK IT UP   Each student throws two beanbags. Or students multiply their points together. Change the target size, shape, or distance.

GEAR IT DOWN   Enlarge the target areas. Have each student add up his or her score.

ASSET ACTION

Integrity (asset 28) and honesty (asset 29)—Explain the connection between honesty (and integrity) and playing by the rules. In Beanbag Addition, playing by the rules means that students follow the teacher's instructions and tally their scores honestly.

COORDINATED SCHOOL HEALTH LINKS

Mutual trust is a cornerstone of social health, which is an essential part of classroom health education. In Beanbag Addition, players need to trust that no one is inflating her or his scores.

Beanbag Barrage

CONTENT CONNECTIONS   Throwing accuracy

READY FOR ACTION

- Give each student one hoop and two beanbags.
- Pairs of students place their hoops on the ground 8 feet (2.4 meters) apart. Facing her or his partner and holding two beanbags, each student stands behind her or his hoop (see figure 11.3).

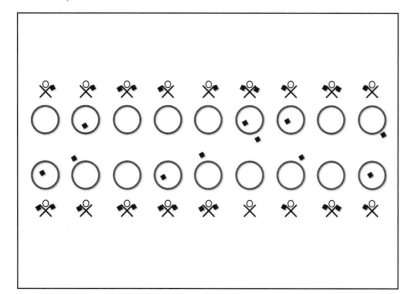

Figure 11.3   Beanbag Barrage diagram.

LET'S PLAY   On signal, players try to throw their beanbags into their partner's hoop. Students must stay outside and behind their hoop. Students can bat away, catch, or pick up and throw any beanbag that lands inside their hoop or their play area. They can leave their hoop to chase the thrown beanbags. On the stop signal, students count the beanbags in their partner's hoop.

CRANK IT UP   Place the hoops in two parallel lines. After each round, have one side of partners move to the right. Students then will have new partners. If students keep score, the total number of beanbags that land inside the hoop determines the winner.

GEAR IT DOWN   Have partners take turns throwing at one hoop from a starting line. Vary the distance with both partners taking turns throwing and retrieving. Eliminate hoop guarding (batting away or catching the beanbag).

ASSET ACTION

Teacher tip—The ability to form friendships is vitally important for a young person's development. Define friendship skills like listening and sharing. Tell your students about the importance of friendship in your life. Share stories and anecdotes about your friends, things you've done with them, and why they mean so much to you.

COORDINATED SCHOOL HEALTH LINKS

Have beanbags represent a negative influence or choice (such as peer pressure, junk food, alcohol, or drugs) that students bat away from their hoops. In a fun twist, have beanbags represent good things (such as adequate sleep, healthy foods, or respect for others) that students acquire if they catch a beanbag. Classroom teachers can use Beanbag Barrage to reinforce their own lessons on related topics.

Beanbag Fitness Challenges

CONTENT CONNECTIONS   Muscular endurance, eye–hand coordination, flexibility

READY FOR ACTION   One beanbag per student

LET'S PLAY   The teacher calls out an activity from the following lists, followed by "Ready. Go!" Students then perform that activity.

Mid-body (students are seated)

- Foot toss—Place a beanbag on your feet, throw it upward, and catch it with your hands.
- Around the leg—Lift one leg, and pass the beanbag under or around that leg; repeat with your other leg.
- Biking—Place a beanbag between your feet. Support your body with your hands on the floor behind your back. Bring the beanbag in toward your abdomen and back out without the feet touching the ground.
- Scissors—Lying on your back, move your legs scissors-fashion and pass the beanbag between them.

Upper Body (students are in a push-up position)

- Bag taps—Tap the beanbag with alternating hands.
- Beanie slaps—Push the beanbag from side to side with alternating hands.
- Push around—With your right hand, push the beanbag in a circle around your left hand. Switch hands.
- Touch all—Pick up the beanbag, touch your head with the beanbag, and place the beanbag back where it was. Switch hands. Repeat, touching different body parts.
- Juggle—Repeatedly toss the beanbag from one hand to the other.

CRANK IT UP   Students jog around the room for 30 seconds and then perform one of the "Let's Play" activities for 30 seconds.

GEAR IT DOWN   Students walk while balancing the beanbag on different parts of their body. The teacher calls out a toss-and-catch challenge (see Beanie Bag of Tricks on page 147) or one of the easier activities from "Let's Play."

ASSET ACTION

High expectations (asset 16)—Show students that you expect them to do their best. Encourage them to set personal goals such as increasing the number of repetitions during mid-body activities. Setting and achieving smaller goals builds a foundation for achieving larger goals, such as self-management, in many life endeavors.

COORDINATED SCHOOL HEALTH LINKS

Ask students to practice the upper-body activities in Beanbag Fitness Challenges at home with family members. A sock can be used in place of a beanbag.

Beanbag Rotation

CONTENT CONNECTIONS   Muscular endurance, aerobic health

READY FOR ACTION

- Give each student a beanbag in one of five colors or labeled with the number 1, 2, 3, 4, or 5 if colored beanbags are not available.
- Students are scattered in general space.
- Use exercise charts in which a color or number represents a particular activity, with each chart having a different code. (Hint: It is easy to create other charts by simply moving the exercise activities to a different color.) For example, one chart might be coded as follows:
  - Blue (1)—jumping jacks
  - Red (2)—curl-ups
  - Green (3)—push-ups
  - Yellow (4)—stretches
  - Orange (5)—free choice
- Have music on hand.
- For "Crank It Up," use poly spots and basketballs.

LET'S PLAY   While music plays, students walk around the room and swap beanbags with each student they meet. When the music stops, students move to personal space. The teacher holds up the exercise chart. On her or his signal, students perform the exercise that corresponds to their color or number. After a couple of rounds, switch to a chart with a different color or number code so that each student will perform a new activity.

CRANK IT UP   Put poly spots of various colors on the floor. Replace the beanbags with basketballs. Create a chart of basketball tricks (see Globetrotter Games, page 103). While the music plays, students dribble the ball. When the music stops, students stop on a poly spot and perform a basketball trick corresponding to that spot's color or number. The teacher can either call out the tricks or use a chart.

GEAR IT DOWN   Use beanbags of only two colors (e.g., red beanbags and blue beanbags). When the music stops, students toss and catch their beanbag and then perform color-coded tricks such as the following:

- Red—Toss, clap, and catch.
- Blue—Toss, touch your head with both hands, and catch.

For other options, see "Beanie Bag of Tricks," page 147.

 ASSET ACTION

Teacher tip—Building social skills is a major goal of physical education. Encourage students to greet one another by name and to say, "Thank you," after they swap beanbags.

COORDINATED SCHOOL HEALTH LINKS

Have students play Beanbag Rotation with each beanbag color representing a different healthy food. Here are examples:

Red—meat

Green—vegetables

Yellow—fruit

Blue—dairy

Students swap beanbags. When the music stops, all students toss and catch beanbags. When the teacher names a food, students with a beanbag corresponding to that type of food sit down and wait for another food to be called. For example, if the teacher calls, "Broccoli," all students with green (vegetables) beanbags sit; if he or she calls, "Hamburger," all students with red (meat) beanbags sit down. If the teacher says, "Milk," all students with blue beanbags sit.

Beanie Bag of Tricks

CONTENT CONNECTIONS

Tossing, catching, throwing, eye–hand coordination

READY FOR ACTION

- One beanbag per student
- Music
- Students scattered in general space
- For "Crank It Up": deck rings, basketballs, or fluff balls

LET'S PLAY   As directed by the teacher, students perform the following activities:

One Student

- One hand—Alternating between right hand and left hand, toss the beanbag up and down.
- Juggle—Toss the beanbag from hand to hand.
- Toss, catch behind—Toss the beanbag overhead and catch it behind your back.
- Claps—Toss the beanbag up, clap your hands one or more times, and catch.
- Under—Toss the beanbag under a lifted leg, and catch.
- Header—Put the beanbag on your head, lean forward or backward so that the beanbag falls off, and catch it.
- Back balance—Toss the beanbag up, and catch it on your back.
- Footsies—Balance the beanbag on one foot, toss the beanbag with that foot, and catch.
- Rebound—Toss the beanbag overhead, and jump up to catch it.
- Shake and bake—Get down on all fours, put the beanbag on your back, and shake it off.

Partners

Partners may choose one of the following actions to perform:

- Quick toss—Partner 1 stands with his or her back to partner 2; at the signal "Go!" partner 2 tosses the beanbag, and partner 1 turns around to catch it.
- Travel—While sliding, students toss (and catch) the beanbag with two hands.

Groups of Three

- Split second—With their hands on their laps, two partners sit facing each other. A third student stands and drops the beanbag. The sitting players attempt to catch or cover the beanbag with their hands.
- Double vision—The three students in each group form a triangle. Each of the two students at the triangle's base has a beanbag. One of these students tosses to the player at the triangle's apex. That player returns the beanbag to the thrower. The action is repeated with the student at the other base tossing to the player at the apex.

CRANK IT UP   Use deck rings, basketballs, or fluff balls instead of beanbags. Allow students to create, name, draw, post, and demonstrate their newly created activities.

GEAR IT DOWN   Ask students to place a beanbag on their head and walk around the room avoiding others. When the music stops, they work on simple tossing and catching. Encourage students to stay in control and stay within their own space.

ASSET ACTION

Interpersonal competence (asset 33) and cultural competence (asset 34)—Beanie Bag of Tricks provides great opportunities for cooperation and respect. Tell students that accepting the differences among people, respecting others' opinions, and cooperating with others are assets that will serve them well in many real-life situations. Draw connections between what they're learning in your class and what's happening in their lives, in the community, and in the world.

COORDINATED SCHOOL HEALTH LINKS

Encourage students to create beanbag activities that can be played at home. Playing beanbag games with their family will help students stay interested in physical activities learned at school and will help connect school and home into one support system. At home, beanbags can be made of old or rolled-up socks.

Fleet Feet

CONTENT CONNECTIONS   Rolling skills, throwing accuracy, dodging

READY FOR ACTION

- Divide the playing area in half with a line.
- Place beanbags on the centerline (one beanbag per two students).
- Divide the students into two teams. The students on each team move to their area's back boundary line (see figure 11.4).

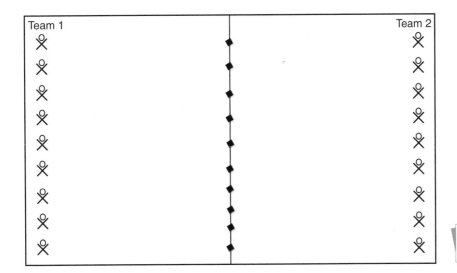

Figure 11.4
Fleet Feet diagram.

LET'S PLAY   At the signal, students move to the centerline, pick up a beanbag, and attempt to slide it on the floor to the other team's side and tag an opponent on the foot with it. A tagged student walks around the perimeter of the game to the opponent's side for further play.

CRANK IT UP   Instead of changing sides of the court as in "Let's Play," tagged students must perform a reentry task before returning to their side to play.

GEAR IT DOWN   Pairs of students practice sliding a beanbag back and forth to each other. Students also can slide a beanbag down a line to a partner, slide it under a partner's straddled legs, or slide it to tag a cone.

ASSET ACTION

Peaceful conflict resolution (asset 36)—Disagreements are a normal part of life for young people and adults. Fleet Feet is an excellent activity to remind students that arguing and fighting are poor ways to handle disagreements, since the activity is contingent on students being honest about whether they have been tagged in the foot or not. Tell them that the need to resolve conflicts peacefully isn't limited to PE sports and games. Solving a problem or conflict peacefully is important at school, home, and in their future workplace.

COORDINATED SCHOOL HEALTH LINKS

Resolving conflicts peacefully promotes physical, emotional, and social health. In Fleet Feet, students try to eliminate others from the game. To turn the competition into a way of fostering peaceful conflict resolution, the teacher can set the competition within a context of friendship: "We start the game as friends, and we end it as friends."

Four-Color Tag

CONTENT CONNECTIONS   Chasing, dodging, fleeing, tagging

READY FOR ACTION

- Beanbags of four different colors
- One beanbag per student
- Students scattered in general space
- Music

LET'S PLAY   While music plays, students carry their beanbag and walk in general space. When the music stops, students freeze, and the teacher calls out a color. All students with a beanbag of that color become taggers. Tagged students remain in the game and continue to try to avoid being tagged. They may tally the number of times they're tagged. Ask taggers to tag as many different students as possible. Play in timed rounds suited to students' abilities and fitness levels.

CRANK IT UP   Designate a fitness area for students who have been tagged and are waiting to reenter the game. Have students do an assigned activity when they're tagged.

GEAR IT DOWN   Before the students walk at the beginning of the game, announce the beanbag color that designates a student a tagger. The taggers move to the perimeter of the play area and the remaining students walk until the teacher says, "Ready, tag!"

ASSET ACTION

Integrity (asset 28) and responsibility (asset 30)—Ask students to say what fairness means to them. Have them give examples of playing the game fairly without mentioning names. Promote student integrity and responsibility by emphasizing that students need to be honest and accurate when they tally the number of times that they've been tagged.

COORDINATED SCHOOL HEALTH LINKS

Tie beanbags to health issues by having particular beanbag colors represent particular foods, body parts, or items in other health-related categories. For example, different beanbag colors can represent different foods (see Beanbag Rotation on page 145 for ideas.)

Hasty Helpers

CONTENT CONNECTIONS   Aerobic health, tossing, catching

READY FOR ACTION

- Four foam balls
- Four beanbags
- For "Crank It Up": basketballs or other balls

LET'S PLAY   Students spread out in general space. Designate four students as taggers, and give each of them a foam ball. Designate four students as "hasty helpers," and give each of them a beanbag. At the signal, taggers try to tag students with their foam ball. Tagged students freeze in place. A hasty helper who spots a frozen student moves close to that student and gently tosses her or him a beanbag. If the student catches the beanbag, he or she unfreezes and takes over as a hasty helper. If the student doesn't catch the beanbag, the helper picks it up and looks for another student to help. Taggers may not tag helpers.

CRANK IT UP   Use balls instead of beanbags, and add skills. For example, helpers can bounce-pass basketballs to frozen students.

GEAR IT DOWN   Keep the same taggers for a designated amount of time. Select new taggers from among students who are playing the game correctly. Have students first play the game at a walking pace, as a simple tag game without helpers. Students freeze and count to 25 before resuming play.

ASSET ACTION

Caring school climate (asset 5), community values youth (asset 7), and safety (asset 10)—When young people feel safe at home and at school, the environment is rich in asset-building potential. To help young people feel safe at school, encourage teachers, administrators, and staff members to get to know students and to watch out for their safety. As a teacher, what can you do to facilitate a safe and caring environment for students in the game and throughout the school environment?

COORDINATED SCHOOL HEALTH LINKS

Hasty Helpers can reinforce lessons about safe behavior. For example, taggers can represent some unsafe behavior that students should avoid, such as pushing other students, not washing one's hands, or eating foods high in fat, sugar, or cholesterol.

The hasty helpers can represent ways of preventing or treating injury, such as bandages, ointments, or helmets.

Hot Potato

CONTENT CONNECTIONS   Tossing, catching

READY FOR ACTION

- Students form groups of five or six.
- Each group forms a circle and gets a beanbag. For "Gear it Down", use a large ball.
- In groups, form one big circle (see figure 11.5).
- For "Crank It Up," use popular music and different equipment, such as basketballs or soccer balls.

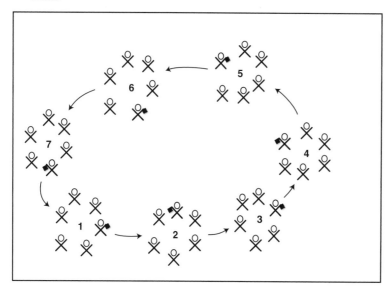

Figure 11.5
Hot Potato diagram.

LET'S PLAY   Within each group, students toss the beanbag around their circle while the teacher chants, "Hot potato, hot potato. Who's got the hot potato? If you've got the hot potato, you move on." When the chant ends, every student holding a beanbag gives it to the player on the right and moves counterclockwise to play in the next circle.

CRANK IT UP   Replace the chant with popular music. Use different equipment (e.g., a basketball or soccer ball), and change the type of toss or pass that is used.

GEAR IT DOWN   Use a large ball instead of a beanbag so that catching is easier. When the chant ends, students holding a ball must walk with it once around their circle before play resumes.

 ASSET ACTION

Interpersonal competence (asset 33) and cultural competence (asset 34)—Hot Potato promotes interaction and friendship by having students work in circle formation and in small groups. Such interaction helps students to feel comfortable with others of any national origin or ethnicity. Encourage students to welcome new players.

 COORDINATED SCHOOL HEALTH LINKS

Change the Hot Potato chant so that it focuses on healthy food choices. For example, have them chant, "Broccoli, broccoli, who's got the broccoli? If you've got the broccoli, you're healthy." Share this game with classroom teachers so that they can use it to reinforce nutrition lessons.

Stop, Bop, and Drop

CONTENT CONNECTIONS   Eye–hand coordination, tossing, catching, muscular endurance

READY FOR ACTION

- One beanbag per student
- Music
- For "Crank It Up": basketballs

LET'S PLAY   While music plays, students walk with a beanbag in their hands. Intermittently, the teacher calls out one of the following signals. Students perform the designated action for 30 seconds and then resume walking around the room.

- Stop—Perform a beanbag trick. (See "Beanie Bag of Tricks," page 147).
- Bop—Jog in place with high knees while moving the beanbag in a figure-eight pattern under and around your legs.
- Drop—Drop to the floor, get into a push-up position, place the beanbag on the floor, and push it from side to side (see Beanbag Fitness Challenges, page 144).

CRANK IT UP   Add tossing to a partner or juggling. Use basketballs instead of beanbags, and perform basketball tricks (see Globetrotter Games, page 103).

GEAR IT DOWN   Students place their beanbag on one shoulder and walk around the playing area. At the signal, students perform toss-and-catch activities that build spatial skills. For example, they might toss and catch the beanbag at a low level or put it on their back and shake it off.

ASSET ACTION

Teacher tip—Walk through the cafeteria during lunch, and compliment the students on responsible behavior and healthy food choices. Let them sign a poster board in the gym entitled "Caught You Being Responsible."

COORDINATED SCHOOL HEALTH LINKS

Ask students to play Stop, Bop, and Drop at home. A sock or paper ball can be used instead of a beanbag. Also suggest that students teach the game to family members.

Trading Spaces

CONTENT CONNECTIONS   Reaction time, dodging, agility

READY FOR ACTION

- Place in a circle one beanbag per student, each bag of different colors. (For more activity, use several circles.)
- One student, the chaser, stands in the middle of the circle.
- All other students stand by a beanbag.
- Have music on hand for "Crank it Up. "

LET'S PLAY   The teacher calls out a color. Students who are standing by a beanbag of that color trade places with one another student of the same color bag. The chaser tries to tag students who are trading places. Students tally the number of times that they're tagged. Change taggers often.

CRANK IT UP   When the teacher starts the music, all students quickly walk clockwise around the circle. Students may not pass to one another. When the music stops, the students stop, find the nearest beanbag, and perform Beanbag Fitness Challenge (see page 144) before the teacher calls the next trading of places.

GEAR IT DOWN   Eliminate the chaser. Ask students to trade colors. When the teacher calls a color that doesn't correspond to any of the beanbags, all students trade places.

ASSET ACTION

Achievement motivation (asset 21)—Introduce students to Web sites, such as Packy Play Fair, that have asset-building themes (see References and Resources). These Web sites can motivate kids so that they become committed to learning, bond to their school, and realize the importance of playing fair.

COORDINATED SCHOOL HEALTH LINKS

Share Trading Spaces with classroom teachers so that they can have students play it during recess.

Dice

12

The two main causes of the obesity epidemic are poor diet and insufficient physical activity.

Dice games—a new way to teach health and fitness!

Alphabet Soup

CONTENT CONNECTIONS   Balance, flexibility, shapes

READY FOR ACTION

- One die
- Students scattered in general space
- Music
- For "Gear It Down": alphabet cards

LET'S PLAY   While music plays, students skip around the area. When the music stops, the teacher rolls the die. Students quickly form groups with as many members as the number shown on the die. The teacher calls out a letter, and group members jointly form that letter while standing, lying on the ground, or using both postures.

CRANK IT UP   Announce one or two letters, which students use to form a word.

GEAR IT DOWN   Hold up alphabet cards, and have each student form the letters by himself or herself. Group students in two or threes, and have the groups form simple words that you call out—such as *cat, dog,* or *and.*

ASSET ACTION

Positive peer influence (asset 15)—Young people need the positive influence of peers and adults. The positive aspects of friendships and peer groups increase motivation and lead to improved academic performance. With teacher guidance, Alphabet Soup can provide an experience of positive peer influence because students work in groups.

COORDINATED SCHOOL HEALTH LINKS

In Alphabet Soup, younger students might need some peer help in forming letters. Have some students act as helpers. Encourage other teachers to also use peer helping. Extending the peer helper model to the regular classroom can become the impetus for developing a coordinated school health program.

Dice Jump-Off

CONTENT CONNECTIONS   Jumping rope, jumping, landing

READY FOR ACTION

- Students are paired and scattered around the room.
- Each pair has one jump rope and one die.
- For "Gear It Down," use lines or ropes on the floor.

LET'S PLAY   Each student rolls the die. The partner with the higher number adds the two numbers and tries to jump that many times without a miss in order to earn one point. If the student doesn't succeed, her or his partner tries (either using the same number or rolling for another).

CRANK IT UP   Students sum the numbers and then double the total. If they jump successfully, they get two points.

GEAR IT DOWN   Students use lines or ropes on the floor when jumping. To score, they must jump continuously to avoid stumbling or touching the line or rope.

ASSET ACTION

Peaceful conflict resolution (asset 36)— The ability to resolve conflicts peacefully is an asset that increases in value throughout life. Discuss with the class how class disputes can be resolved peacefully. In Dice Jump-Off students might disagree regarding the correct answers to the math problems. Encourage them to go through the addition step by step. If they can't agree, they can ask another person for help in settling the dispute. Younger students can play Rock, Paper, Scissors. Have the students suggest scenarios involving conflicts that the class discusses and resolves. Tell the students that one thing they can do to be a peacemaker is to speak softly when trying to resolve a conflict. If they speak in an angry tone, people will not want to listen to them.

COORDINATED SCHOOL HEALTH LINKS

Dice Jump-Off contributes to students' academic success by reinforcing math skills learned in class. It also encourages cooperation between math and PE teachers, a step to building coordinated efforts.

Dice Multiples

The creativity of SES PE student Leslie Vaden helped to spark the idea for this activity.

CONTENT CONNECTIONS   Aerobic health, muscular endurance, flexibility

READY FOR ACTION

- Pairs of students scattered around the play area
- One die per pair
- A sheet of grade-appropriate equations for each pair
- For "Crank It Up": basketballs

LET'S PLAY   One partner rolls the die twice and multiplies the two numbers that the die displayed. The roller announces what he or she believes to be the total, and the partner checks the answer using the equation sheet. If the answer is correct, the roller chooses an exercise for both partners to perform. If not, both students walk or jog around the perimeter.

CRANK IT UP   Increase the duration of the exercises or make them more difficult. Add skill work such as basketball shooting.

GEAR IT DOWN   Have students add rather than multiply. Also, students can perform teacher-designated exercises rather than choose their own exercises.

ASSET ACTION

Caring school climate (asset 5)—A caring school climate is important because young people do better in school when they feel they are valued and cared for. To promote a caring school climate, you can plan to play Dice Multiples and bring students, teachers, administrators, and staff together for fun and fellowship. You also can start a lunchtime, study hall, or after-school discussion group for students who want to "just talk."

COORDINATED SCHOOL HEALTH LINKS

Dice Multiples provides a fun way of connecting fitness to classroom math instruction. Share these games with the after-school activity directors at your school or in your school district.

Dice Trios

The combined creativity of SES PE students August Zimmerman and William Nguyen helped to spark the idea for this activity.

CONTENT CONNECTIONS   Aerobic health, muscular endurance

READY FOR ACTION

- Groups of 3 scattered around the play area
- One die per group
- An exercise chart such as table 12.1.

Table 12.1   Fitness Exercise Chart

High	Medium	Low
Jogging in place 20 times	15 jumping jacks	10 curl-ups
Bicycling 15 times	25 line jumps	10 push-ups

LET'S PLAY   Each group member rolls a die. The student who rolls the highest number selects a fitness activity (e.g., jogging in place or the bicycle exercise) from the "High" column of the exercise chart, the student who rolls the middle number selects from the "Medium" column, and the student who rolls the lowest number selects from the "Low" column. All group members then perform the selected exercises simultaneously, followed by a new round.

CRANK IT UP   After all members of a group have rolled a die, they perform the exercise and jog one lap. Then the high roller in the group moves clockwise to the next group and plays with new partners.

GEAR IT DOWN   Divide the room into three areas: high, medium, and low. When all groups have completed their die rolling, high rollers go to the "high" area, middle rollers to the "medium" area, and low rollers to the "low" area. Each of the three groups then performs an exercise announced by the teacher before returning to their team.

ASSET ACTION

Achievement motivation (asset 21) and school/learning engagement (asset 22)—Dice Trios reinforces math skills. People learn in different ways. Dice Trios is especially helpful to students who learn more easily within a context of exercise and play than within a standard classroom environment.

COORDINATED SCHOOL HEALTH LINKS

Discuss with other teachers how Dice Trios can be incorporated into math lessons or exercise breaks.

Dice-Ercise

CONTENT CONNECTIONS

Aerobic health, muscular endurance, flexibility

READY FOR ACTION

- An exercise chart that lists three exercises each for numbers 1 through 6
- Students in small groups
- One die per group

LET'S PLAY One student at a time rolls the die and leads his or her team in the exercise that corresponds to the rolled number. No exercise may be repeated. If the die number corresponds to an exercise that already was performed, the roller makes up an exercise for the group to perform.

CRANK IT UP Before leading an exercise, the student who rolls the die jogs once around the gym while the other group members jog in place.

GEAR IT DOWN Either the teacher or a student volunteer rolls the die and leads the class in each exercise.

ASSET ACTION

Teacher tip—Dice-Ercise cultivates leadership skills. Discuss with your students the qualities of a good leader and note positive qualities about good leaders in society.

COORDINATED SCHOOL HEALTH LINKS

Send parents a letter about Dice-Ercise and how it relates to building assets in their children. Then use assets as springboards for discussions in conferences with parents and students with the goal of establishing a coordinated school health program.

Exercise Surprise

CONTENT CONNECTIONS   Aerobic health, muscular strength, flexibility

READY FOR ACTION

- Students scattered in general space
- A poster with a numbered list of exercises such as the following:
    1. Curl-ups
    2. Push-ups
    3. Jumping jacks
    4. Jogging in place
    5. Straddle stretches (sitting with the legs in a V)
    6. Scissor jumps (one foot in front, one foot in back, foot positions switched while in the air)
- Music
- For "Crank It Up": balls

LET'S PLAY   Each student chooses one exercise from the list and performs that exercise while the music plays. When the music stops, the teacher or a student volunteer rolls a die to reveal the secret exercise. Students who performed the exercise whose number is the same as the rolled number receive one point. Students should play for several rounds.

CRANK IT UP   Increase the exercise time. Change the exercises to ball handling tricks or other activities that develop skills, such as jump rope tricks.

GEAR IT DOWN   Students walk around the play area. At the teacher's signal, they freeze. The teacher rolls a die, and the students perform the exercise whose number corresponds to the number rolled.

ASSET ACTION

Teacher tip—It's important for children to be excited about learning inside and outside of school. Children who are actively engaged in learning feel more connected to their school. By being supportive and providing many enjoyable exercise choices, PE teachers can create a warm, welcoming environment that encourages this engagement.

COORDINATED SCHOOL HEALTH LINKS

Exercise Surprise provides an excellent opportunity to discuss health-related fitness. Invite the parents to come to school for "Movin' Monday." Before playing Exercise Surprise, ask students to teach each guest the proper way to perform the exercises.

Four-Sided Fitness

CONTENT CONNECTIONS   Aerobic health, muscular endurance, flexibility

READY FOR ACTION

- Place cones numbered 1, 2, 3, and 4 in the room's corners.
- Put one exercise card on top of each cone. Use your own cards or Let's Get Physical cards (see appendix B).
- Students are scattered in general space.
- Have music on hand.

LET'S PLAY   While music plays, students jog randomly in the middle of the activity area. When the music stops, they go stand next to whichever cone they choose. The teacher rolls a die. If the die shows 1, 2, 3, or 4, students at the corresponding cone sit down and stretch while all other students perform the exercise shown on the card at their cone. If the die shows 5, all students exercise. If it shows 6, the teacher chooses any exercise and performs it for the class.

CRANK IT UP   Have students skip or slide rather than jog, and increase the duration of the cone exercises.

GEAR IT DOWN   Students move counterclockwise from cone to cone and perform the exercise designated at each cone. The teacher rolls a die to determine how they'll move. For example, 1 could represent "Skip," 2 "Hop," and 3 "Walk backward."

ASSET ACTION

Adult role models (asset 14)—Students need positive role models to emulate. In Four-Sided Fitness the teacher acts as a positive role model when she or he performs exercises for the class. Likewise, students notice teachers who drink water instead of sugary beverages.

COORDINATED SCHOOL HEALTH LINKS

Have students invite their parents to play Four-Sided Fitness with them. Tuck a brief newsletter into each child's homework folder that emphasizes the importance of exercise and encourages parents to ask their child how to play Four-Sided Fitness.

Odds and Evens

CONTENT CONNECTIONS Aerobic health, muscular endurance

READY FOR ACTION

- One pair of dice
- Pairs of students standing on opposite sides of the centerline facing each other with one giant step between them (see figure 12.1)

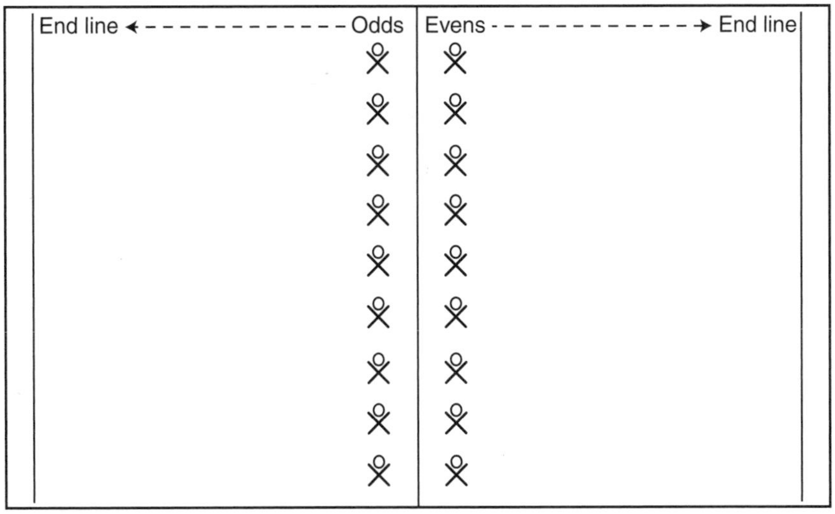

Figure 12.1 Odds and Evens diagram.

LET'S PLAY Designate one line of students "odds" and the other line "evens." Roll the dice, and announce the two numbers shown on the dice. Students mentally add the numbers. If the total is even, the "evens" turn and run to their endline, and their partners try to tag them before they cross the finish line designated by the teacher. If the total of the rolled numbers is odd, the students' roles are reversed.

CRANK IT UP Students play the game in a large outside play area in groups of three. One student in each group rolls a die, and the other two students play as described in "Let's Play." Students rotate after each round. Award points for tags. Add other math operations such as subtraction and multiplication.

GEAR IT DOWN Students do exercises instead of playing tag. For example, the "evens" might do curl-ups and the "odds" march in place.

ASSET ACTION

Planning and decision making (asset 32)—The quick pace of Odds and Evens gets students thinking ahead and making decisions. What will they do if the number is even? What will they do if it's odd? What pathways will they use when running and chasing? What strategies will they use? The students need to make quick decisions based on which number is rolled and what their partner does. They should notice the tactics that their partner uses to escape or chase and plan countermoves.

COORDINATED SCHOOL HEALTH LINKS

Link Odds and Evens to health topics. Designate one side as dairy and the other side as whole grains. Students try to catch a certain number of servings. Classroom teachers can implement Odds and Evens for their own lessons.

Roll 15

CONTENT CONNECTIONS   Aerobic health, muscular endurance, flexibility

READY FOR ACTION

- Groups of three scattered around the room
- One die per group
- For "Crank It Up": jump ropes

LET'S PLAY   Group members take turns rolling a die. During each round each member adds her or his score as she or he tries to get as close as possible to the number 15. A player may stop rolling at any time during a round if he or she thinks that his or her score is closest to 15. The player with the sum closest to 15 wins the round, selects an exercise, and decides how many times it will be performed. All members of the group then perform the exercise before the die is rolled again.

CRANK IT UP   Increase the duration of the exercises. List jump rope tricks. The winner can choose the trick and the duration. Change the winning number.

© Human Kinetics

GEAR IT DOWN   Each student rolls the die twice and adds up their score. The player with the highest score wins.

ASSET ACTION

Interpersonal competence (asset 33) and responsibility (asset 30)—To work well together, team members must respect one another. When students play Roll 15, remind them of this. Ask them to describe respectful, responsible behavior with regard to Roll 15.

COORDINATED SCHOOL HEALTH LINKS

Roll 15 fosters students' ability to accept and get along with others (social health). Stress the importance of caring, respect, and cooperation in all of your activities. Students should be asked about games that they play away from PE.

Copy 'N' Go

Do you emphasize cooperation, fair play, and responsible participation during physical activity sessions?

Every activity in this chapter uses a reproducible from appendix B.

Alpha Action

CONTENT CONNECTIONS   Physical activity featuring verbs and adverbs; locomotor skills; flexibility; aerobic health; muscular endurance

READY FOR ACTION

- One copy of the Alpha Action task cards for the teacher (see appendix B, page 241).
- Students scattered in general space
- For "Gear It Down": alphabet cards with a letter on the front and an action on the back

LET'S PLAY   The teacher announces a letter and an action keyed to that letter using the Alpha Action task sheet as a guide. At the signal the students perform that action. For example, "A: Act like a kangaroo," "B: Bounce like a ball."

CRANK IT UP   Give students a movement word such as *skip, jump,* or *hop,* and have them make other movement words that start with each of its letters. For example, students could create the following words from *skip*: **s***lide,* **k***ick,* **i***nchworm,* **p***rance.* For an additional challenge, have the students construct a phrase or sentence that contains the new words in any order in plural or singular form (e.g., "Inchworms can't kick or prance, but they can slide.")

GEAR IT DOWN   Create alphabet cards with a letter on the front and an action on the back. Show students the letters, and have them form the letter with their body. Demonstrate an action, and ask students to imitate it.

ASSET ACTION

School/learning engagement (asset 22)—Alpha Action helps young students develop English language skills and skills that can help them become more successful in school.

COORDINATED SCHOOL HEALTH LINKS

Teaching English skills through physical education fosters cooperation between PE and classroom teachers.

Cardio Challenge

CONTENT CONNECTIONS   Aerobic health, muscular endurance, flexibility

READY FOR ACTION
- One Cardio Challenge task card per student or pair of students (see appendix B, page 242).
- Students scattered in general space
- Cones
- Step benches

LET'S PLAY   Give each student or pair a task card. Students perform the exercises and movements on each card in order and then return the card to the teacher before taking another.

CRANK IT UP   Expand the play area by increasing the distance between cones. Have students perform the exercises on each card twice. Ask each student to write his or her own workout.

GEAR IT DOWN   Have the students form small groups with one reader. Read the tasks for each group to perform, or have a good reader lead the group members. If you like, ask classroom teachers which students are good readers.

ASSET ACTION

Healthy lifestyle/restraint (asset 31)—Ask students how the particular activities in Cardio Challenge promote aerobic or heart health.

COORDINATED SCHOOL HEALTH LINKS

Ask the students to create a "cardio challenge" at home and to discuss heart health with their parents. It's important for children to receive coordinated health messages and adult support.

Fitness Frolic

Fitness Frolic reprinted by permission from R. Rainey.

CONTENT CONNECTIONS Listening, following directions, aerobic health, muscular endurance

READY FOR ACTION

- Students scattered in general space
- Fitness Frolic task sheet for the teacher's use (see appendix B, page 244)
- Music

LET'S PLAY While music plays, the teacher calls out fitness tasks, which students perform as quickly as possible as described on the task sheet. Encourage students to group quickly by choosing classmates close to them.

CRANK IT UP Students who do not form a group before the allotted time is up must go to a designated area and race-walk one time around the perimeter before returning to the big group.

GEAR IT DOWN Give only one or two commands from the Fitness Frolic sequence. Teach the partner activities, and allow students to play with one partner until they've learned the routines.

© Human Kinetics

ASSET ACTION

Teacher tip—Activities that require young people to listen and follow directions build personal responsibility. Expect students in your class to act responsibly, and praise them for doing so. Stress the importance of getting to assigned places in the gym or playground on time.

COORDINATED SCHOOL HEALTH LINKS

Teacher tip—With teachers and parents, discuss ways to build social skills and assets, especially personal responsibility, acceptance of others, and friendship skills. Make acceptance and appreciation of others a motto for your classroom or gym. Discuss with school administrators the possibility of a school motto related to acceptance of others.

Heart Smart

CONTENT CONNECTIONS   Aerobic health, muscular endurance

READY FOR ACTION

- Students scattered in general space
- One Heart Smart task card for the teacher's use (see appendix B, page 246)

LET'S PLAY   The teacher calls out one activity at a time from Heart Smart task cards, and the students perform those activities.

CRANK IT UP   Using a Heart Smart task card, list factors that contribute to heart disease and discuss with students how these factors can cause heart attacks and other potentially fatal heart problems. Link these factors to healthy habits that prevent heart disease.

GEAR IT DOWN   Tell students about the heart. For example, you might say, "The heart is an organ inside your chest. It's the size of your fist. The heart pumps blood to your entire body. The blood circulates to all of your cells, including your muscle cells." Have students perform actions linked to your description. For example, they might jump on the word *pump* or make a fist when they hear the word *heart*. You also can have students create their own actions.

ASSET ACTION

Healthy lifestyle/restraint (asset 31)—Heart Smart engages children in active learning about heart health. Connect physical activity to reducing the risk of heart disease.

COORDINATED SCHOOL HEALTH LINKS

Ask classroom teachers to help each student cut a heart shape out of red construction paper. Students can write the title "Be Heart Smart" at the top of the heart and write a short statement stating what a person can do to be "heart smart." Classroom teachers can post these heart notes around the school halls, in the cafeteria, in the nurse's office, or in the administration area.

I Say Go

CONTENT CONNECTIONS   Aerobic health, muscular endurance, agility, coordination, following directions, sequencing

READY FOR ACTION

- An I Say Go task card for the teacher's use (see appendix B, page 248)
- Beanbags
- Students scattered in general space
- Index cards for "Crank It Up"

LET'S PLAY   Using an I Say Go task card, the teacher slowly gives a three-step command and then says, "Go." Students perform the command in sequence.

CRANK IT UP   Create sample cards to show the students. Give the students index cards, and have them write and perform their own three-step commands, but limit the number of repetitions that students can include on their card. Students can trade cards with other students and attempt those three-step commands.

GEAR IT DOWN   Give students only one line of a command at a time. For example, instead of saying all of task 1 say only, "Shake your hands three times. Go."

ASSET ACTION

Creative activities (asset 17) and personal power (asset 37)—To promote creative thinking, empower students, and increase their sense of self-worth, ask students to create their own "Go" card. Expand this strategy during other lessons by having students create new games, exercises, and dance moves.

COORDINATED SCHOOL HEALTH LINKS

Share the I Say Go task cards with classroom teachers. Suggest that they have students touch objects on their desk or in the room rather than perform the "I Say Go" movement tasks that require more space. For example, students might perform the command, "Shake your hands, clap two times, put your book on your head, and put your pencil on the left side of your desk."

Lucky Draw

CONTENT CONNECTIONS   Aerobic health, flexibility, strength

READY FOR ACTION
- Several decks of cards in front of the room
- Designated exercise areas around the room, depending on equipment used
- Students grouped in threes or fours, spaced away from the equipment
- One Lucky Draw task sheet per group (see appendix B, page 249)
- Jump ropes, scooters, cones, and basketballs for "Crank It Up"

LET'S PLAY   One student from each group draws a card from the front of the playing area and brings it to her or his group. All group members perform the activity together. Then another group member draws a card. Play continues for an amount of time designated by the teacher.

CRANK IT UP   Change the task sheet so that students practice sport skills such as basketball dribbling, jump rope tricks, or volleying skills. To provide a varied workout, include different types of skills.

GEAR IT DOWN   Each student draws a card from the front of the room. Students find the equipment they need and go to their own personal workspace. The teacher modifies the activities for the entire group of students or individuals as needed according to developmental levels. For example, instead of shooting baskets, a student might bounce and catch the ball at his or her spot or shoot at a trash can target.

ASSET ACTION

Cultural competence (asset 34)—In Lucky Draw, students work in groups. Group efforts promote cultural competence. Students have the opportunity to get to know people whose backgrounds and experiences differ from their own. A teacher can encourage and promote cultural competence by requiring mixed groups.

COORDINATED SCHOOL HEALTH LINKS

Discuss Lucky Draw with the students. Ask them how many different activities they performed that they also could do during recess or at home. Invite them to share other activity ideas that could work. As a homework assignment, have them play Lucky Draw outside of school with family or friends.

Summer Shuffle

CONTENT CONNECTIONS   Aerobic health, flexibility, muscular endurance, cooperation

READY FOR ACTION

- Students scattered in general space
- Summer Shuffle task sheet for the teacher's use (see appendix B, page 250)
- For "Gear It Down": beach music

LET'S PLAY   The teacher gives one command at a time from the Summer Shuffle task sheet, and students perform each command.

CRANK IT UP   Challenge the students to perform the actions quickly. Remind students that performing the incorrect action or not being able to find a group means they have to move to the edge and "tread water" (pretend to swim). Students who tread water may do any swimstroke in their sideline space. They may reenter the main game when they have correctly performed the swimming stroke 20 times.

GEAR IT DOWN   Have students "swim" around the area while beach music plays. When the music stops, call out a one-student command from the list. Repeat easier commands often.

© Human Kinetics

ASSET ACTION

Interpersonal competence (asset 33) and cultural competence (asset 34)—To foster empathy and social competence, ask students, "Did you welcome all students into your group? How does it feel when you can't find a group?" Remind students to always include and accept everyone.

COORDINATED SCHOOL HEALTH LINKS

Use Summer Shuffle as a lead-in to a discussion of weather-appropriate clothing and protection against the summer sun. Discuss the body's response to heat and sunlight. (See www.kidshealth.org.)

Winter Wonderland

CONTENT CONNECTIONS   Aerobic health, quickness, flexibility, muscular endurance, cooperation

READY FOR ACTION
- Students scattered in general space
- Winter Wonderland task sheet for the teacher's use (see appendix B, page 251)

LET'S PLAY   The teacher gives one command at a time from the Winter Wonderland task sheet, and students perform each command.

CRANK IT UP   Challenge the students to perform movements quickly. Eliminate students who perform the wrong action or cannot find a group. For more activity without elimination, designate a second game area, and ask those who perform incorrectly, or are left without a group, to continue to play in this area.

GEAR IT DOWN   Students jog around the area and intermittently perform one-person activities that the teacher calls out from the task sheet.

ASSET ACTION

Cultural competence (asset 34)—Providing activities that increase students' acceptance of the differences among people is important. Many PE activities can help develop cultural competence. However, discussion also helps develop this important asset. For instance, you can ask students to tell the class about the winter activities and celebrations.

COORDINATED SCHOOL HEALTH LINKS

Use Winter Wonderland as a lead-in to a discussion of weather-appropriate clothing and protection against winter cold. Discuss the body's response to cold. (See www.kidshealth.org.)

Spinners

Go, Team!

Inactive people can improve their health and well-being by regularly engaging in moderate exercise.

See appendix B for instructions on making your own spinner!

Color Detectives

CONTENT CONNECTIONS   Locomotor skills, spatial skills, aerobic health, flexibility, muscular endurance, cooperation

READY FOR ACTION

- Game spinners (one for every three to five students) on a table in the middle of the room (see appendix B, page 252 for instructions on how to make a spinner)
- Colored cones, hoops, and poly spots scattered around the activity area
- For "Crank It Up": music

LET'S PLAY   The teacher designates a locomotor movement that all students will use during the activities. Students spin, search for an object of the color that matches where the spinner landed, touch the object, and return to spin again. For example, if the player's spin lands on red, she will search for a red cone, touch it, and return to her spot. (Demonstrate the way in which students should properly tap an object during play.) After several turns, the students spin twice and move to touch the colors in the order of the spin sequence. For example, if the first spin was red and the second was yellow, the students would touch something red and then something yellow before returning to their original spot.

CRANK IT UP   Play music while the students are playing color detectives. Periodically stop the music, and ask the students to stretch. For more space and movement and therefore a more aerobic activity, students can go outside to play. Before spinning again, students can perform exercises of 10 to 20 counts.

GEAR IT DOWN   Use one spinner. Students stretch or exercise while waiting for the teacher to call the color that has been spun. The teacher spins and says, "Students with blue shirts, touch something red. Go."

ASSET ACTION

Responsibility (asset 30)—In Color Detectives, students are individually responsible for completing each task. They have to decide where to go, how to move safely, what objects to search for, and how to handle the spinner properly.

COORDINATED SCHOOL HEALTH LINKS

Send Color Detectives instructions to the classroom or home. Ask students to create their own spinner and use it during recess or at home. Also ask PTA members to make spinners to be used in class (see page 252 in appendix B), and invite them to come try them.

Go Loco

CONTENT CONNECTIONS

Aerobic health, locomotor skills, muscular strength, endurance

READY FOR ACTION

- Spinners (one for every three to five students) in the center of the room
- A circular jogging track marked by cones
- A locomotor chart, in a central location, showing that red = skip, green = hop, yellow = gallop, and blue = walk
- For "Crank It Up": Let's Get Physical cards (see appendix B)

© Human Kinetics

LET'S PLAY   Beginning at a starting line, students spin and travel once around the circular track using the locomotor movement indicated by spin color.

CRANK IT UP   After each lap, students look at the Let's Get Physical card that the teacher is holding and perform the depicted stretch for 20 seconds before spinning again. Another option is to use muscular endurance and strength cards instead of stretch cards.

GEAR IT DOWN   The teacher divides the class into two groups. Instead of having the students spin, he or she spins for group 1 while group 1 performs the designated locomotor movement and group 2 stretches. When group 1 gets back from the task, the teacher spins for group 2 while group 1 stretches.

ASSET ACTION

Teacher tip—Quality PE lessons take preparation and sound class management strategies. Planning increases the chances that students will be safe, follow instructions, have fun, and experience success.

COORDINATED SCHOOL HEALTH LINKS

Go Loco provides a chance to discuss the importance of health-related fitness components, especially aerobic health.

Obstacle Options

CONTENT CONNECTIONS   Aerobic health, locomotor skills, muscular endurance

READY FOR ACTION

- Divide students into groups of three or four, and assign each group a work area.
- Give each group a spinner.
- Create an equipment zone marked with four cones (red, blue, orange, green).
- At each cone, place varied equipment—such as hoops, small jumping rings, poly spots, domes, cones, ropes, and hurdles—that will be used to create an obstacle course. (See figure 14.1.)

Red cone	Blue cone	Orange cone	Green cone
△	△	△	△
– Hoops	– Hurdles	– Polyspots	– Coffee cans
– Ropes	– Balance boards	– Domes	– Cardboard strips
– Cones	– Polyspots	– Blocks	– Jumping rings
Group 1	Group 2	Group 3	Group 4
⊕	⊕	⊕	⊕
Group 5	Group 6	Group 7	Group 8
⊕	⊕	⊕	⊕

Figure 14.1
Obstacle Options diagram.

LET'S PLAY   The teacher shows students how to build a simple obstacle course using various types of equipment. One at a time, the students within each group spin one at a time, go to the matching color zones, choose one piece of equipment, and bring it back to their team. For example, a student who spins red might pick a hoop, rope, or cone to bring to her or his team (see figure 14.1). Each team then builds an obstacle course. Upon completion of the course, team members move through that course safely and under control, one at a time.

CRANK IT UP   Allow students to try obstacle courses built by other teams. Remind them to leave each course intact for the next group.

GEAR IT DOWN   Instead of having students use equipment, have them form an obstacle with their own body. For example, one student might stand in a straddle while a second student crawls under her or his legs, or one student might curl up in a ball while another jogs around him or her. For additional fun and challenge, arrange jumping rings on the floor in a variety of patterns and have students hopscotch through them after crawling through another student's legs.

ASSET ACTION

Interpersonal competence (asset 33) and peaceful conflict resolution (asset 36)—When students work as a team to construct an obstacle course, they develop interpersonal competence and the ability to resolve conflicts peacefully. Remind students of acceptable ways to solve conflicts during this activity.

COORDINATED SCHOOL HEALTH LINKS

Introduce the lesson by explaining that an obstacle is something that makes it more difficult for someone to reach a goal. Discuss obstacles to good health such as unhealthy diets and insufficient physical activity and how students can overcome these obstacles.

Run and Gun

The creativity of SES PE students Johnny Taylor and Travis Kinard helped spark the idea for this activity.

CONTENT CONNECTIONS
Jogging, sprinting, aerobic health, basketball shooting and passing

READY FOR ACTION

- In the absence of gym lines, create lines equidistant apart with cones or chalk.
- Two feet (0.5 meter) behind each starting line, place one spinner for every three to five students.
- Place poly spots or Xs on the floor for students to shoot from.
- Provide 1 basketball for every 2 students.
- At each basket place a sign that indicates red = free throws, yellow = lay-ups, green = spot shots (shots made from the poly spots or Xs), and blue = toss to self and shoot.
- For "Gear It Down," use beanbags to toss at hoops and trash cans for targets instead of basketballs and basketball hoops.

LET'S PLAY
Students spin and look at their spin's number and color. The number indicates how many times a student must run to and from particular lines. The color indicates the type of shot the student will practice after completing the line run. For example, a student who spins "Red 2" runs to the first line, then back to the starting line, then to the second line, then back to the starting line. The student then advances to the basket that has a red sign and practices free throws. Practice at a particular basket continues until the teacher asks students to spin again. For large classes, it is advisable to limit the number of shots at a basket to 2 or 3 per turn, and then spin again.

CRANK IT UP
Students dribble during the line run and switch from right hand to left hand every time they change directions. Students form pairs, and one partner spins while the other practices ball handling or dribbling tricks on the side.

GEAR IT DOWN
Instead of shooting basketballs, students toss beanbags at hoops or targets (such as trash cans). Students spin and go to a target area.

ASSET ACTION
School/learning engagement (asset 22), achievement motivation (asset 21), and responsibility (asset 30)—Run and Gun challenges students to do their best. They are responsible for following instructions, remembering the numbers and colors when spinning, moving safely, and taking turns. Ask students if they saw anyone behaving responsibly, and what that responsible behavior was.

COORDINATED SCHOOL HEALTH LINKS
In order to teach students about aerobic health, have them check their heart rate during Run and Gun's various activities. For example, they might check their heart rate after running to line 2. Messages about aerobic health can be coordinated with parents and classroom teachers.

Strive to Survive

CONTENT CONNECTIONS

Locomotor skills, muscular endurance, flexibility

READY FOR ACTION

- One spinner
- In each corner, a cone the same color as one color on the spinner (red, blue, green, yellow)
- Students scattered in general space
- Music

© Human Kinetics

LET'S PLAY   While music plays, the students move around the room using the locomotor movements that the teacher verbally designates. When the music stops, each student chooses a corner (a safe island) and goes there. The teacher spins. All students who are in a corner whose cone is the same color as the designated spinner color must go to the room's middle (the jungle) and perform one of the following activities:

- Alligator crawl—Crawl on your belly dragging your feet.
- Hot coals—Run in place quickly with high knees as if to avoid the hot coals.
- Shark attack—Sit down and pretend to row away fast.
- Mountain climb—Get in push-up position and run feet.
- Crab creep—Walk like a crab.

CRANK IT UP   Prolong the game's locomotor and exercise segments.

GEAR IT DOWN   While in the "jungle," students signal for help by stretching and waving with their arms overhead instead of doing the activities listed in "Let's Play."

ASSET ACTION

Healthy lifestyle/restraint (asset 31)—Discuss healthy food and exercise habits in relation to Strive to Survive. Ask students how they might stay fit and eat well on an island or in a jungle.

COORDINATED SCHOOL HEALTH LINKS

Change Strive to Survive to a nutrition game. Place food pictures or names of foods in the middle of the play area. As he or she enters the jungle area, each student chooses a depicted or named food and guesses whether or not that food is healthy. This activity could be shared with cafeteria workers who could quiz students when they are in line to purchase food.

Wheel of Fitness

CONTENT CONNECTIONS   Locomotor skills, muscular endurance

READY FOR ACTION

- One four-colored parachute
- One spinner
- Twelve hula hoops
- Twelve jump ropes
- Music
- For "Crank It Up": a chart of sport skills, 12 basketballs, 12 volleyballs, 12 footballs, 12 paddles with balls

LET'S PLAY   Place the parachute on the ground. While music plays, the students walk or jog around the parachute. When the music stops, the students stop and the teacher spins the game spinner. The teacher calls out the designated color and either announces an activity corresponding to that color or has students use a poster listing color-coded activities (e.g., red = hula hoop; yellow = jump rope forward; green = jump rope backward; blue = put the hoop on the ground and jump in and out). All students standing by the designated color on the parachute leave the area and perform the designated activity until the next round.

CRANK IT UP   Substitute activities from a chart of sport skills (e.g., red = basketball shooting; blue = volleying to self; yellow = football throws to the wall; green = paddle-and-ball tap-ups to self.)

GEAR IT DOWN   Substitute parachute activities—for example, red = make waves; blue = hold on, jump up and down, and shake the chute; green = hold on and do toe touches; yellow = merry-go-round (hold on and slide to the right). The entire group performs the activity using the parachute.

ASSET ACTION

Bonding to school (asset 24) and achievement motivation (asset 21)—In a PE setting, students benefit from exercise and activity choices. In Wheel of Fitness, a color can represent a predetermined exercise or the teacher can allow students to perform an exercise of her or his choice. Allowing more activity choices increases children's fun and helps reinforce or build assets related to commitment to learning.

COORDINATED SCHOOL HEALTH LINKS

Ask students if Wheel of Fitness is a game that they would be interested in playing at recess or in an after-school program. Coordinated school health activities, whether in a PE class or after-school program, won't hold a child's attention unless he or she has fun, remains at least moderately active, and has a choice of activities. Offer to share the parachute and spinners with other teachers and after school programs.

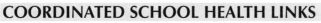

Zone Fitness

CONTENT CONNECTIONS   Locomotor skills, aerobic health, muscular endurance, flexibility

READY FOR ACTION

- The middle of the room should contain one spinner for every three to five students.
- Post a chart of color-coded exercises: red = push-ups; green = stretches; yellow = curl-ups; blue = jumping jacks.
- The play area should contain four exercise zones marked by four cones of the same colors as those on the exercise chart.
- For "Crank It Up," provide jump ropes or other equipment.

LET'S PLAY   Students take turns spinning; go to the cone of the color indicated by the spin; and, trying to maintain good form, perform the exercise indicated by the chart until the teacher says, "Spin again."

CRANK IT UP   Increase the time that students spend at each exercise station (cone). Give them a choice of exercises. Have students jog a lap after completing each exercise and before spinning again. Post jump rope or sport skills instead of exercises.

GEAR IT DOWN   Each student spins and goes to the appropriate corner. The teacher designates the exercises that each group performs at the cones. Instead of health-related exercises, you can have students do animal movements such as crawling like an alligator, walking like an elephant, or hopping like a kangaroo.

ASSET ACTION

Responsibility (asset 30)—Responsibility is important in making choices and decisions. Praise students who act responsibly while doing the tasks set by Zone Fitness, and set clear and fair consequences for irresponsible behavior.

COORDINATED SCHOOL HEALTH LINKS

Physical activity settings provide many opportunities for personal growth in various health dimensions. Give students choices in Zone Fitness and other activities to stimulate personal growth.

Poly Spots

15

Can you spot the opportunities to develop assets?

Using poly spots is a great way to build social competencies and meet physical education national standards!

Body Boogie

CONTENT CONNECTIONS   Warm-up, flexibility, muscular endurance

READY FOR ACTION

- Have colored poly spots: blue, red, and a mix of other colors.
- Have one poly spot for each student.
- Using a permanent marker, divide each poly spot into quadrants. Write a letter, a color, the name of an exercise, and a sport on the poly spot. (If you don't want to write on poly spots, use index cards placed on poly spots.)
- Scatter the poly spots around the room.

LET'S PLAY   Younger students or larger classes may share polyspots. When the teacher says, "Go!" students perform the following sequence:

1. Leave your poly spot, and touch four other poly spots before you return home.
2. Use your body to form the letter written on your poly spot.
3. Slowly jog, find and leap over 10 different poly spots, and freeze.
4. Skip home.
5. Touch three poly spots. At the third, do push-ups until the teachers says, "Stop."
6. Find a new poly spot and balance on it.
7. Perform the exercise written on it.
8. Spell your poly spot color by forming the letters with your body. Say the letter while you spell it with your body three times.
9. Walk backwards avoiding the polyspots until the teachers says, "Stop."
10. Find a new poly spot.
11. If the color written on the poly spot is blue, jump up and down. If it's red, hop on one foot. If it's another color, stretch. (This command can be changed for poly spots of different colors.)
12. Pretend you're surfing on your poly spot.
13. Sit down and stand up on eight different spots.
14. Return to your home poly spot.
15. Pretend to do the sport that's written on it.
16. Jump side to side over three different polyspots.

CRANK IT UP   Have students create new actions and describe them to you. Try different combinations with the class. Ask partners to give each other a task.

GEAR IT DOWN   Allow students to stay on their own poly spot. Have them do a variety of actions. Include jumping up and down on the poly spot, jumping from side to side, jumping front to back, hopping, and balancing. With younger students, include levels (high, medium, low) and spatial relationships (beside, behind, in front). For example, have students jump up and down at a low level in front of their poly spot.

ASSET ACTION

Achievement motivation (asset 21), school/learning engagement (asset 22), and bonding to school (asset 24)—Body Boogie gives students practice in spelling. PE activities that include academic skills help students to do well in school.

COORDINATED SCHOOL HEALTH LINKS

Creating a safe, caring school environment is a good way to start a coordinated school health program or to strengthen an existing program. Effective coordination of school activities to enhance student health can begin with caring and cooperation. Ask students if Body Boogie would be a fun activity to do during recess or in the classroom.

Connect the Dots

CONTENT CONNECTIONS   Aerobic health, muscular endurance, agility, kicking, throwing, catching, dribbling

READY FOR ACTION

- Number 10 poly spots 1 through 10. Use two or more sets, depending on the class size.
- Place each set of poly spots within a different area; randomly scatter that set's poly spots within the area.
- For "Crank It Up," provide basketballs.
- For "Gear It Down," use poly spots with letters of the alphabet rather than numbers.

© Human Kinetics

LET'S PLAY   Students start on a poly spot and jog to the next poly spot in order of the poly spots' numbers. After students are warm and familiar with the procedure, they do the following:

- At poly spot 1, do one push-up; at poly spot 2, do two push-ups; and so on up to 10 push-ups at poly spot 10. Repeat with other exercises such as curl-ups.
- Soccer dribble to each poly spot and stop the ball with one foot on top. While standing on the poly spot, tap the ball from side to the side with your instep as many times as the number on the poly spot.
- In pairs, throw a ball from number to number. (Player 1 starts at spot 1, player 2 at spot 2. Player 1 passes to player 2, player 1 runs to spot 3, and player 2 passes to player 1 at spot 3. Player 2 then runs to spot 4, and so on.)

CRANK IT UP   Students dribble a basketball and stop on each poly spot, kneel down, and dribble as many times as the number on the poly spot. Students can also alternately do push-ups and curl-ups, as described in the first "Let's Play" sequence.

GEAR IT DOWN   Replace the numbers with letters. Students move from letter to letter in alphabetical order. When the teacher says "Freeze," each student stops and, with her or his body, forms the letter on the poly spot.

ASSET ACTION

High expectations (asset 16), achievement motivation (asset 21), and personal power (asset 37)—Instead of requiring students to conform to some absolute standard, Connect the Dots encourages them to assess their progress in reaching goals. Students perform an increasing number of push-ups. The teacher can remind them that they succeed if they simply do as many push-ups as they can and work at increasing that number.

COORDINATED SCHOOL HEALTH LINKS

The push-ups in Connect the Dots require muscular endurance, a component of health-related fitness. Ask students, "Why is muscular endurance important in everyday life? How do push-ups increase muscular endurance? How is muscular endurance related to health? Why are push-ups good for the upper body?"

Dot Dash

CONTENT CONNECTIONS   Chasing, fleeing, dodging, tagging

READY FOR ACTION

- Scatter poly spots around the playing area, one for every two to three students.
- If necessary, change the number of poly spots to ensure active participation. Use the students' developmental levels as a guide.
- For "Crank It Up," use Let's Get Physical cards or beanbags.

LET'S PLAY   This is a walking tag game. Choose several taggers. Students are safe when they're standing on a poly spot. Only one student at a time is allowed on any particular poly spot. Taggers may tag anyone not on a poly spot. Students on poly spots must leave if another student comes to them and says, "Spot, please." Tagged students jog once around the perimeter and then go to the reentry area, where the teacher guides them back into the game by pausing and saying "Go."

CRANK IT UP   Reduce the number of poly spots. Change the reentry task to a Let's Get Physical exercise (see appendix B) or Beanbag Fitness Challenges (see page 144).

GEAR IT DOWN   Eliminate the taggers. One student stands up front without a poly spot. The rest of the students stand on their own poly spot. On signal the students on poly spots try to change places with one another while the student who was up front tries to find an unoccupied poly spot. Students may not return to the same poly spot. When a student cannot find a spot, she or he may come to the front for help.

ASSET ACTION

Peaceful conflict resolution (asset 36)—Dot Dash tests students' ability to resolve conflicts quickly and peacefully. The game requires that players try to get to a poly spot before someone else does and avoid being tagged. A simple way to resolve conflicts in this game is by taking turns or playing Rock, Paper, Scissors.

COORDINATED SCHOOL HEALTH LINKS

Modify Dot Dash to focus on nutrition information. Taggers can represent unhealthy foods. As in real life, students should try to stay away from unhealthy foods. You might use foam balls to represent high-fat foods and to teach children to stay away from sugar-coated snacks and fried foods.

Dot Duos

CONTENT CONNECTIONS   Locomotor skills, muscular endurance, flexibility, aerobic health

READY FOR ACTION

- One poly spot for every two students, placed in a large circle with at least 2 feet (0.6 meter) between poly spots
- Students in two circles, one inside the other (see figure 15.1).
- Music
- For "Crank It Up": exercise cards, dance cards, balls suitable for dribbling

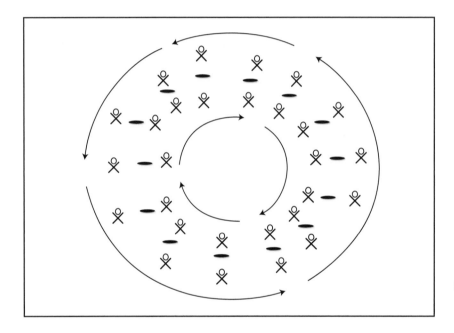

Figure 15.1   Dot Duos diagram.

LET'S PLAY   While music plays, students jog around their circle, following the student in front of them. The inside circle moves clockwise, the outside circle counterclockwise. When the music stops, students stop and find a nearby poly spot and partner. The teacher calls out a simple endurance exercise or stretch activity for partners to perform.

CRANK IT UP   Place exercise cards, dance cards, or alternate actions under the poly spots (see Operation Cooperation, page 49). Students look under the poly spots and perform an activity specified on a card until directed to stop. When students have found a partner, they can dribble a ball and pass and catch.

GEAR IT DOWN   Partners walk or jog side by side around the circle's circumference. When the music stops, the teacher leads the students in an exercise.

ASSET ACTION

Interpersonal competence (asset 33), cultural competence (asset 34), and adult role models (asset 14)—An enjoyable physical activity setting offers students the chance to form friendships. Dot Duos is a good activity to use to emphasize friendship skills in your class. Encourage your students not to limit their friendships to people of their own age, gender, ethnicity, or national origin. Serve as a role model by treating all people in a friendly, respectful way.

COORDINATED SCHOOL HEALTH LINKS

An important point in health education is that health is multidimensional and includes social health. Remind students that making friends (social health) is closely tied to physical and emotional health. Ask them how the use of activities like Dot Duos helps them make friends (by presenting the opportunity to work with others).

Dot to Dot

CONTENT CONNECTIONS
Aerobic health, muscular endurance, flexibility

READY FOR ACTION
- Poly spots (one or more per student) scattered around the activity area
- Music

LET'S PLAY   While music plays, students walk through general space, avoiding the poly spots. When the music stops, the teacher calls out a body part and a number (e.g., "Elbow 6"). When the teacher says, "Go," the students safely touch six different poly spots with one elbow. The last poly spot touched becomes their home until the teacher calls out another body part and number. Students must allow others to touch their home spot when others are looking for a spot to touch.

CRANK IT UP   Students crab-walk to each poly spot, where they do a crab push-up before touching the poly spot with the designated body part (see page 225, appendix B, for the Let's Get Physical card showing this exercise.) Teach students about bones and muscles by referring to body parts with scientific terms such as *patella* and *biceps*. Change the way students move between poly spots. For example, they might hop, jump, or do an animal walk.

GEAR IT DOWN   Call out numbers only. Students walk and touch that many poly spots. When they arrive at the last poly spot, they touch it with the designated body part. Once students understand the routine, have them walk and touch five poly spots with that body part. Change the body part, but have students continue to touch five poly spots in each round. Students could also pick up the spot and touch it to the body part that the teacher calls out.

ASSET ACTION
Honesty (asset 29)—Ask the students if they were honest when they played Dot to Dot. Did they play by the rules? Ask students, "What is one way that you can be honest while playing Dot to Dot?" Students might answer, "I touched the number of spots that the teacher instructed me to touch."

COORDINATED SCHOOL HEALTH LINKS
Dot to Dot reinforces the rules that you expect students to follow in your PE class. You can give parents copies of these rules and of the developmental assets framework and explain links between the assets and your rules.

Hot Spot

CONTENT CONNECTIONS   Aerobic health

READY FOR ACTION

- Two fewer poly spots than the number of players are scattered around the play area with at least 2 feet (0.5 meter) between poly spots.
- Two hoops are placed in the front of the room.
- For "Crank It Up," provide beanbags or basketballs.

LET'S PLAY   A student volunteer stands inside a hoop (the "hot spot") at the front of the room. Every other class member stands on a poly spot. When the teacher says, "Hot Spot," all students try to move to a new poly spot while the student volunteer tries to move to a vacant poly spot. The student who is left without a poly spot comes to the front and stands inside the hoop.

CRANK IT UP   Students can move with a beanbag on their head or while dribbling a basketball. To increase the challenge of finding a poly spot, remove some of the poly spots.

GEAR IT DOWN   Hot Spot can be challenging for younger students learning spatial awareness. Call time after short intervals, and count from 10 down to 1. At the end of the countdown, the teacher or classmates can help students that are having difficulty finding a spot. It also helps to place extra spots in the area and eliminate the "hot spot" in the front.

ASSET ACTION

Adult role models (asset 14)—Tell the students that just as poly spots are scattered around the play area, adults are scattered around the school who can make a difference in their lives. Make an effort to expose your students to role models of different genders, ages, ethnicities, and socioeconomic backgrounds. Invite parents to come talk to your class.

COORDINATED SCHOOL HEALTH LINKS

In a coordinated school health program, parents and teachers work together to show students that adults value, support, and care for them. When kids receive support from parents, teachers, and other adults in the community, their chances of success increase. Share Hot Spot with parents and the community. Urge adults to play Hot Spot with children so that everyone is involved.

Spots Are Wild

CONTENT CONNECTIONS   Cooperation, ball rolling, bowling

READY FOR ACTION

- With chalk or tape, mark a highly visible line that divides the play area in half.
- Scatter an equal number of poly spots around each half.
- Provide one medium-sized ball for every three to four students.
- Divide the students into two teams, with one team on each side of the play area.
- For "Crank It Up," use cones and bowling pins.
- For "Gear It Down," add marked lines, bowling pins, or hurdles.

LET'S PLAY   Students stay on their side of the play area and try to roll balls over the opposing team's poly spots. Rolling a ball over a poly spot earns a student one point. Balls may be stopped before they reach a poly spot. All balls that cross the centerline are retrieved by the opposing team and rolled back to the other side.

CRANK IT UP   Scatter poly spots around the play area, and place one cone per team around the perimeter. Teams of three to four students stand behind a cone. One team member at a time stands to the side of the cone and rolls the ball, trying to roll it across the poly spots during a timed interval (45-60 seconds). Each student retrieves his or her ball and returns to his or her home cone to continue rolling until the allotted time elapses. Keep individual best or team scores, or assign a point value to each poly spot color. After each round, each team totals its members' points. While student 1 rolls a ball, students 2 and 3 record points. Student 4 practices bowling at a cone placed behind her or his team (see figure 15.2).

For an extra challenge, replace poly spots with bowling pins.

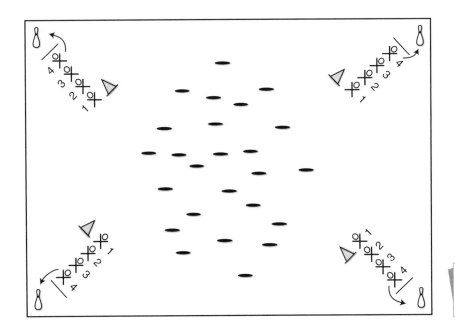

Figure 15.2 Spots Are Wild "Crank It Up" diagram.

GEAR IT DOWN   In pairs, students roll a ball down a line, over a poly spot, at a bowling pin, or under a hurdle. Create ball-rolling work stations or circuits using the above ideas.

ASSET ACTION

Caring (asset 26) and honesty (asset 29)—Ask the students how they might show a Spots Are Wild teammate that they care about him or her. Explain that honest counting during the game demonstrates caring because it shows fairness and respect for others.

COORDINATED SCHOOL HEALTH LINKS

Place pictures of foods high in fat or sugar on some of the poly spots or bowling pins. Ask students to bowl over these foods to score extra points. After the class, post the pictures in the hallways under the title "Strike Down Fat and Sugar."

Stop the Clock

CONTENT CONNECTIONS   Aerobic health, muscular endurance

READY FOR ACTION

- Poly spots, one for each student.
- Arrange four to six bowling pins in a circle at the center of the room.
- Scatter poly spots at least 3 feet (1 meter) from the circle so that they fill the play area outside the circle (see figure 15.3).
- Give each student a number, and have her or him stand on a poly spot.
- Have music on hand.

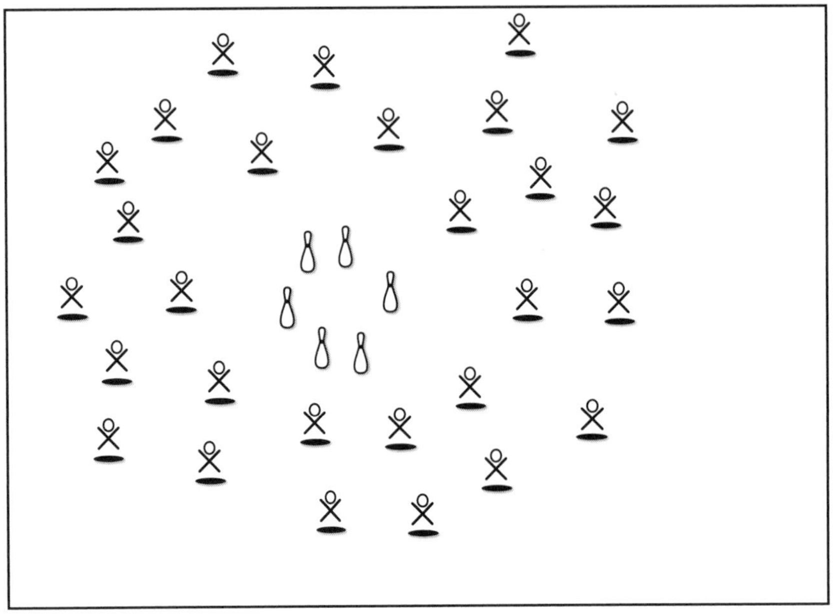

Figure 15.3   Stop the Clock diagram.

LET'S PLAY   The teacher announces an exercise to be performed when the music stops. While music plays, the students jog randomly within the area outside the bowling-pin circle, dodging poly spots. When the music stops, all students move to stand on a poly spot. The teacher calls out a number. The student with that number goes to the circle, lays or knocks down each bowling pin in succession, and then returns to the first pin and stands each pin back up. All other students perform the designated exercise using their best form. When all of the bowling pins are back up, the pin setter shouts, "Stop!" and the exercise round is over. Play for several rounds.

CRANK IT UP   Have all students jog or jump in place before you call out a number.

GEAR IT DOWN   Eliminate the bowling pins. When you call out a color, all students whose shirt or dress is that color begin to skip or quickly walk around the perimeter of the exercise area. When all students have returned to their starting position, they sit on a poly spot and the exercising stops.

ASSET ACTION

Personal power (asset 37) and caring (asset 26)—The pin setter in Stop the Clock can influence how long the other students exercise. Talk to your students about "the power of one" (in this case, the pin setter) to make a difference in life. Tell them true stories of people who have had a positive effect on others' lives. Ask students if they have used their "power of one" to help others—for example, by volunteering in the community or adopting a stray dog.

COORDINATED SCHOOL HEALTH LINKS

Show students the U.S. Department of Agriculture food pyramid, and stress the connection between good eating habits and physical activity. Tell them that knocking down pins represents knocking down bad food choices. Ask a student to knock the pins down and slowly set them back up. As each pin is set back up, the other students call out a healthy food.

Stretch City

CONTENT CONNECTIONS   Flexibility, aerobic health

READY FOR ACTION

- Poly spots of different colors (one poly spot per student) scattered around the play area
- A stretch area called "Stretch City"
- Posted at Stretch City, a list of four stretching exercises (for ideas, see Let's Get Physical cards in appendix B)
- Music

LET'S PLAY   A student volunteer or the teacher stands in front of the room with his or her back to the class. While music plays, students move in open space. When the music stops, each student stands on a poly spot. The student in front calls out a color. All students standing on a poly spot of that color immediately move to Stretch City, where they select a stretch from the poster and perform it while the music starts again. Students stay in Stretch City until students in the next group arrive to take their place. The teacher can either call out colors or have a different student do so at each round.

CRANK IT UP   Play Stretch City Survival. All students stay in Stretch City and continue to stretch until only five students are left in the game. These five survivors get to choose colors in the next game. Use Let's Get Physical exercises instead of stretches.

GEAR IT DOWN   Students who are standing on a poly spot of the announced color come to the front of the room and lead the class in a teacher-designated stretch. The entire class stretches together.

ASSET ACTION

Peaceful conflict resolution (asset 36)—Ask students how they could peacefully resolve the conflict if two students playing Stretch City wanted the same poly spot. Establish a conflict resolution corner where students can go to talk and work out their differences.

COORDINATED SCHOOL HEALTH LINKS

Stretch City promotes flexibility, a health-related fitness component. Ask students how stretching improves flexibility and how flexibility relates to health.

Target Fitness

CONTENT CONNECTIONS Tossing, throwing, aerobic health, muscular endurance, flexibility

READY FOR ACTION

- Scatter poly spots of different colors around the play area—one for every three students.
- Use cones to indicate a starting line.
- Provide each student with a beanbag (see figure 15.4).
- Display a Spot Exercise Color poster such as the following:
  - Blue—curl-ups
  - Red—push-ups
  - Green—jumping jacks
  - Yellow—pike stretch (sitting with the legs together)
- For "Gear It Down," use hoops or other large targets.

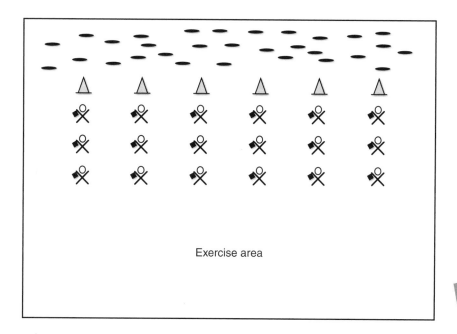

Figure 15.4 Target Fitness diagram.

LET'S PLAY Standing by a cone, students toss their beanbag at a poly spot. The student then retrieves the beanbag. If any part of it has landed on the poly spot, the student performs the exercise keyed to the poly spot's color 10 times in the exercise area. Students may hit each color only once, but they are allowed to change lines to throw at a color they need. If the beanbag has missed the poly spot, the student gets back in line to try again. After each exercise, the student tosses at a new color and continues until all colors are completed.

CRANK IT UP Students play in pairs. If a student misses the target, they hand their beanbag to their partner and jog one time around the perimeter before the partner takes his or her turn. Another option is to continue the play for an extended period, encouraging the children to throw at colors that represent an area of personal weakness. For example, a student who could use some practice doing push-ups would aim for red poly spots.

GEAR IT DOWN   Create a large circle of cones. Place hoops or other targets larger than poly spots in the middle of the cone circle. Each student has a beanbag and all walk in a circle around the perimeter of the cones. When you say, "Freeze. Ready. Throw," students toss their beanbag at any target, retrieve the beanbag, and return to the walk line. Call out a stretch or exercise before asking the children to walk and repeat the activity.

ASSET ACTION

Honesty (asset 29)—Remind students that being honest means that people can trust them. Tell students that Target Fitness requires honesty. When their beanbag lands on a poly spot, they're "on their honor" to perform the specified exercise 10 times.

COORDINATED SCHOOL HEALTH LINKS

Teacher tip—Developmental assets related to social skills include honesty, caring, cultural competence, peaceful conflict resolution, and interpersonal competence. Any activity in which such social assets are mentioned provides an opportunity to discuss the dimensions of health. Many people think of health as only physical health. Explain to students that social skills such as making friends and being honest are part of social health. Talk about different types of health.

Food Labels and Pictures

When you establish your school health team, include parents, classroom teachers, the school nurse, the cafeteria manager, and an administrator.

Food labels help us lead healthy lives!

Food Fact Fitness

CONTENT CONNECTIONS   Aerobic health, muscular endurance, flexibility, healthy eating

READY FOR ACTION

- Four quadrants designated *zero, low, medium,* and *high*
- Two piles of food labels and a pile of Let's Get Physical exercise cards in the front of the room (see figure 16.1)
- Music
- The following list posted in a visible location:

Quadrant Fat Content

Zero = 0

Low = 1 to 6

Medium = 7 to 13

High = 13+

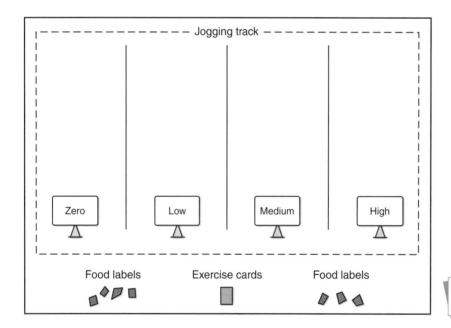

Figure 16.1   Food Fact Fitness diagram.

LET'S PLAY   While music plays, each student draws a food label and jogs around the perimeter of the play area. When the music stops, each student reads her or his food label and then goes to the zero, low, medium, or high quadrant, depending on the level of fat in the named food. For the purposes of this activity, use the Quadrant Fat Content list:

The teacher or a student volunteer draws a Let's Get Physical card for each quadrant. The card describes an exercise to be performed in that quadrant for one minute.

CRANK IT UP   For a fitness workout, have each quadrant represent a health-related fitness component, and place a pile of Let's Get Physical cards that match the component in each quadrant. Each student draws two cards and performs the designated exercises before the next round.

GEAR IT DOWN   A student volunteer draws a food label and asks the class to guess the fat content. Students then stand in whichever quadrant they think represents the correct answer. Give the students the correct answer, and have them exercise as a group before another label is drawn. Simplify the game for younger students by asking if the fat content is either high or low.

ASSET ACTION

Teacher tip—An important part of the support structure in a young person's life comes from adults besides her or his parents. Ideally three or more adults provide support. The PE teacher can help build this important asset by having an open-door policy for students who want to talk. Be available as often as you can before and after school. Offer to mentor students during your planning time.

COORDINATED SCHOOL HEALTH LINKS

Ask students to discuss Food Fact Fitness with their parents and to bring a food label from their home pantry. Create a bulletin board for the cafeteria, hallway, or gym that teaches the basics about food labels.

"Go Away, Fat" Relay

CONTENT CONNECTIONS

Aerobic health, muscular endurance, reading nutrition labels

READY FOR ACTION

- Food labels, at least six per team
- One scooter per team of 3 or 4
- Several hoops in the middle of the room, each with a variety of food labels in them
- A displayed chart with six exercises numbered 1 through 6

© Human Kinetics

LET'S PLAY   In relay formation, the members of each team sit behind a scooter. One team member at a time sits on the scooter, scoots to a hoop of his or her choice, chooses one food label, and returns to his or her team. Under this student's leadership, the team performs the first exercise on the chart as many times as the number of fat grams in one serving of the food. For example, they would perform the exercise for eight repetitions if one serving contained 8 grams of fat. With each round, students perform the next exercise on the chart. (Limit the number of times that an exercise is repeated because some foods are loaded with fat.)

CRANK IT UP   During each round, designate a body part, such as the arms, and let students choose any exercise for that body part that they've learned in class. Challenge them to create and name new exercises. If a team member selects the label of a high-fat food, his or her team jogs once around the perimeter.

GEAR IT DOWN   The teacher chooses a food label and shows it to the class. If the class decides that it has a high fat content, they jump high. If they decide it has a low fat content, the students sit and stretch.

ASSET ACTION

Healthy lifestyle/restraint (asset 31)—Being physically active and having healthy eating habits are two important components of a healthy lifestyle. "Go Away, Fat" Relay provides a unique setting in which to develop these healthy lifestyle components.

COORDINATED SCHOOL HEALTH LINKS

Healthy eating and physical activity are at the heart of disease prevention. As an extension of "Go Away, Fat" Relay, show the students the food pyramid, and discuss the importance of physical activity and good eating habits. Ask the cafeteria manager to post the food pyramid in the cafeteria so that students have a visual reminder of the choices that lead to healthy eating. Another good place to post a food pyramid is the teacher's lounge.

Inside the Pyramid

CONTENT CONNECTIONS   Aerobic health, classifying foods

READY FOR ACTION

- Food labels or pictures (see www.mypyramid.gov for the current USDA food pyramid)
- Whistle
- For "Crank It Up": a large food pyramid drawn on the ground or created with long jump ropes

LET'S PLAY   When the music is on, students move around the activity area using designated locomotor skills. The teacher then blows a whistle a number of times, and the students form groups consisting of that many students. For example, if the teacher blows the whistle three times, students form groups of three.

After students are familiar with the procedure, give each student a food picture or label. Now students must group by USDA food group. For example, if the teacher blows the whistle three times, the students form groups of three in which each member's food picture or label refers to the same food group. A grain group might consist of students whose food pictures or labels refer to bread, cereal, and rice. Students who can't locate a group come to the front, and the teacher asks the class which groups those students should join. Students trade pictures or labels and listen for the next set of whistle blows.

CRANK IT UP   Draw a large food pyramid on the ground or create it using long jump ropes that delineate each section of the pyramid. At each round, students stand in the pyramid section that corresponds to their food picture or label.

GEAR IT DOWN   Instead of playing the whistle game, students skip while holding their food picture or label. On signal, students freeze and then find another student whose depicted food is in the same category as their own. Start with only two food groups, such as fruits and vegetables, and add the other groups when students demonstrate an understanding of fruit and vegetable groups. Use different categories, such as food color, first letter of the name of the food, or category. Have students swap food pictures or labels often.

ASSET ACTION

Healthy lifestyle/restraint (asset 31)—Poor diet and inadequate physical activity are health risks. Nutrition-related physical activities such as Inside the Pyramid teach good habits in a fun way.

COORDINATED SCHOOL HEALTH LINKS

Send copies of the USDA food pyramid with the boxes representing servings in each section home with the students (see www.mypyramid.gov for the pyramid). Each time students eat a food, they put a check mark inside the pyramid section that represents the group to which that food belongs. Food pyramid instruction in PE, especially if coupled with parental involvement, can be a first step toward establishing a coordinated school health program.

Junk Food Dodge

CONTENT CONNECTIONS   Chasing, dodging, tagging, healthy eating

READY FOR ACTION   Pictures or labels of healthy and unhealthy foods

LET'S PLAY   Four to six students represent healthy snackers. Each of these students has a picture of a healthy snack food, such as bananas, celery, and low-fat yogurt. Four other students represent junk-food junkies. Each of these students has a picture of an unhealthy snack food, such as doughnuts, potato chips, and packaged sweets. The students play tag with the junk-food junkies trying to tag students other than the healthy snackers. Because they lack energy, tagged students freeze until a healthy snacker gives them her or his snack. Unfrozen healthy snackers try to help their frozen friends by handing them a healthy snack picture.

CRANK IT UP   All students can be tagged. Students tagged by a junk-food junkie must walk once around the play area, pass by the teacher, and tell her or him their favorite healthy snack before reentering the game.

GEAR IT DOWN   Teach students about high-calorie foods rather than concentrating on various categories of food-label information, such as fat, protein, and carbohydrate content. Simplify the game by playing without trading the healthy snacks. Give students red foam balls to represent junk food and green balls to represent healthy food. When tagged by a red ball, the tagged student freezes until tagged by a green ball. Change the junk food and healthy food taggers often.

ASSET ACTION

Positive family communication (asset 2) and parent involvement in schooling (asset 6)—Consider telling parents what their children have learned about food labels. Encourage them to use this game to teach their children about healthy food choices.

COORDINATED SCHOOL HEALTH LINKS

Connect Junk Food Dodge's health message to students' tendency to snack. Show students pictures of other foods, and ask them which foods would make the healthiest snacks. Ask students what snacks are sold in the cafeteria and which would be the best choices. Invite your school's food service manager to your class to watch Junk Food Dodge.

Label Locomotion

CONTENT CONNECTIONS   Locomotor skills, nutrition

READY FOR ACTION

- Scatter food pictures or labels around the room.
- Students form a circle around the pictures or labels.

LET'S PLAY   On signal, the students move counterclockwise around the room using a teacher-designated locomotor movement. At the stop signal, they pick up the nearest food picture or label. If the food is high in fat, the student skips around the room with the picture or label. If the food is low in fat, the student walks. If the food is fat free, the student freezes. (To help students judge whether a food is low or high in fat, the teacher can assign food numbers. For example, a food numbered 5 or less would be low in fat.)

CRANK IT UP   For a fitness workout, use higher-intensity exercises. Movements linked to high-fat foods should be upright (e.g., jogging or jumping jacks). Movements linked to fat-free or low-fat foods should be close to the ground (e.g., curl-ups or push-ups). For safety, joggers should move outside the play area, and ground exercisers should stay inside the area.

GEAR IT DOWN   Show a food label, and read the fat content to the class. Tell the class whether the food is low or high in fat and how they should move. This is a good time to practice animal movements.

ASSET ACTION

Positive family communication (asset 2)—Adults need to support young people and create asset-rich environments at home and at school. Such support should include in-depth conversations with young people on many subjects. Encourage this support by giving homework assignments that include student–parent conversations. For example, you might have students interview their parents and say, "We learned about food labels today. What are the health risks associated with eating too much high-fat food?"

COORDINATED SCHOOL HEALTH LINKS

Find out when classroom teachers are teaching nutrition, and schedule Label Locomotion for the same day or week. Use label activities to review healthy eating principles.

Nutriball

CONTENT CONNECTIONS   Ball handling, throwing, catching, nutrition

READY FOR ACTION

- One ball for each pair of students
- A set of nutrition questions (for nutrition information, visit www.catchtexas.org, www.dole5aday.com, or www.kidshealth.org)
- Food labels or pictures
- Music

LET'S PLAY   While music plays, pairs of students practice a ball skill (basketball pass, soccer pass, partner curl-ups, or partner push-ups). When the music stops, the teacher asks a nutrition question. Each pair works together to determine an answer. Award two points for each correct answer and one point for each partially correct answer. Allow time for discussion. Partners keep score using an honor system. Here are some nutrition questions that you might ask:

- Can you name three fruits that are green?
- Is the food shown on this label higher in protein or in fat content?
- Is the food on this label a fruit or a vegetable?
- What is the calorie count per serving for the food shown? (To make the question easier, use a multiple-choice or true–false format.)
- What is one piece of information you can obtain by reading this label?
- Does this food contain more carbohydrate or protein?
- Which food contains more sugar: broccoli or a soft drink?
- Where would you find this food on the food pyramid?

CRANK IT UP   Change the type of exercises. Ask questions about sport skills. For example, you might ask, "What step is missing or incorrect in this overhand throwing sequence: face the target, arm back, step with the opposite, throw, and follow through?"

GEAR IT DOWN   Instead of asking students questions, show them a food label or picture and state a nutrition fact related to the label or picture before changing the skill.

ASSET ACTION

Interpersonal competence (asset 33)—Contemporary PE activities offer opportunities to teach or reinforce assets or social skills. This is especially true of activities, such as Nutriball, that entail partnering.

COORDINATED SCHOOL HEALTH LINKS

Modify Nutriball so that it focuses on fruits and vegetables, and have students play it during "Five a Day" national campaigns. Also have students play Nutriball during Nutrition Month. Ask the cafeteria staff to create a "Rainbow of Foods" bulletin board in the cafeteria. This bulletin board would emphasize the importance of eating a variety of fruits and vegetables of several different colors.

Nutrient Treasure Hunt

CONTENT CONNECTIONS Aerobic health, muscular endurance, identifying nutrients in foods, reading and analyzing labels

READY FOR ACTION

- Place food labels at 10 to 12 stations around the room.
- Put a felt-tip pen at each station.
- Have students form groups of two, three, or four.
- Give each group a Nutrient Treasure Hunt worksheet (see appendix B, page 253).
- For "Crank It Up," use a whistle.

LET'S PLAY Teach students how to read the nutrition information on food labels. The student groups rotate to each station and use the posted label to fill in the Nutrient Treasure Hunt worksheet. After writing down the answer, group members stay together, race-walk once around the perimeter, pass the station they just completed, and go to the next station. They may also use the labels to answer questions that the teacher asks about food content. The teacher can have students locate foods. For example, he or she might say, "Find the food that has 7 percent saturated fat, 112 calories per ounce, and 3 grams of carbohydrate per serving."

CRANK IT UP Periodically blow a whistle and either call out an exercise or have students put their worksheet on the floor and jog or perform a muscular endurance exercise for 15-second intervals.

GEAR IT DOWN Show the students two pictures or labels, and then designate an exercise based on the correct answer to a question. For example, you might say, "Which of these foods has more sodium? Jog if you think it's food number 1; jump if you think it's food number 2."

ASSET ACTION

- **Healthy lifestyle/restraint (asset 31) and achievement motivation (asset 21)**—Nutrient Treasure Hunt stimulates a child's imagination. It's a fun way to teach them about a healthy lifestyle and motivate them to develop such a lifestyle.
- **Parent involvement in schooling (asset 6)**—Ask students to discuss food labels with their family and to bring a label from home to use in Nutrient Treasure Hunt.

COORDINATED SCHOOL HEALTH LINKS

Give students an assignment for the next time they're in a fast-food restaurant: Have them ask the restaurant for its customer-geared nutrition information; also have them share that information with their family or classroom teacher. Create a bulletin board of food labels in the hallway, classroom, or cafeteria, and title it "Read any good labels lately?"

Nutrition Addition

CONTENT CONNECTIONS   Analyzing foods' nutritional value, jumping

READY FOR ACTION

- A pile of food labels in the front of the room
- For "Crank It Up": a list of exercises divided into *Flexibility, Strength,* and *Cardiorespiratory*

LET'S PLAY   Make sure that students have some basic knowledge of food labels. Have each student choose a label and take it to her or his personal space. Ask students to look for the fat information on the label. On signal, all students do as many jumping jacks as the grams of fat indicated on the label. The students stay together and exercise while the teacher counts aloud. If any students have labels indicating very high fat contents, the teacher might want to have them stop jumping after a certain amount of time and ask them how many grams of fat their label indicated. Students sit down and stretch when they've completed their jumping. Students whose labels indicate zero fat can sit down immediately. Ask students who did the most jumping jacks to stand up and show their foods. Then ask students who jumped only a few times to show their foods. Play the game using different categories of nutrition information, such as protein and carbohydrate content.

CRANK IT UP   Students choose an exercise from a list of exercises divided into *Flexibility, Strength,* and *Cardiorespiratory*. For flexibility, a student could choose to do a straddle stretch (seated with legs apart), modified hurdle stretch (seated with one leg straight, one leg bent with the sole of the foot touching near the knee), or runner's stretch (standing with one foot in front and one in back). Change the exercise category after each gram-count jumping round has been completed. Connect calorie intake and required activity level: The more calories you consume, the more activity you must perform to burn calories.

GEAR IT DOWN   A student volunteer chooses a food label and, with the teacher's help, tells the class the amount of fat in the food item. That student can then come up front and lead the class in the appropriate number of jumping jacks.

ASSET ACTION

Planning and decision making (asset 32)—Tell students that it is important to plan and make wise choices. Ask them what choices Nutrition Addition helps them make and how.

COORDINATED SCHOOL HEALTH LINKS

Have students share Nutrition Addition with their family, or have them use some of the food labels to determine the fat content of lunch foods that they bring with them or get in the cafeteria.

Strive for Five

CONTENT CONNECTIONS   Aerobic health, flexibility, healthy eating

READY FOR ACTION

- Food labels/pictures facedown in the middle of the play area
- A circle of cones around the perimeter
- Students sitting in small relay teams behind the cones and facing the middle of the play area
- Music

LET'S PLAY   Explain to students why fruits and vegetables are essential to a healthy diet. Mention that fruits and vegetables are high in vitamins, minerals, and fiber; low in fat; and completely free of cholesterol. Discuss the importance of eating at least five servings of fruits and vegetables every day (see www.dole5aday.com). Students stretch when the teacher calls out the name of a fruit and do jumping jacks when she or he calls out the name of a vegetable.

CRANK IT UP   While music plays, team members do all of the following one at a time: jog counterclockwise once around the pile of food labels/pictures; return to the team cone; touch it; return to the pile of food labels/pictures; draw a label; bring the label back to the team. This process continues until all food labels/pictures have been used. While waiting for their turn, team members sit, organize the labels/pictures by USDA food category, and stretch. Students then organize into breakfast, lunch, dinner, and snacks for one day. Tell students to make sure that they have at least five servings of fruits and vegetables; ask them what foods they might be missing. Groups sitting next to each other can discuss their choices.

GEAR IT DOWN   Limit the food labels/pictures to fruits and vegetables. Allow each student to pick his or her favorite fruits or vegetables. Remind them to try to eat five a day.

ASSET ACTION

Healthy lifestyle/restraint (asset 31)—Like other food label games, Strive for Five is excellent for teaching good nutrition through physical activities. You might want to invite parents to your class to observe Strive for Five, which shows what contemporary physical education is all about. Invite parents to class during National 5 a Day week in September and play Strive for 5.

COORDINATED SCHOOL HEALTH LINKS

Give the classroom teacher a simple project that students can complete. Each student traces his or her hand and writes the name of, or draws, a fruit or vegetable on each finger. The teacher posts the drawings in the hallway, gym, or cafeteria. Later, students write what they learned about Five a Day on the back of their original drawing and take the drawing home to share with their parents.

APPENDIX

A

Sample Lesson Plan and Concept Lessons

The Essentials of a Quality Physical Education Lesson

By Jim Roberts, 1998 National Elementary Teacher of the Year, Crismon Elementary School, Mesa, Arizona

THE FOUR-PART LESSON FORMAT   The suggested four-part lesson format includes (1) an introductory or warm-up activity, (2) a fitness activity, (3) a lesson or skill focus, and (4) a closing or game activity. This format prepares students for activity, ensures moderate to vigorous activity, teaches skills, and implements the skills in an applied setting. Each of the four lesson parts is described in greater detail in the sections that follow.

INTRODUCTORY (WARM-UP) ACTIVITY

Each lesson begins with an introductory or warm-up activity with a duration of 2-5 minutes. In most cases, some type of gross, unstructured movement (usually locomotor movement based) is included during this introductory activity.

The introductory activities are an important part of the lesson format and are used for the following purposes:

1. They serve as a physical warm-up by preparing children's bodies for physical activity.

2. Introductory activities can introduce or focus on some portion of the lesson objectives. The warm-up can be used to establish anticipatory set or to review previously learned skills.

3. They provide opportunities to review class management skills such as stopping on signal, moving with spacing and under control, and the like. The warm-up activity often sets the tone for the rest of the lesson. If a class is well-managed during the warm-up activity, then it is much more likely that this quality behavior will continue throughout the remainder of the lesson. The fact that most introductory activities require limited instruction allows for the focus on shaping class behavior.

4. An effective introductory activity gives students immediate activity as they enter the activity area. Students want to be able to move immediately rather than having to sit and listen to lengthy instructions. It is better to get children moving vigorously first and then give more lengthy instructions when they are ready to recover.

FITNESS ACTIVITY

The second part of the lesson devotes approximately 6-10 minutes to fitness by using activities that cultivate health-related fitness and activity habits.

Fitness activities should provide children with opportunities to develop health-related fitness and to experience a variety of exercises and exercise routines. It is important that children develop an understanding of the various types or components of fitness and personally experience exercises that will impact each component. Choices should be highlighted so that children begin to understand that there are a variety of exercises or activities that improve each component of fitness. Exercises and fitness development concepts and knowledge should be systematically integrated into these experiences.

Fitness activities should also help children develop activity habits and positive attitudes toward exercise and activity. The ultimate test of our effectiveness in teaching children to become fit is not in what they do during their time with us, but instead in what they do when they are not in a physical education setting. Physical educators must continually focus on the attitudes of children and on the development of habits that include exercise and activity on a regular basis.

These seven principles should guide the development of quality fitness routines:

1. Target all five components of health-related fitness to ensure a well-rounded workout.

2. Use a variety of fitness routines. Using a diverse array of fitness routines, as opposed to a year-long program of regimented calisthenics, will help ensure appeal to the interests of all children.

3. Alternate aerobic (cardiorespiratory) exercises with strength and flexibility exercises. Use a variety of aerobic exercises such as locomotor movements, rope jumping, aerobic games, and

jumping and hopping variations. Alternate these aerobic activities with upper-body strength, abdominal strength, and flexibility activities.

4. Be a role model. When adults participate in and model fitness activities, children see that the adults around them value an active lifestyle. The children themselves then come to value an active lifestyle.

5. Base workloads on time intervals rather than number of repetitions. When working on upper body strength, for example, never ask all children to repeat a particular body-strength exercise the same number of times. Instead specify an amount of time (e.g., 30-45 seconds), and then ask them to perform to the best of their ability. Even better is to allow children to select the exercise or activity that will improve the targeted fitness component during the allocated time. You should not expect all children to perform the same workload.

6. Use music tapes for motivation and to time intervals. Music increases motivation to move. By creating tapes that alternate between music and silence (e.g., 40 seconds of music followed by 40 seconds of silence), we can build in time frames for various exercise focuses.

7. Never use exercise as punishment. Doing so gives children the harmful message that push-ups, running, sit-ups, and the like are things that people are forced to do when they misbehave. The opportunity to exercise should be viewed as a privilege and an enjoyable experience. By being effective salespeople, we sell children on the joy of activity and the many benefits of physical fitness.

LESSON OR SKILL FOCUS

The lesson focus takes up approximately 15 to 20 minutes of the allocated time and contains the primary learning experiences that help students develop physical skills. Repetition and refinement of physical skills in a success-oriented setting lie at the heart of this lesson component. The emphasis is on teaching the process of performing skills correctly.

The following principles should guide skill development and instruction:

1. Use instructional cues. Cues are short descriptive phrases that call to the learner's attention key points of skill technique. Children learning new skills need a clear understanding of critical skill elements because motor learning and cognitive understanding of the skill are developed simultaneously. Cues must be precise and accurate, short and to the point. For longer or more complex cues used in partner or group settings, it may be helpful to create a written list of cues that partners or groups can use as guides to skill practice.

2. Maintain a productive class environment. A variety of management protocols must be in place before instruction related to skill practice begins. Children must be taught these protocols and given opportunities to practice them early in the school year. Review and additional practice should be provided as needed. Management protocols that should be systematically taught include starting and stopping signals with and without equipment, finding partners quickly (toe to toe), moving with reasonable quickness, working and moving in one's own space, forming groups quickly, getting into a variety of formations (lines, circles, squads) quickly, and listening skills. In addition to these management procedures, teachers should have a system in place for dealing with disruptive or otherwise inappropriate behavior. This system should include a set of rules and consequences.

3. Use effective teacher behaviors. A number of teacher behaviors have been shown to improve the productivity of the physical education environment. A few of these behaviors are detailed below.

   a. Teacher movement—Teachers who systematically move through the teaching area are much less likely to leave groups of children isolated. Children who are isolated do not receive instructional feedback and are more likely to become disruptive or get off task. Teachers should deliver instruction from a variety of spots within the teaching area rather than from only one spot or side of the facility.

   b. Avoid overtalking and overteaching. Deliver instructions in short, concise pieces and then let children perform the directed task. Modifications, additions, and clarifications can always be added after children begin the activity. Children's relatively short attention spans do not allow for long, in-depth explanations. Children can quickly reach a state of information overload and begin to tune out teachers who talk too long.

c. Use appropriate instructional feedback and verbal interaction. When giving children feedback, be specific. Children need to know precisely what makes a skill performance high quality. Negative feedback or reprimands should be delivered privately. Express reprimands in terms of the child's behavior, not the child himself or herself. Children who are embarrassed by their teachers are apt to dwell on the teacher's behavior instead of thinking about their own misbehavior.

d. Monitor student performance and behavior. Have "eyes in the back of your head." Be aware of the entire class at most times. Scan the class following a direction to ensure a quick response by students and to allow for expeditious attention to potential problems. A "nip it in the bud" attitude will go a long way toward preventing disruptions and toward correcting misunderstandings quickly.

4. Use appropriate skill progressions. For every student, balance success and challenge by teaching skills in a progression from simple to complex and from easy to more difficult. Children who are not provided with an opportunity to experience success often become frustrated. Children who experience success too easily, without challenge, often become bored. Using a progression of skills or providing two or four choices of skills of differing degrees of difficulty can help create a continuous balance between success and challenge for all children.

5. Maximize participation. Enough equipment should be on hand for all children to practice skills simultaneously. Children do not learn by standing in line and waiting for a turn. Equipment should be spread out along one side or the entire perimeter of the teaching area to ensure efficient and safe acquisition and return of equipment. Reduce direction time to the minimum that is necessary and increase activity and practice time to the available maximum.

6. Demonstrate and model skills. Use teacher and student demonstrations. A picture is worth a thousand words. Teachers who model the behavior and skills that are expected of students come across as more genuine and believable.

7. Facilitate personal best or goal achievement. By using statements such as "See how many times you can..." or "Count how many you get in a row," we can increase students' motivation and engagement in practicing the targeted skill. By providing children with a challenge or goal, we help them to focus their efforts on performing the skill more accurately and with more concentration.

8. Teach responsible student behavior. Use a system, such as Don Hellison's "Levels of Behavior" system (Hellison, 1995), that teaches and provides opportunities for children to develop personal and social responsibility. Physical education and activity settings provide unique opportunities to teach these skills, but learning is not automatic. The learning of responsible behavior must be planned for. Responsible behavior must be systematically taught and integrated into the presented activities.

9. Use a variety of teaching styles to more effectively meet the needs of all children. More direct teaching styles suit efficient delivery of instruction, whereas more indirect styles promote student exploration and discovery. When attempting to use new teaching styles, keep in mind that it may take time for children to learn and get accustomed to the new format. Children should be given opportunities to make decisions and work independently, regardless of their current ability and desire to do so.

10. Design effective practice sessions. Practice is the key to motor learning. Practice needs to focus on quality of movement or correct technique. Place more emphasis on process than on product. A focus on process (using proper technique, using critical elements, incorporating learning strategies) should eventually lead to improvements in the product (how far, how accurate, how many). Research indicates that using practice sessions spread out over the course of the year is more effective in teaching skills than trying to teach a skill from start to

finish within a shorter time period. By presenting a skill, providing practice opportunities, and revisiting the skill later, we decrease frustration and increase learning. The use of varied practice experiences (e.g., different equipment, different speeds, different settings) has also been shown to improve skill acquisition.

CLOSING

The closing activity should be highly enjoyable and leave children wanting more. It can stress and reinforce skills that were practiced during the lesson focus by applying them to a game-like activity. Alternatively, the closing activity can be an unrelated game that children participate in simply for enjoyment. A more physically demanding lesson can be ended with a relaxing, less demanding game or closure activity that allows children to return to the classroom feeling calmer.

Whatever its intended objectives, the closing game or activity should not be held over the heads of children as a reward. It is an important part of a quality physical education lesson and should not be used to bribe children to behave.

CLOSING THOUGHTS   Regardless of the type of lesson format that is used, it is important that the principles delineated above are considered and implemented in order to improve the efficiency and effectiveness of each physical education lesson. The objectives of quality physical education programs are numerous and broad. The lesson format and teaching principles described in the preceding sections can be used to enhance the achievement of these objectives by providing a guiding structure for most physical education lessons.

Five-a-Day Week Celebrations

OBJECTIVE   Teach students the importance of eating fruit and vegetables

RESOURCES

www.dole5aday.com

www.5aday.com

www.mypyramid.gov

READY FOR ACTION

IN THE CAFETERIA

- Create a bulletin board for the Five a Day Question of the Day.
- Each day post a new question. Ask students to write their answer down in their journals or guess the answer and listen to the next day's morning announcements for the answer.

Sample questions:

1. How many green vegetables can you name?
2. Name three fruits that you can eat unpeeled.
3. How many ways can you think of to cook potatoes?
4. How many colors are on your plate today?

The cafeteria manager places a plate or bowl of fruits and vegetables on display for the students to see during the week. On Friday she or he hides the display and asks the students to name all the fruits and vegetables they remember seeing on the plate or in the bowl. Students write their guesses on pieces of paper and drop them into a salad bowl by the cashier. Students who have answered correctly are drawn and their names are posted on the 5-a-Day Question Board the following week. Small treats or other prizes may be given. Many district food service personnel have prizes available.

Place pieces of different colored construction paper on a bulletin board. Ask the cafeteria manager to write the name of a food served in the cafeteria during the week on a matching color. For example, he or she might write "Banana" on the yellow paper and "Tomato" on the red paper.

ON MORNING ANNOUNCEMENTS

Choose five students to make announcements about particular fruits and vegetables. Have each of them make one announcement on a particular day of the week. For example, a student might announce, "Eating five to nine servings of fruits and vegetables a day provides health benefits," "Fruits and vegetables are rich in vitamin C," or "Exercising and eating fruits and vegetables every day promotes good health." Other announcements could include information about specific fruits or vegetables, skits, or songs (for some ideas, visit the Dole 5 a Day Web site at www.dole5aday.com).

LET'S PLAY

IN PHYSICAL EDUCATION

Play the following games:

1. Strive for Five from chapter 16
2. Nutriball from chapter 16 (played with fruit and vegetable "Who am I?" questions)
3. Fruit and Vegetable Take a Stand (below)

FRUIT AND VEGETABLE TAKE A STAND

When the teacher calls out a fruit, students jump up and down. When the teacher calls out a vegetable, they sit and stretch their legs in a V straddle. After the game, draw a large rainbow on chart paper. Ask each student to draw her or his favorite fruit or vegetable on the chart by the part of the rainbow that is the same color as that fruit or vegetable. For example, a student who chooses an apple would draw an apple above the rainbow's red arc. Title the chart "I Can Eat a Rainbow," and post it in the hallway.

IN THE CLASSROOM OR AT HOME

Draw a picture of 5 for health. (See Strive for 5 on page 209). Give each student a piece of paper. Ask the students to trace their hand; draw, color, and label a fruit or vegetable on each finger; write in the center of the hand, "I will strive for five;" and sign that pledge. Post the drawings in the hallway, or have students take them home, ask all family members to sign the pledge, and bring back their drawing with the signatures.

Super Foods for Super Bodies Celebration

OBJECTIVE   Use the NFL Super Bowl week to focus on healthy eating and physical activity.

RESOURCES

www.kidshealth.org

www.mypyramid.gov

LET'S PLAY IN THE CAFETERIA   Working with the cafeteria staff, hold a writing contest in which students write a paragraph on the slogan "Super Foods for Super Bodies." The cafeteria and PE staff judge the paragraphs and post the winners on the cafeteria bulletin board. The food service department gives prizes to the winning students. Many district food service managers have access to prizes from food vendors. These prizes can include balls, Frisbees, pencils, bottled water, fruit, and backpacks. Ask the cafeteria manager to put football decals by super foods (foods high in nutrients) on the cafeteria menu, or create a Super Foods bulletin board.

LET'S PLAY IN PHYSICAL EDUCATION

LESSON 1

With your PE class, discuss six essential nutrients and their importance (see www.kidshealth.org).

Play a nutrition version of a scooter board relay. Place food pictures or cards in the middle of the room. Divide the class into small groups who sit around the perimeter. One at a time, team members scoot into the middle, pick up a food picture or card, and return to their group. The group then places the depicted foods in piles according to their nutrients. Discuss the nutrients in the foods. For younger students, focus on the importance of eating fruits and vegetables.

LESSON 2

Discuss the health benefits of physical activity, particularly fitness exercises.

Create a Super Six Exercise circuit. Post a list of 8-10 exercises on the bulletin board. Discuss with students which exercises develop which health-related fitness components. Let students choose 6 of the exercises. Place the name of each exercise at a station and ask students to rotate through them using a circuit approach. For example, stay at each station for one minute, rest 15 seconds, then rotate to the next station.

LET'S PLAY IN THE CLASSROOM   Ask classroom teachers to give students some writing time to participate in the "Super Foods for Super Bodies" writing contest discussed in the "Let's Play in the Cafeteria" section.

LET'S PLAY AT HOME   Send a brief note home to parents about the Super Foods for Super Bodies celebration held at school. Ask students to discuss with their parents the nutrients in the food they choose at home. Ask students to tell parents who watch the Super Bowl that they should consider taking a quick walk or doing exercises during the halftime performance, or add some fruits or vegetables to the snacks served during the game.

APPENDIX

B

Reproducibles

Stick Figure Worksheet

Let's Get Physical!

Upper-Body Moves

WALL PUSH-AWAYS

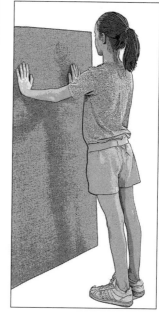

From *PE Connections: Helping Kids Succeed Through Physical Activity* by Thomas Fleming and Lisa Bunting, 2007, Champaign, IL: Human Kinetics.

Let's Get Physical!

Upper-Body Moves

FLAT TIRE   Over a span of 10 counts, slowly go flat.

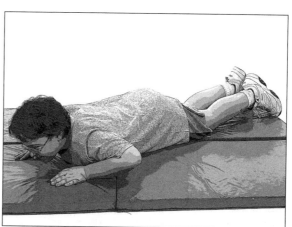

From *PE Connections: Helping Kids Succeed Through Physical Activity* by Thomas Fleming and Lisa Bunting, 2007, Champaign, IL: Human Kinetics.

Let's Get Physical!

Upper-Body Moves

KNEE PUSH-UPS

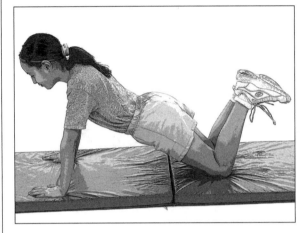 

From *PE Connections: Helping Kids Succeed Through Physical Activity* by Thomas Fleming and Lisa Bunting, 2007, Champaign, IL: Human Kinetics.

 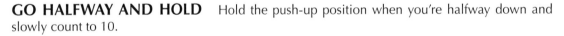

Let's Get Physical!

Upper-Body Moves

GO HALFWAY AND HOLD   Hold the push-up position when you're halfway down and slowly count to 10.

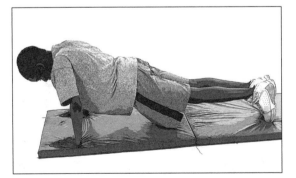 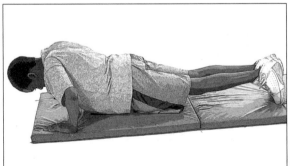

From *PE Connections: Helping Kids Succeed Through Physical Activity* by Thomas Fleming and Lisa Bunting, 2007, Champaign, IL: Human Kinetics.

Let's Get Physical!

Upper-Body Moves

BENCH PUSH-UPS

From *PE Connections: Helping Kids Succeed Through Physical Activity* by Thomas Fleming and Lisa Bunting, 2007, Champaign, IL: Human Kinetics.

Let's Get Physical!

Upper-Body Moves

CHAIR PUSH-UPS

From *PE Connections: Helping Kids Succeed Through Physical Activity* by Thomas Fleming and Lisa Bunting, 2007, Champaign, IL: Human Kinetics.

Let's Get Physical!

Upper-Body Moves

TUMMY PUSH-UPS   Lie on your tummy with the arms bent and hands at the shoulders (like the arm position for a push-up). Push up on arms, keeping your tummy on the floor.

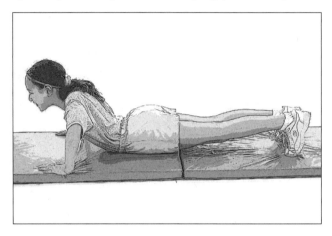

Let's Get Physical!

Upper-Body Moves

CRAB KICKS

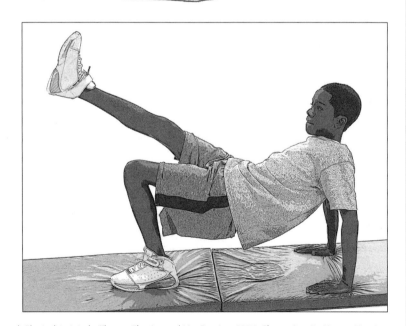

Let's Get Physical!

Upper-Body Moves

CRAB PUSH-UPS

From *PE Connections: Helping Kids Succeed Through Physical Activity* by Thomas Fleming and Lisa Bunting, 2007, Champaign, IL: Human Kinetics.

Let's Get Physical!

Mid-Body Moves

HELP YOURSELF CURL-UPS   Holding onto your legs, pull yourself up and down.

From *PE Connections: Helping Kids Succeed Through Physical Activity* by Thomas Fleming and Lisa Bunting, 2007, Champaign, IL: Human Kinetics.

Let's Get Physical!

Mid-Body Moves

CURL, LOOK, AND HOLD   Hold for five counts.

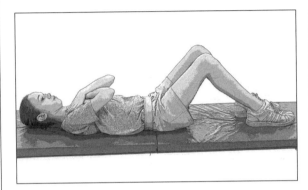
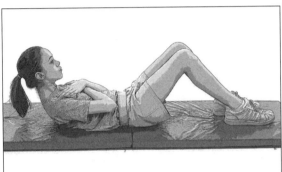

From *PE Connections: Helping Kids Succeed Through Physical Activity* by Thomas Fleming and Lisa Bunting, 2007, Champaign, IL: Human Kinetics.

Let's Get Physical!

Mid-Body Moves

CURL AND SLIDE   Curl while you slide your hands on the floor toward your heels.

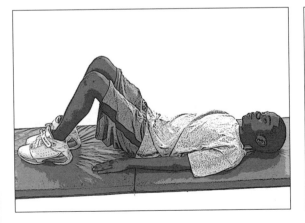

From *PE Connections: Helping Kids Succeed Through Physical Activity* by Thomas Fleming and Lisa Bunting, 2007, Champaign, IL: Human Kinetics.

Let's Get Physical!

Mid-Body Moves

BENCH CURL-UPS   Curl to touch the steps or bench.

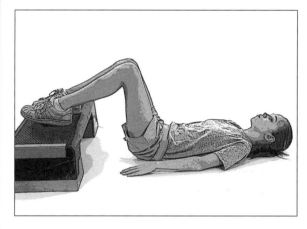

From *PE Connections: Helping Kids Succeed Through Physical Activity* by Thomas Fleming and Lisa Bunting, 2007, Champaign, IL: Human Kinetics.

Let's Get Physical!

Mid-Body Moves

CLIMB-THE-ROPE CURLS   Pretend to climb a rope with your hands.

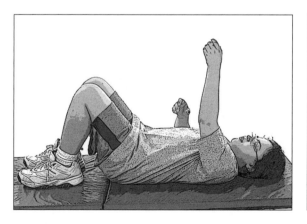
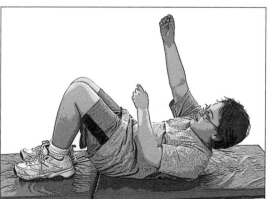

From *PE Connections: Helping Kids Succeed Through Physical Activity* by Thomas Fleming and Lisa Bunting, 2007, Champaign, IL: Human Kinetics.

Let's Get Physical!

Mid-Body Moves

BIKE AND TWIST Twist so that your elbow goes to the opposite knee.

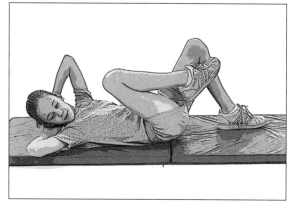

From *PE Connections: Helping Kids Succeed Through Physical Activity* by Thomas Fleming and Lisa Bunting, 2007, Champaign, IL: Human Kinetics.

Let's Get Physical!

Mid-Body Moves

SUPERWOMAN/SUPERMAN Lie on your tummy with your arms on the floor straight overhead. Lift the arms and legs, balancing on your tummy.

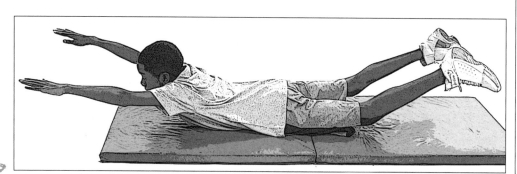

From *PE Connections: Helping Kids Succeed Through Physical Activity* by Thomas Fleming and Lisa Bunting, 2007, Champaign, IL: Human Kinetics.

Let's Get Physical!

Mid-Body Moves

JACKKNIFE

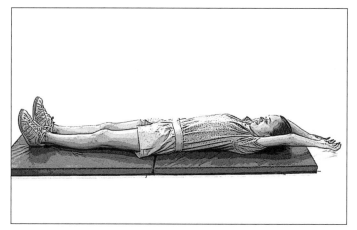

From *PE Connections: Helping Kids Succeed Through Physical Activity* by Thomas Fleming and Lisa Bunting, 2007, Champaign, IL: Human Kinetics.

Let's Get Physical!

Mid-Body Moves

CORE BODY BALANCE

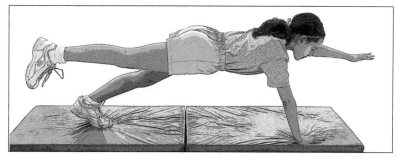

From *PE Connections: Helping Kids Succeed Through Physical Activity* by Thomas Fleming and Lisa Bunting, 2007, Champaign, IL: Human Kinetics.

Let's Get Physical!

Lower-Body Moves

JUMPING JACKS

From *PE Connections: Helping Kids Succeed Through Physical Activity* by Thomas Fleming and Lisa Bunting, 2007, Champaign, IL: Human Kinetics.

Let's Get Physical!

Lower-Body Moves

HOPS

From *PE Connections: Helping Kids Succeed Through Physical Activity* by Thomas Fleming and Lisa Bunting, 2007, Champaign, IL: Human Kinetics.

Let's Get Physical!

Lower-Body Moves

PRETEND JUMP ROPE

Let's Get Physical!

Lower-Body Moves

LINE JUMPS   Jump front to back or side to side.

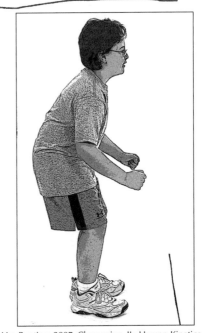

Let's Get Physical!

Lower-Body Moves

JOG IN PLACE

From *PE Connections: Helping Kids Succeed Through Physical Activity* by Thomas Fleming and Lisa Bunting, 2007, Champaign, IL: Human Kinetics.

✂ -

Let's Get Physical!

Flexibility

STANDING LEG STRETCH

From *PE Connections: Helping Kids Succeed Through Physical Activity* by Thomas Fleming and Lisa Bunting, 2007, Champaign, IL: Human Kinetics.

Let's Get Physical!

Flexibility

BUTTERFLY

From *PE Connections: Helping Kids Succeed Through Physical Activity* by Thomas Fleming and Lisa Bunting, 2007, Champaign, IL: Human Kinetics.

Let's Get Physical!

Flexibility

UPPER-ARM STRETCH

From *PE Connections: Helping Kids Succeed Through Physical Activity* by Thomas Fleming and Lisa Bunting, 2007, Champaign, IL: Human Kinetics.

Let's Get Physical!

Flexibility

BACK STRETCH

From *PE Connections: Helping Kids Succeed Through Physical Activity* by Thomas Fleming and Lisa Bunting, 2007, Champaign, IL: Human Kinetics.

Let's Get Physical!

Flexibility

SIDE LEG STRETCH   For improved body alignment, lie on your side and hold your ankle to stretch.

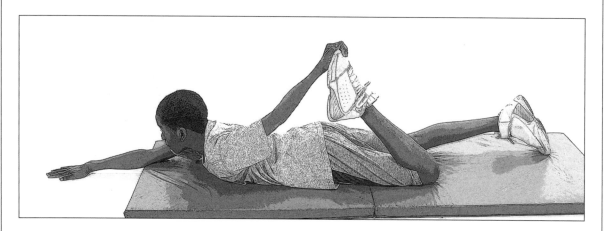

From *PE Connections: Helping Kids Succeed Through Physical Activity* by Thomas Fleming and Lisa Bunting, 2007, Champaign, IL: Human Kinetics.

Let's Get Physical!

Flexibility

STANDING LEG STRETCH

From *PE Connections: Helping Kids Succeed Through Physical Activity* by Thomas Fleming and Lisa Bunting, 2007, Champaign, IL: Human Kinetics.

Let's Get Physical!

Flexibility

PIKE

From *PE Connections: Helping Kids Succeed Through Physical Activity* by Thomas Fleming and Lisa Bunting, 2007, Champaign, IL: Human Kinetics.

Let's Get Physical!

Flexibility

STRADDLE

From *PE Connections: Helping Kids Succeed Through Physical Activity* by Thomas Fleming and Lisa Bunting, 2007, Champaign, IL: Human Kinetics.

Let's Get Physical!

Flexibility

SIT 'N' HOOK

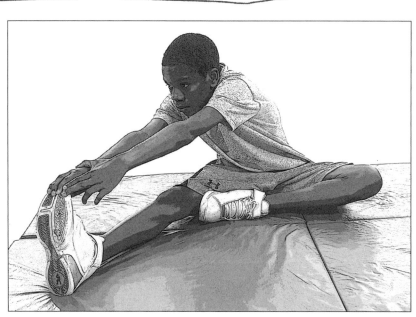

From *PE Connections: Helping Kids Succeed Through Physical Activity* by Thomas Fleming and Lisa Bunting, 2007, Champaign, IL: Human Kinetics.

Let's Get Physical!

Flexibility

ON YOUR MARK

From *PE Connections: Helping Kids Succeed Through Physical Activity* by Thomas Fleming and Lisa Bunting, 2007, Champaign, IL: Human Kinetics.

Let's Get Physical!

Flexibility

PULL 'N' HOLD

From *PE Connections: Helping Kids Succeed Through Physical Activity* by Thomas Fleming and Lisa Bunting, 2007, Champaign, IL: Human Kinetics.

Let's Get Physical!

Flexibility

RAG DOLL Cross your legs and arms. Hang and relax.

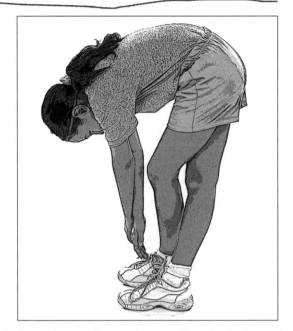

From *PE Connections: Helping Kids Succeed Through Physical Activity* by Thomas Fleming and Lisa Bunting, 2007, Champaign, IL: Human Kinetics.

Let's Get Physical!

Flexibility

BACK TUCK

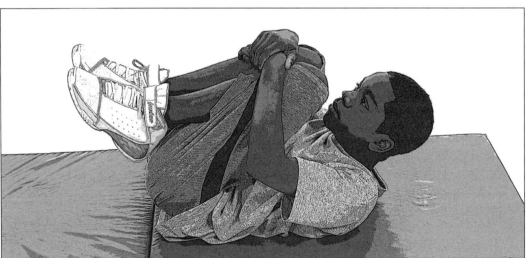

From *PE Connections: Helping Kids Succeed Through Physical Activity* by Thomas Fleming and Lisa Bunting, 2007, Champaign, IL: Human Kinetics.

Let's Get Physical!

Flexibility

EAR TO SHOULDER

From *PE Connections: Helping Kids Succeed Through Physical Activity* by Thomas Fleming and Lisa Bunting, 2007, Champaign, IL: Human Kinetics.

Let's Get Physical!

Flexibility

SIDE STRETCH

From *PE Connections: Helping Kids Succeed Through Physical Activity* by Thomas Fleming and Lisa Bunting, 2007, Champaign, IL: Human Kinetics.

Fitness Code Chart

 = Hop around on one foot

 = Jog inside the hoop

 = Push-ups

 = Curl-ups

 = Stretch

 = Jump in and out of hoop

 = Crab push-ups or crab walk

 = Scissor jumps

From *PE Connections: Helping Kids Succeed Through Physical Activity* by Thomas Fleming and Lisa Bunting, 2007, Champaign, IL: Human Kinetics.

Alphabet Action Tasks

A Around, Above, Act

B Balance, Bounce, Bend

C Crabwalk, Crawl, Curl, Climb, Crunch, Clap

D Dance, Dash, Drop, Down

E Exercise, Extend, Expand

F Float, Fly, Fall, Freeze

G Gallop, Go, Give

H Hop, Hit a Ball

I Inchworm, Ice Skate

J Jump, Jumping Jack, Jog

K Kick, Kangaroo

L Leap, Lunge, Lift

M Melt, Move, Make Your Body Look Like an *M*

N Navigate

O Open, Over

P Prance, Pounce, Push, Pop

Q Quick Time, Quiver, Quickly

R Run, Race-Walk, Roll, Reach

S Sit, Slide, Swim, Skip, Swing, Sway, Scurry, Soar, Stomp, Spin, Shake

T Turn, Travel, Twist, Tiptoe

U Under, Up

V Volley, Vibrate

W Walk, Waddle, Wiggle

X X-Jump

Y Yell Your Favorite Color, Animal, or Food

Z Zigzag Walks, Zip Around

From *PE Connections: Helping Kids Succeed Through Physical Activity* by Thomas Fleming and Lisa Bunting, 2007, Champaign, IL: Human Kinetics.

Cardio Challenge Task Card 1

1. Jog two laps around the cones.

2. Step up and down on the steps or benches 10 times.

3. Skip down the gym once.

4. Do 15 jumping jacks.

5. Do 10 push-ups.

6. Gallop two laps around the cones.

7. Do 15 karate kicks.

8. Jog in place 30 times.

9. Do eight scissor jumps.

10. Walk one lap around the cones.

From *PE Connections: Helping Kids Succeed Through Physical Activity* by Thomas Fleming and Lisa Bunting, 2007, Champaign, IL: Human Kinetics.

Cardio Challenge Task Card 2

1. Touch something green.

2. Jog one lap around the cones.

3. Do 10 knee lifts.

4. Slide two laps around the cones.

5. Do 10 curl-ups.

6. Hop on one foot 10 times.

7. Do 20 line jumps.

8. Gallop one lap around the circle.

9. Do five jumping jacks.

10. Sit and stretch for 25 counts.

From *PE Connections: Helping Kids Succeed Through Physical Activity* by Thomas Fleming and Lisa Bunting, 2007, Champaign, IL: Human Kinetics.

Cardio Challenge Task Card 3

1. Do 10 jumping jacks.

2. March in place 40 times.

3. Do 15 seal walks.

4. Jump a line 14 times.

5. Skip three laps around the cones.

6. Jog in place 20 times.

7. Pretend to hula hoop 30 times.

8. Stretch in a straddle for 10 seconds.

9. Jump and twist 14 times.

10. Do 10 push-ups.

Cardio Challenge Task Card 4

1. On your back, bicycle with your knees 15 times.

2. Skip one lap around the cones.

3. Pretend to jump rope 20 times.

4. Slide between two cones eight times.

5. Walk backward around the cones once.

6. Hop on your right foot 10 times; hop on your left foot 10 times.

7. Do 25 jumping jacks.

8. Do 10 push-ups.

9. Skip around the cones three times.

10. March 50 times.

Fitness Frolic Individual Tasks

- Hit the Trail—Walk freely in the area.

- Jog

- Slide

- Jumping Jacks

- Jump and Twist—Jump up and down, while twisting your arms from side to side.

- March

- Raise the Roof—March and pulse press your palms up toward the ceiling.

- Kanga Jump—Jump up and down in one spot.

- Knee lift—Alternate knee lifts.

- Step Clap—Step side to side, and clap on each step.

- Super Star—Jump to stand with your feet apart, arms up, hands open, and fingers spread.

- Space Jam—Facing your partner, do your own dance moves at your spot.

Fitness Frolic Partner Tasks

- Circle Two—Join hands with another and walk, slide, or jog.

- High-Five Jump—Facing a partner, jump and high-five right, high-five left, high-five both hands.

- Double Fives—Facing a partner, jump and high-five continuously.

- Follow the Leader—While one leads and one follows, skip, gallop, slide, jog, and walk.

- Follow the Leader Switch—Partners do Follow the Leader. At the signal, "Switch," change directions so that the other partner leads.

- Move on Up—On signal, the partner in back moves to the front and leads.

- Partner Kanga—Partners face the same direction. The back partner's hands are on the front partner's shoulders. Partners jump up and down like a pogo stick.

- Kanga Switch—Partners do Follow the Leader Switch and switch on the teacher's signal, this time with a kanga jumping action.

- Twist and Shout—While holding each other's hands and turning, partners go under each other's arms. They say, "Hey!" after each rotation.

- Do-si-do—Facing each other, partners jog and clap while moving around each other.

- Ab Blast—In a sit-up position, partners touch toes; do a curl-up, high five, and go back down.

From *PE Connections: Helping Kids Succeed Through Physical Activity* by Thomas Fleming and Lisa Bunting, 2007, Champaign, IL: Human Kinetics.

Fitness Frolic Groups-of-Four Tasks

- Tunnel—Two people form a tunnel; two others go through. Then the pairs reverse tasks.

- Jump and Jam—Facing inward, four people form a square. They take turns jumping to the opposite side.

- Four-Person Follow the Leader—Three people follow a leader, with each of the four taking turns at being the leader.

Fitness Frolic Whole-Class Tasks

- Circle All—Everyone walks or jogs in a big circle, following the student in front.

- Super S—Everyone walks or jogs, following the teacher or student leader who is moving in a variety of paths.

- Hit the Highway—Walk counterclockwise in a large circle side by side in pairs. On the signal "Inside, reverse," all students in the inner circle turn around and move in the opposite direction until they meet their partner. On the signal "Outside, reverse," all students in the inner circle do the same.

From *PE Connections: Helping Kids Succeed Through Physical Activity* by Thomas Fleming and Lisa Bunting, 2007, Champaign, IL: Human Kinetics.

Heart Smart Tasks 1

- **Blood**—Clasp your hands above your head to create a circle representing a blood cell.

- **Circulation**—Walk around the play area, pretending to be a blood cell.

- **Pump**—Two students perform alternating toe touches (one hand up in the air, one down on the opposite foot).

- **All Body Parts**—Shake and move your whole body.

- **Muscles**—Make muscle poses with flexed biceps.

- **Lungs**—Side by side, two students do push-ups.

- **Atrium**—Move to the front of the play area, and clasp your hands over your head to form the letter *A*. Add the words *right* and *left* to atrium and ventricle, and move to the right or left side of the play area.

- **Ventricle**—Move to the back of the play area. Sit on the floor with your legs apart and straight to form the letter *V*.

- **Valve**—Do jackknife sit-ups (lie on your back and lift your arms and legs in the air to form a *V* while balancing on your bottom).

- **Septum**—Everyone stands on the play area's middle line or center.

- **Aorta**—Six or more pairs join hands to form a tunnel.

- **Lub Dub**—Do jumping jacks.

- **Artery**—Walk away from the center of the play area.

- **Vein**—Walk toward the center of the play area.

From *PE Connections: Helping Kids Succeed Through Physical Activity* by Thomas Fleming and Lisa Bunting, 2007, Champaign, IL: Human Kinetics.

Heart Smart Tasks 2

- **Cholesterol**—A group of seven forms a line by linking elbows and move slowly forward by shuffling their feet.

- **High Blood Pressure**—Jump as high as you can.

- **Smoking**—Cover your mouth and walk while coughing.

- **Stress**—Jog while waving arms overhead.

- **Junk Food**—Bend over slightly, and walk sideways while holding your abdomen.

From *PE Connections: Helping Kids Succeed Through Physical Activity* by Thomas Fleming and Lisa Bunting, 2007, Champaign, IL: Human Kinetics.

I Say Go Task Card

TASK 1
- Shake your hands three times.
- Clap your hands six times.
- Pretend to sweep the floor.

TASK 2
- Stomp your feet.
- Turn around twice.
- Pat your belly.

TASK 3
- Walk and touch a wall.
- Put your hands on your head.
- Whistle and march 10 times.

TASK 4
- Take a deep breath.
- Face the back wall.
- Touch your toes eight times.

TASK 5
- Make a fist.
- Blink your eyes five times.
- Walk backward around a circle.

TASK 6
- Put a beanbag on a line.
- Jump seven times.
- Tug your ear.

TASK 7
- Spin your arms 12 times.
- Clap your hands 10 times.
- Spell your name out loud.

TASK 8
- Jump rope 10 times.
- Say your last name three times.
- Sit and stretch.

TASK 9
- Blink your eyes.
- Hum "Happy Birthday."
- Snap your fingers 10 times.

TASK 10
- Skip on a line.
- Hop on your right foot three times.
- Curl up on the floor.

TASK 11
- Go to the poster board.
- Write your name.
- Turn around three times.

TASK 12
- Draw a circle in the air.
- Knock on the floor four times.
- Gallop in a circle.

TASK 13
- Shake hands with two friends.
- Sit down and row a boat.
- Tap your head five times.

TASK 14
- Laugh.
- Do 10 jumping jacks.
- Scratch your chin.

TASK 15
- Toss your beanbag five times.
- Stand on one foot for 10 counts.
- Sit on the floor.

TASK 16
- Whistle while you clap five times.
- Slap your knees four times.
- Spell your teacher's name.

TASK 17
- Hop once on your left foot.
- Reach for the sky eight times.
- Count to five, and freeze.

TASK 18
- Do five push-ups.
- Skip around the cones.
- Touch something red.

From *PE Connections: Helping Kids Succeed Through Physical Activity* by Thomas Fleming and Lisa Bunting, 2007, Champaign, IL: Human Kinetics.

Lucky Draw Task Sheet

King—Jog two laps around the cones, or do 15 jumping jacks.

Queen—Do 8 push-ups on the ground or 15 push-ups at the wall (standing with your hands on the wall and pushing away).

Jack—Slide or skip one lap around the cones.

10—March up and down a bench 10 times.

9—Do 20 wall jumps (face the wall, jump up, and tap the wall lightly with both hands).

8—Do toe-touch stretches for 15 counts.

7—Do 25 speed jumps with a rope, or do your favorite jump rope trick 15 times.

6—Do 20 right-foot hops and 20 left-foot hops.

5—Do 10 stretchband biceps curls or 10 curls using a sand-filled water bottle.

4—Do 15 side or front-and-back jumps over a line.

3—Do 5 crab push-ups or 10 crab-position leg kicks.

2—Scooter one lap around the cones.

Ace—Shoot at a basketball goal five times, or get a drink of water and draw another card.

From *PE Connections: Helping Kids Succeed Through Physical Activity* by Thomas Fleming and Lisa Bunting, 2007, Champaign, IL: Human Kinetics.

Summer Shuffle Tasks for One Student

- **Hot Sand**—Run on tiptoe, keeping your knees high.
- **Swim**—Backstroke while walking.
- **Sunblock**—Lie on your back, and cover your face with your hands.
- **Ride the Waves**—Balance on a line, pretending to surf.
- **Flip-Flops**—Alternately walk on all fours and walk like a crab, flipping back and forth.
- **Crabs**—Crabwalk in a circle.
- **Seagulls**—Standing in one place, flap your arms while moving up and down.
- **Surfboard**—Lie straight as a board.

Summer Shuffle Tasks for Two Students

- **Sun**—One student makes a sun shape (circle); the other stands behind in a frozen jumping jack to depict sun rays.
- **Umbrella**—One student kneels to represent the stalk of an umbrella; the other stands behind and forms the top of an umbrella with his or her arms.
- **Sand Castle**—One student curls into a circle representing a moat; the other stands in the middle of the circle with her or his hands crossed at the chest, representing the castle.

Summer Shuffle Tasks for Three Students

- **Paddle a Canoe**—Two students sit on the floor, facing each other, and hold hands to form a canoe. A third student stands in the middle and pretends to paddle.
- **Tent**—Standing with their arms raised, two students form a bridge. A third student stands in the middle, representing the pole of a tent.

Summer Shuffle Tasks for Four Students

- **Waves**—Students stand shoulder to shoulder in a line and raise and lower their arms, imitating waves.
- **Beach Ball**—Students lie on their tummies in a circle. With their arms overhead, they touch the ankle of the person in front of them.
- **Dig a Sand Tunnel**—Students line up, shoulder to shoulder, in push-up position with their bottoms raised slightly to form a tunnel. One at a time, students crawl through the tunnel and resume push-up position at the other end. Each student goes through the tunnel until a new command is called.

From *PE Connections: Helping Kids Succeed Through Physical Activity* by Thomas Fleming and Lisa Bunting, 2007, Champaign, IL: Human Kinetics.

Winter Wonderland Tasks for One Student

- Bells—Stand and shake your body.
- Snow Boot—Lie on back, feet up in the air.
- Candy Cane—Stand up; bend over with arms curved forward.
- North Pole—Move to the north side of the room.
- South Pole—Move to the south side of the room.
- Bow—Sit with legs crossed and arms crossed across chest.
- Candle—Stand with hands clasped and flickering above head.
- Gum Drops—Curl up in a small ball.
- Toy Soldiers—March in place and salute.
- Blinking Lights—Jump up with hands extended above shoulders; hands open and close.
- Shovel Snow—Pretend to shovel and fling snow over your shoulder.
- Brrrrrr!—Shiver.

Winter Wonderland Tasks for Two Students

- Ice Skating—Two students stand side by side and shuffle their feet as if skating.
- Snowboarding—One student lies down, pretending to be a snowboard; the other straddles him or her.
- Reindeer—Two students in follow-the-leader formation. The student in front has antlers, and the student in back has hands on the shoulders of the leader and is slightly bent over.
- Snowball—Two students join hands, form the shape of a bridge, and turn under (wring the dishcloth).

Winter Wonderland Tasks for Three to Five Students

- Sled—Sit in a line, and scoot together across the floor. (three students)
- Train—Standing in a line, holding the elbows of the student in front, slowly chug around the room. (four students)
- Wreath—Sit and form a circle. Join hands and hold them overhead. (five students)
- Star—While seated in a straddle, touch feet of adjacent student. (five students)

From PE Connections: Helping Kids Succeed Through Physical Activity by Thomas Fleming and Lisa Bunting, 2007, Champaign, IL: Human Kinetics.

Spinner

To make a spinner, you need a paper clip bent like this,

three or four tagboard circles, 6 inches (15 centimeters) in diameter,

6 in (15 cm)

Punch holes with a pencil point.

and an arrow this size cut from cardboard.

3/4 in (2 cm)

4 in (10 cm)

Cut three small tagboard squares. Use them as washers. Spinners really won't spin without them.

1/2 in (1 cm)

To change the face of your spinner, remove the arrow and drop a new circle over the old one.

Be creative by adding colors or numbers to the spinners to meet class or activity needs.

Adapted, by permission, from M. Burns, 1978, *Good time math event book* (New York: McGraw-Hill Companies). © The McGraw-Hill Companies.

From *PE Connections: Helping Kids Succeed Through Physical Activity* by Thomas Fleming and Lisa Bunting, 2007, Champaign, IL: Human Kinetics.

Nutrient Treasure Hunt

1. Food _____
   Fat _____

2. Food _____
   Fat _____

3. Food _____
   Fat _____
   Sugar _____

4. Food _____
   Sodium _____

5. Food _____
   Vitamin C _____

6. Food _____
   Carbohydrate _____

7. Food _____
   Protein _____

8. Food _____
   Sugar _____

9. Food _____
   Calories _____

10. Food _____
    Calcium _____

Which of the first three foods contained the most fat? _____

_____

Which of the foods had a nutritional value that surprised you? _____

_____

From *PE Connections: Helping Kids Succeed Through Physical Activity* by Thomas Fleming and Lisa Bunting, 2007, Champaign, IL: Human Kinetics.

APPENDIX

C

Suggestions for Modifying Physical Education Activities

The contemporary model for physical education provides a foundation of active participation for all students in a variety of activities. Designing and planning PE lessons for large groups, small groups, and individual students is challenging. If students are to succeed, PE teachers must offer activities that are safe, challenging, enjoyable, and developmentally appropriate. This task can be daunting to an activity planner. Students enter the physical education (activity) arena in large numbers and with varying degrees of readiness, ability, and experience. Activity settings must be adapted to meet children's needs, expectations, and abilities. Skilled teachers adapt the curriculum as needed and use a variety of instructional methods.

To accommodate the wide range of abilities and experiences among students, teachers can modify or change the equipment, the actions that students perform during an activity, the amount of space and boundaries for the movements, and the time used and force applied during movements. For suggestions on modifying games and other activities to encourage students' full participation, see the "Crank It Up" and "Gear It Down" sections of each activity in part II of this book.

Accommodate students with disabilities so that they can participate in activities. Many of the modifications that appear in "General Suggestions for Activities" (page 256) can be implemented for increased participation for all students, including those with disabilities. Each student's competencies and level of performance should be considered individually. You'll find suggestions for meeting individual needs in "General Adaptations for Specific Skills" (page 256). When a student with a disability is placed in a general physical education or activity setting, the teacher should work with the school support team to provide the best setting for the student. It is also important for teachers and others who direct activities to understand the student's disability and avoid involving the student in contraindicated activities. Web sites such as www.twu.edu/inspire and www.pecentral.org offer helpful information on disabilities and working with students who have disabilities.

Inclusive physical activities allow everyone in the class to fully participate and succeed, regardless of age, experience, physical limitations, and ability level. Modifications and adaptations, such as those suggested here, can assist the activity planner.

General Suggestions for Activities

Equipment

Changing the equipment used in an activity can increase the chances of successful participation. You can do any of the following:

- Change the size or weight of the equipment (e.g., increase a target's size, lower a target or goal, use a trash can or milk crate instead of a basketball goal, or hang a hula hoop over the rim of an existing basketball goal to imitate a high target).
- Change a ball's size or weight.
- Change a ball's color or texture.
- Use bright colors for targets and cones.
- Change the size of the racket or bat.
- Lower the basketball goal or net.
- Use suspended balls.

Student Actions

Simplify the way that students are expected to move in an activity.

- In chasing games, reduce locomotor patterns to walking. In jump rope activities, allow students to place the rope on the ground in a straight line and jump back and forth over it instead of turning it.
- Use body parts other than those normally specified.
- Modify the body positions (e.g., allow students to sit in a chair or on the floor when appropriate).

Boundaries and Space

Change the size of the play area or the space needed to perform the activity.

- For younger students, increase the size of the play area.
- Decrease the play area for students who are more adept at dynamic movement.
- Include a marked safe zone or play area within the regular boundaries to more closely monitor students who lack coordination or balance.
- Use larger or more brightly colored cones to mark areas.

- Vary the distance to targets or goals, the distance needed for moving, or the distance needed for completing the task.
- Give options when varying the distance that students are required to move or jump. For example, students can try to leap 1 foot (about 30 centimeters) and increase the distance when they succeed.

Speed, Effort, Time

The speed or effort can be modified.

- Slow the activity.
- Use stationary tasks instead of combining locomotion with skills.
- Use a variety of tempos when appropriate.

General Adaptations for Specific Skills

Aerobic Fitness

- Decrease the time of participation.
- Give additional rest.
- Reduce distances.
- Instead of having students do total-body exercises, have them exercise only their arms or feet.
- Encourage students of low motor ability to march or walk rather than do locomotor movements.
- Give the option of using the arms.

Balance

- Provide peer assistance or a bar for support.
- Teach eye focus on one spot.
- Provide a soft surface to work on.
- Widen the base of support.

Ball Rolling

- Use two hands instead of one.
- Roll from a seated position.
- Push the ball off the lap.

Bouncing and Dribbling

- Use larger balls.
- Try different kinds of balls.
- Allow students to bounce and catch rather than repeatedly bounce.

- Students in wheelchairs can hold the ball on their laps while being pushed.
- Allow students to bounce and catch in a stationary position.

Catching

- Use Velcro balls and mitts.
- Use balloons and beach balls.
- Use scoops for catching.
- Vary the distance between partners.
- Use larger balls.

Coordination

- Slow the tempo of the movements.
- Concentrate on safety.
- Work in stationary positions.
- Break the movement into doable parts.

Hula Hoops

- Circle the hoop around your neck or arms.
- Join hands with a peer and, together, spin the hoop around your joined arms.

Jumping

- Instead of jumping, step over low objects or repeatedly step on and off a step or folded mat.
- Instead of doing jumping jacks, either place your hands on your hips and jump slowly or keep your feet stationary and move your arms.

Jumping Rope

- The student jumps over a rope on the floor.
- The student holds a rope folded in half by the handles, then jumps and turns the rope as if he were jumping over the rope.
- Slip pipe insulation over a rope, and ask the student to walk over the encased rope.
- Cut a jump rope in half. The student holds one half in each hand and turns each half.
- The student jumps to the beat without a rope while you clap.
- The student and a peer assistant hold the rope while the student jumps rope.

Kicking

- Have the student use a large or deflated ball.

- Provide the student with hand support as she or he kicks from a stationary position.
- Have the student kick while seated in a chair.

Muscular Strength and Endurance for the Mid-Body

- Assist the student doing curl-ups by holding the legs or knees. The student can reach to touch the helper's hand instead of performing a full curl-up.
- Encourage modifications of the curl-up. For example, students can perform look-throughs (lying on the back with the knees bent and lifting the head and shoulders to look through the knees).

Muscular Strength and Endurance for the Upper Body

- Students try to support their body weight in a push-up position for 10 counts.
- Students perform modified push-ups.
- Students do a "seal" (lie on the belly, place the hands under the chest, and gently push the upper body off the ground).
- Students do wall push-ups (stand by a wall, put hands on the wall, and push up and down).

Striking

- Use larger balls.
- Strike with the hand.
- Strike off a tee or other stationery object.
- Use a lighter bat.
- Use a foam paddle.
- Suspend a balloon and strike it with a hand.
- Use paddles and balls with larger striking surfaces.

Throwing and Tossing

- Change the size of the object.
- Push or strike suspended balls of different sizes.
- Push or strike an object down a ramp or off a tee.
- Use a smaller object.
- Use beanbags for an easier grasp.

Volleying

- Use balloons or beach balls.
- Use lighter balls.
- Hold the ball, and let the student hit it out of your hand.

- Using a jump rope and two cones, create a low "net." Have the student throw a ball over this.
- Have the student hit a balloon to a partner on the other side of the rope-and-cones "net."

References and Resources

References

Adler, E. (1998, April 6). Does P.E. stand for "pretty exciting"? *The Kansas City Star.*

Benson, P.L. (1997). *All kids are our kids: What communities must do to raise caring and responsible children and adolescents.* San Francisco: Jossey-Bass.

Benson, P.L., Galbraith, J., & Espeland, P. (1998). *What kids need to succeed: Proven, practical ways to raise good kids.* Minneapolis: Free Spirit.

Blair, S.N. (1995). Exercise prescription for health. *Quest, 47,* 338-353.

Blair, S.N. (2005, February 07). Letter from Steven N. Blair, president and CEO of the Cooper Institute (Dallas, TX) to Thomas Fleming.

Blair, S.N., Kohl, H.W., Paffenbarger, R.S., Jr., Clark, D.G., Cooper, K.H., & Gibbons, L.W. (1989). Physical fitness and all-cause mortality: A prospective study of healthy men and women. *Journal of the American Medical Association, 262*(17), 2395-2401.

Bogden, J.F. (2003). *How schools work and how to work with schools: A primer for professionals who serve children and youth.* Alexandria, VA: National Association of State Boards of Education.

Caine, R.N., & Caine, G. (1991). *Making connections: Teaching and the human brain.* Arlington, VA: Association for Supervision and Curriculum Development.

Carnegie Council on Adolescent Development. (1989). *Turning points: Preparing American youth for the 21st century.* New York: Carnegie Corporation.

Centers for Disease Control and Prevention. (April 2006). *Overweight and obesity: Obesity trends.* Retrieved on May 9, 2006. from www.cdc.gov/nccdphp/dnpa/obesity/trend.

Centers for Disease Control and Prevention. Tobacco-related mortality fact sheet. Retrieved May 09, 2006. from www.cdc.gov/tobacco/factsheets/Tobacco_Related_Mortality_factsheet.htm.

Curriculum Development and Supplemental Materials Commission. (2004). *Health framework for California public schools: Kindergarten through grade twelve.* Sacramento: California Department of Education.

Fleming, T.M. (1989). *The aerobic years: A historical analysis of the work of Kenneth H. Cooper and his influence in promoting healthy lifestyles.* Unpublished doctoral dissertation, Texas A&M University.

Fleming, T.M. (1999). Child and Adolescent Trial for Cardiovascular Health (CATCH). *Texas Association of Health, Physical Education, Recreation, and Dance Journal, 67*(2), 41.

Fleming, T.M. (2001, Winter). Revenge of the dodge ball victims. *Texas Association of Health, Physical Education, Recreation, and Dance Journal, LXIX,* (2)9.

Fleming, T.M. (2006). *Helping students succeed through coordinated school health.* Orlando, FL: Harcourt School Publishers.

Hellison, D. (1995). *Teaching responsibility through physical education,* pages 10-21. Champaign, IL: Human Kinetics.

Hoelscher, D.M., Kelder, S.H., Murray, N., Cribb, P.W., Conroy, J., & Parcel, G.S. (2001). Dissemination and adoption of the Child and Adolescent Trial for Cardiovascular Health (CATCH): A case study in Texas. *Journal of Public Health Management Practice, 7*(2), 90-100.

Human Kinetics. WOW! World of Wellness Health Education Series. Retrieved on April 7, 2006 from http://www.wowhealth.org.

Kirby, S.D. (1997). Developing social skills: Making the case for teaching social skills. *Teaching Elementary Physical Education, 8*(5), 9.

Kolbe, L.J. (2002, Autumn). Education reform and the goals of modern school health programs. *State Education Standard*, 4-11.

Lemonick, M.D. (2004, June 7). How we grew so big. *Time*, 59-60, 84.

Lohrmann, D.K., & Wooley, S.F. (1998). *Health is academic: A guide to coordinated school health programs*. New York: Teachers College Press.

McNeely, C.A., Nonnemaker, J.M., & Blum, R.W. (2002). Promoting school connectedness: Evidence from the National Longitudinal Study of Adolescent Health. *Journal of School Health, 72*(4), p. 138.

National Association for Sport and Physical Education (2004). *Moving into the future: National standards for physical education* (2nd ed.). Reston, VA: Author.

Nygard, Green, and Koonce. World of Wellness Health Education series. Champaign, IL: Human Kinetics, 2005.

Poag, S. (2000). Focus group findings: Research for the Health and PE Center for Educator Development. Austin, TX: Education Service Center Region XV and Texas Education Agency.

Scales, P.C., Sesma, A., Jr., & Bolstrom, B. (2004). *Coming into their own: How developmental assets promote positive growth in middle childhood*. Minneapolis: Search Institute.

Search Institute. The Asset Approach: 40 Elements of Healthy Development. Retrieved on May 26, 2006 from www.search-institute.org.

Search Institute. Making a difference for young people: The power of one, pp. 2-3. Retrieved March 18, 2005 from www.search-institute.org/assets/individual/ThePowerOfOne.html.

Search Institute. Why are the 40 developmental assets important? Retrieved on May 10, 2006 from www.search-institute.org/assets/importance.html.

Starkman, N., Scales, P.C., & Roberts, C. (1999). *Great places to learn: How asset-building schools help students succeed*. Minneapolis: Search Institute.

Texas Essential Knowledge and Skills for kindergarten to grade 12 (September 1997). *Texas Administrative Code*, Title 19, Part 2, Chapter 16.

Texas Administrative Code (TAC), Title 19, Part III, chapter 116. Texas essential knowledge and skills for physical education. www.tea.state.tx.us/rules/tac. Retrieved May 10, 2006.

Texas Congress. *Physical Activity Programs for Elementary School Students*. 77th Texas Legislature, Bill 19. (March 22, 2002).

U.S. Department of Health and Human Services (DHHS) (1996). *Physical activity and health: A report of the surgeon general*. Atlanta, GA: DHHS, Centers for Disease Control and Prevention, and National Center for Chronic Disease Prevention and Health Promotion.

Weir, T. (2000, May 7). The new PE. *USA Today*.

Welch, R. (2004). *Building assets is elementary: Group activities for helping kids ages 8-12 succeed*. Minneapolis: Search Institute.

Physical Education Resources

Teaching Elementary Physical Education. Champaign, IL: Human Kinetics. (800-747-4457)

One of the premier periodicals on elementary physical education, this bimonthly journal focuses on current ideas in physical education. Each issue consists of more than 30 pages on topics such as lifetime fitness, developmentally appropriate activities, assessment, integration, and implementing the standards of the National Association for Sport and Physical Education. PE success stories relate to adapted PE, assessment, and healthy lifestyles. Human Kinetics' Web site is www.humankinetics.com.

www.aahperd.org/naspe

Appropriate Practices for Elementary School Physical Education (2000) is a National Association for Sport and Physical Education (NASPE) position statement. It can be accessed at the NASPE home page under "Publications." Appropriate Practices in Physical Education is the heart of quality PE and a useful tool for practitioners. An appropriate practice incorporates the best-known procedures, derived from both research and teaching experience, into instruction that maximizes opportunities for learning and the success of all children.

The NASPE position statement *Appropriate Practices for Middle School Physical Education* (2001) helps PE teachers assist middle school students in the transition from childhood to young adulthood. It explains and outlines quality physical education that meets the needs of middle school students with diverse needs.

The 2004 NASPE publication *Moving Into the Future: National Standards for Physical Education* (2nd ed.) is a must-read document for a PE professional. It answers the basic question, "What should students know and be able to do?"

www.catchtexas.org

Coordinated Approach to Child Health (CATCH) PE activity boxes and guidebooks for K through 8, Centers for Health Promotion and Prevention Research, 7320 N. Mopac, Suite 300, Austin, TX 78731 (866-346-6163).

The Web site is easy to navigate and includes links to curriculum materials, training and support, and implementation and coordination topics such as "How to Get Started Using CATCH," "The History of CATCH," and information on what other CATCH schools are doing.

www.pecentral.org

This may be the most comprehensive Web site for health and physical education. The wide range of topics and links reflects PE Central's goal of "providing the latest information about developmentally appropriate PE programs for children and youth." "Lesson Ideas" and "Assessment Ideas" are particularly valuable links. More than 900 teachers have submitted over 1,300 ideas about health and PE lessons. The site includes information on research, job openings, and other helpful health and PE Web sites.

www.pelinks4u.org

The home page drop-down menu features topics including "archives" and "teaching unit plans" (there are 47 unit plans, including archery and cross-country skiing). Other home page topics include adapted PE; coaching and sports; elementary PE; health, fitness, and nutrition; interdisciplinary PE; secondary PE; and technology in PE.

www.tea.state.tx.us/rules/tac/ch116toc.html

At this Web site you'll find the guide "Texas Essential Knowledge and Skills for Physical Education" (1997) from the *Texas Administrative Code*, Title 19, Part 2, Chapter 116. "Subchapter A (Elementary)" is a resource guide for K-5, and "Subchapter B (Middle School)" is a guide for 6-8. The guide helps PE teachers incorporate the Texas Physical Education State Standards into their curriculum.

Texas Association for Health, Physical Education, Recreation, and Dance: TAHPERD State Office, 6300 La Calma Dr., Suite 410, Austin, TX 78752-3890 (800-880-7300).

Developmental Assets Resources

Benson, P.L. (1997). All kids are our kids: What communities must do to raise caring and responsible children and adolescents. San Francisco: Jossey-Bass.

This book was written by Search Institute president Peter Benson. Easy to read, it explains the history of developmental assets and how asset building can change young people's lives.

Meeks, L., & Heit, P. (2003). *Totally awesome strategies for teaching health* (Hightstown, NJ: McGraw-Hill).

A five-part book that looks at the framework, health content, and teaching strategies of health education, as well as providing a health resource guide and curriculum guide.

Scales, P.C., Sesma, A., Jr., & Bolstrom, B. (2003). Coming into their own: How developmental assets promote positive growth in middle childhood. Minneapolis: Search Institute.

This book introduces a revised assets framework for children in grades 4 through 6. A chapter is devoted to each of the eight asset categories. The book discusses the similarities and differences among developmental assets in early childhood, middle childhood, and adolescence.

Starkman, N., Scales, P.C., & Roberts, C. (1999). *Great places to learn: How asset-building schools help students succeed.* Minneapolis: Search Institute.

This book offers great suggestions regarding how your school can become an asset-building environment. It includes practical ideas and stories from across the United States of asset building by teachers, school personnel, and communities.

Welch, R. (2004). Building assets is elementary: Group activities for helping kids ages 8-12 succeed. Minneapolis: Search Institute.

This book helps teachers introduce developmental assets to children ages 8 through 12 so that children will build assets in themselves and others. It contains 60 activities that can be applied to various settings, including school classrooms and PE classes.

www.chef.org/age/school.php

The Comprehensive Health Education Foundation promotes health and quality of life through education. The foundation hosts a variety of high-quality training in all aspects of health education including conflict resolution.

www.esrnational.org/cap/index.html

The Kids' Conscious Acts of Peace project offers classroom activities for teaching students how to form and promote peaceable relationships in school and at home.

www.gigglepotz.com/peace.htm

Gigglepotz.com provides materials that help students learn to resolve conflicts peaceably.

www.packyplayfair.com

The goal of this website is to make sportsmanship, fair play, and good behavior as fundamental to raising successful members of society as the three academic "R's" of reading, writing and arithmetic.

www.search-institute.org

This extensive Web site provides the framework of 40 developmental assets, positive experiences and personal qualities that young people need to grow up healthy, caring, and responsible. Links related to schools, parents, and communities offer numerous suggestions for action strategies in many settings.

Search Institute, Banks Building, 615 First Ave. NE, Suite 125, Minneapolis, MN 55413 (800-888-7828).

Coordinated School Health Resources

Marx, E., Wooley, S., & Northrop, D. (Eds.). (1998). *Health is academic: A guide to coordinated school health programs*. New York: Teachers College Press.

This book gives readers a total picture of coordinated school health. Each of its eight chapters focuses on a different component of coordinated school health. The book outlines practical actions that health professionals and members of the school community can take to improve young people's health and educational performance.

www.ccsso.org/publications/details.cfm?PublicationID=59

Council of Chief State School Officers (CCSSO) and the Association of State and Territorial Health Officials. (2003). *Why support a coordinated approach to school health?* School health starter kit (2nd ed.). Washington, DC: CCSSO.

This publication, which suggests ways to improve a school's approach to health, is available from CCSSO (202-336-7035). It provides guidelines for coordinated school health: how to get started, how to identify possible changes, and how to organize support for those changes. The kit is full of resource materials, including a CD-ROM.

www.cdc.gov/healthyyouth/publications/pdf/ten_strategies.pdf

Centers for Disease Control and Prevention. (2003). Ten strategies for promoting physical activity, healthy eating, and a tobacco-free lifestyle through school health programs.

This guide helps schools and communities interested in reducing the health risks associated with inadequate physical activity, unhealthy eating, and smoking. It emphasizes a coordinated approach to risk reduction.

www.healthfinder.gov

An award-winning Web site for consumers, Healthfinder was developed by the U.S. Department of Health and Human Services and other federal agencies. Healthfinder is a key resource for finding the Web's best information on government and nonprofit health and human services. It links to Web sites of more than 1,500 health-related organizations.

www.kidshealth.org

KidsHealth is the largest and most visited Web site providing doctor-approved health information about children. Created by the Nemours Foundation's Center for Children's Health Media,